TWELVE
FEET TALL

TWELVE
FEET TALL

THE AUTOBIOGRAPHY

Tony Ward

with Justin Doyle

**SIMON &
SCHUSTER**

London · New York · Sydney · Toronto · New Delhi

A CBS COMPANY

First published in Great Britain by Simon & Schuster UK Ltd, 2015
A CBS COMPANY
Copyright © 2015 by Tony Ward and Justin Doyle

1 3 5 7 9 10 8 6 4 2

Simon & Schuster UK Ltd
1st Floor
222 Gray's Inn Road
London WC1X 8HB

www.simonandschuster.co.uk

Simon & Schuster Australia, Sydney
Simon & Schuster India, New Delhi

The author and publishers have made all reasonable efforts to contact
copyright-holders for permission, and apologise for any omissions or errors in
the form of credits given. Corrections may be made to future printings.

A CIP catalogue record for this book
is available from the British Library

Hardback ISBN: 978-1-4711-5357-0
Trade paperback ISBN: 978-1-4711-5358-7
eBook ISBN: 978-1-4711-5360-0

Typeset in the UK by M Rules
Printed in the UK by CPI Group (UK) Ltd, Croydon, CR0 4YY

Simon & Schuster UK Ltd are committed to sourcing paper
that is made from wood grown in sustainable forests and supports the Forest
Stewardship Council, the leading international forest certification organisation.
Our books displaying the FSC logo are printed on FSC certified paper.

The definitive work on this journey is dedicated to four extraordinary children and their equally amazing grandma. To Lynn, Richie, Nikki, Ali and Grandma June, this one's for you.

Contents

Acknowledgements

The last decade has made for the most trying in my six decades to date. But that is the way the dice rolled and so myself, my family and friends had to get on with it as best we could. No different I guess to most everybody out there.

And yet over the last three years I found an interest over and above the ordinary in terms of several people urging me to put my life in print. Twice I went close but I had second thoughts.

Then in November 2014 I received a card to my mailbox in St Gerard's.

It went along the lines that 'as a boyhood fan and now a writer of books, if ever you were to commit your thoughts to print, I would be honoured if you would consider the possibility of doing it with me'. I am condensing and paraphrasing what was written.

To cut a long story short, over two months later I made contact with the sender and on the back of two meetings in South County Dublin, the seeds for *Twelve Feet Tall* were sown. For Justin Doyle this was a mission, and one thing I learned early was of some fiery exchanges guaranteed ahead.

I would be lying if I said this has been a smooth journey. In truth, it has been anything but. Yet in the process I have grown to admire and respect Justin so much. What you see is what you get. He wears his heart on his sleeve and calls it as it is.

We have had several heated exchanges in piecing this project together but never did we fall out, as in the end compromise always prevailed. So to Justin and his wife, Paula: my gratitude for patience and perseverance over and above the call of duty.

We will leave it to others to pass final judgement but the end product carries itself.

To Iain MacGregor and everyone at Simon & Schuster, my enormous thanks for all the encouragement and enthusiasm from the get go.

I guess in thanking the following I am opening the proverbial can of worms. It is like the dreaded wedding invitation list; the more you invite, the more you offend. They say in times of crisis you find out who your true friends are and while I did not need a time of crisis to find out mine, I can certainly vouch for its validity.

So to Keith Spencer, Annette Carroll, David and Leslie Boyd, Gordon Laing, John Moloney, Paud Herlihy, John Scally, Mick Quinn, Peter Purcell, Brian O'Brien, Dermot 'D' O'Brien, Dave Phelan, Joe McDonnell, Ken Ging, Ollie Campbell, John Redmond, Dave Courtney, Donal Egan, Ken Ging, Terry and Geraldine Quigley, Lorraine Foy, PJ Cunningham, Hubie Gallagher, Sam Van Eeden, Ray Power and Alina Mihai my sincere thanks for all your help, particularly in most recent years when things got particularly rough.

I want to say a special thank you to Michael and Pamela O'Loughlin, Br Denis Hooper, Victor and Aisling Drummy, Dave and Kay Mahedy, Tom and Eibhlin Geraghty, Ned and Mary Van Esbeck and Micheal and Josephine McMullan.

Michael O'Loughlin, Denis Hooper and Dave Mahedy have long been the blood brothers I never had. Denis and I have been best friends since Junior 2 in St Mary's, and Dave and I since that first day registering at Plassey some forty odd years ago.

As for Michael, for sure he is the twin I never had. He was my scrum half, is my solicitor and godparent (along with his gorgeous wife, Pam) to Ali, and he will forever be the one in whom I trust implicitly for advice and guidance. I have no doubt but that in acknowledging the above I have offended so many more.

To that end, can I say simply: *mea culpa, mea culpa, mea maxima culpa.*

Let me add one extra but very relevant thought. In the final run in to deadline, the sudden and tragic death of the unique voice of Sport on 98FM, Johnny 'Now That's What I Call Sport' Lyons stopped me in my tracks.

There could be no prevaricating. Whatever else, it hammered home the message once again forcibly that life ain't no dress rehearsal.

In memory of Johnny and with the health prognosis good… it is onward and upward.

DELIVERANCE

In the early months of 2012 I sensed something was not right. I was still doing my usual travelling and reporting on rugby matches at home and abroad for my employer, Independent News and Media. But I felt my body was not functioning as it should. I could not put my finger on the exact problem, but I had a strong feeling that there was something wrong somewhere.

When I was passing time between games, a most alarming thing would happen. If I was walking down the street window-shopping, or driving in my car, I would have to run into the nearest shop or pub to have a pee. On one particular day the urge was intolerable. I was in a mad panic as I dashed into a Marks & Spencer's store looking for the toilet. It had been becoming increasingly worse. Until then I would shrug it off. I put it down to a chill or perhaps I was drinking too much liquid. But after the embarrassment of that episode, I decided to make an appointment with my doctor.

On 21 March 2012 I went to see Doctor Ray Power at The Well Clinic in Dublin. I had known Ray a very long time. He was the doctor to so many of us in rugby and he also had a long association with St Mary's where my career began as a schoolboy. Ray was not happy. He actually dished out a short ticking-off because my last medical examination had been on 31 July 2006. He stressed the importance of having a thorough check-up at least every three years. To be honest I just lost track of time amid my sometimes hectic lifestyle. Although I told Ray I felt sure I had visited him in 2009, there was no excuse. It was irresponsible of me and I apologised.

After explaining my concerns and the symptoms, he did two tests. The first one I was dreading. Although I know it is common procedure, he probed through my back passage to try and detect anything abnormal inside my rectum. When he was finished, I knew by the concern on his face, along with his questions, that all was not well. He was very forthright in telling me that he had felt an abnormality; I think he termed it a 'hard and jagged edge'.

The next test was for PSA, or Prostate Specific Antigen. He was concerned that my readings were extremely high and he sent them away for analysis. When the results came back I was immediately sent to see a specialist, Doctor Hubert Gallagher. Ray had informed me that during the 2006 medical my PSA reading was normal at 2.06. However, there were now grounds for grave concerns about my health because the readings had shot through the roof to 9.79. This was serious.

I was well aware from previous medicals over the years that if everything was OK, they would tell you the general findings over the phone. So when I had to travel to the Beacon Clinic just to hear the test results, I braced myself for bad news, if not necessarily the worst. All sorts of things went through my head. What was he going to tell me? Did I have an obstruction or blockage? Did I have some sort of lumpy or collapsed flesh or abscess? Or, worst case scenario, did I have a form of cancer in my lower body?

Thinking about all the endless possibilities was driving me crazy. I had not said much to anyone close to me about my visits to the doctors, but now I felt I needed to. I turned to my eldest daughter, Lynn, as she has always been my rock of sensibility. We have a great bond. Rather than 'mere' father and daughter, we have a relationship that is more like that of close friends. When I told her everything, she insisted on accompanying me to the test results.

Doctor Gallagher – or 'Hubie' as I call him as he is also a long-standing friend and former team-mate – wasted no time. As soon as we were seated he started off by telling me that he concurred with Doctor Ray's findings. He told me there was indeed a distortion or, in everyday language, a lump developing inside. Then his words: 'You have prostate cancer' cut the atmosphere in two.

There was silence in the room. It seemed to last an eternity. I could feel the emotion building in Lynn and see the tears welling. I could sense, despite the moist in her eyes, she was trying to stay strong for me. For my own part, and from God alone knows where, I actually remained measured and calm. I just recall thinking of my favourite film from my teenage years, *Love Story*, when Jenny Cavalleri (played by Ali MacGraw) is told she has cancer. I had seen the film so many times and now I was standing in her shoes. That very moment when the doctor delivered my cancer diagnosis is what I have come to term as 'my Cavalleri moment'.

Going into the clinic that day I had butterflies in my tummy. The same feelings I had experienced throughout my playing career on big match days. These were old and trusted friends in the pit of my stomach. They would envelope me in my hotel room and in the dressing room before big games. They could be make me feel very uncomfortable on certain days, but I did not view them as unfriendly or imposters. On the contrary, they were an essential part of the artillery for big-match build-up. Unwelcome, maybe – but I was very familiar with them. And when the referee blew the whistle for kick-off, they vanished.

So when Doctor Hubie revealed that I had cancer, it bordered on relief to finally know what was actually wrong with me. Now I could get on with my plan for action. My personal game plan, so to speak. But I must admit it was a very strange feeling. It was almost the antithesis of my own personality and make-up. Normally, the smallest things would worry me and this also stretched back to my preparations in the lead-up to match-days. When it comes to stress-induced headaches I am top of the list. But when the important game got underway I was normal. Similarly, when I was told now that I had a very serious form of cancer, it put me somewhat at ease. The little things leading up worried me but the actual revelation had little effect.

I reached over to console Lynn. My heart choked a little as I saw the tears she was working so hard to hold back. That 'C' moment we all fear was having more of an impact on her than it was on me. Of course, I fully understood the enormity of the prognosis. But to me it was just another huge game ahead and, as ever, I would be up for the fight. Later that evening, at home alone, I started to take in and digest everything.

His words were emphatic: 'Prostate cancer … yours is very aggressive … it is at an advanced stage.' I could not sleep. I wanted to get a handle on it. In truth, being alone made it that little bit harder to handle. How was I going to beat this? That burning question was just the beginning of a plague of new worries. The fact I had cancer had been dished out and delivered. So, as far as I was concerned, the big atom bomb had been neutralised. But I knew full well that I had to protect my mental state from all the electrons, protons and neutrons which would batter my mental wellbeing in the coming days, weeks, months and years to worry me. The 'A-Bomb' – in this case the 'Big C' as cancer is more col- loquially known – had been taken care of by way of the doctor's deliverance. But all the unanswered questions going through my brain were the real threats to my chances of survival.

As I lay in bed that night, and over many nights that followed, I thought about how I beat the odds in times past. I thought back to how I confounded people's opinions of me on many previous occasions, on and off the playing field. And yes, there were many times, alone with my thoughts, when I asked: 'Why me?' A myriad of misty images would pass through my mind. I was floating with the ball. I was majestic. I was so fast, so full of vitality – a picture of perfect health.

Moments of near-invincibility on the pitch see Tony Ward burst forth with brown body, dark curly hair and muscular hairy legs. So many pairs of hands of all shapes and sizes reach out to try and grab him. Their efforts fall short. They fail. His extraordinary balance, derived from a natural, well-constructed centre of gravity, makes him so elusive. His trademark jinking – which involved twisting sharply in one direction and then the next before surging clear – means he is a damned elusive pimpernel. Off the pitch so many hands are outstretched looking for autographs; a phalanx of female fans are flailing their arms like pale and golden locks as they try to touch his hair and face. Numerous newspaper headlines label him 'a pin-up boy'.

On my pillow at night, or day-dreaming in my workplace, a smile breaks out on my face at the thoughts and images, but then a bout of melancholy takes over. I am back in the moment – a very real and stark moment. I am confused and I demand answers. Was that really 'me' – Tony Ward? Who am I now? It seems inconceivable that an illness can ravage, pillage and put fitness and vitality to the sword. Will I end up as just an empty shell of myself, confined to a scrap heap and left with mere memories in a scrapbook? Will I weaken and wither and waste away to the point of no return. I go cold at the very thought. My heart beats faster and together with my head spinning I feel like I am going to have a panic attack. Sometimes my heart beats so hard against my chest I feel heart palpitations may follow. Only answers will soothe all this inner torment.

A peaceful calm takes over from the storm. Again and again as I drift into sleep, I return to a powerful and recurring vision. The mighty image of my mother and suddenly I am transported back to my childhood . . . a pleasant and warm calm . . .

CHAPTER 1

WISE & WONDERFUL MOTHER

As a child, one person stood on a pedestal above all others – my mother. She was the tower of strength I looked up to, as well as being my trusted guiding light. My feelings towards her have never wavered. The feeling of love goes without saying, but gratitude is a tiny word in the colossal context of what this remarkable lady did for me.

Ireland in the 1950s was emerging from the ashes. After decades of war, at home and abroad, which followed on from the Great Famine, things began to brighten a little. Many different shades of a great rainbow were about to appear on the horizon. Yes, there was still a cloud over the country with work extremely hard to find. People had to emigrate *en masse* in search of better employment prospects. But the huge depressions of former years, typified by the scourge of TB (tuberculosis), were being eradicated.

The Swinging Sixties were just around the corner and it was against this backdrop that I entered the world. Anthony Joseph Paul Ward was the small bundle delivered in Terenure, Dublin, on 9 October 1954. I would be the only child born to my mother, June Donnelly, and my father, Danny Ward. Only recently I learned a lot more about my father and his life. Before that I knew next to nothing about him except that he was a travelling salesman.

They lived something of a Bohemian lifestyle and were frequently on the move. After living in various Dublin South addresses from Terenure to Sandymount to Rathmines, my father and mother joined the great exodus in 1951 and packed up and moved to England. Intermittently, my mother would come home to Dublin for short breaks and stay in her mother's house in Harold's Cross. When she fell pregnant with me, she made sure she was home for my birth.

We settled in Yorkshire and I fell in love with Leeds. An industrial city in the North of England, and in the beauty of the Yorkshire moors and dales, it was very similar to Dublin. In particular I liked the warmth and friendliness of the people. My long and lasting relationship with Leeds continues today through my passion for, and support of, everything Leeds United. That love affair began in 1965 and continues unabated. I got to know John Giles, an Elland Road legend and one of my sporting heroes in the 1970s. Every year I travel to Eland Road to see 'The Whites' play. And every year means *every* year.

Tragedy struck on St Patrick's Day in 1960 when my father dropped dead after suffering a massive heart attack. I was just five years old, hence the reason I cannot recall too much about him. I know he was born in England and he was a big Arsenal fan. So, in view of my father's birthplace, I was actually eligible to play for England. That thought never entered my head and at no stage did it register among my rugby desires or ambitions.

Recovering from the shock and loss of her beloved husband, my mother returned to Harold's Cross. This time she had me with her. She only intended staying a short while, but we ended up in Dublin for good. With my father gone and my grandfather, Jack Donnelly, a long-term patient in hospital, I was brought up in a house full of women. Granddad was a handy footballer, playing in midfield for St James's Gate, and was known to everyone as 'Dribbler Donnelly'.

Life was a constant financial struggle for my mother, but at least she had the support of her own mother and three sisters. Two of my aunts would subsequently get married, but my mother only had time in her life to provide for me. She worked very hard to try and give me the best life she possibly could. And while she worked, my grandmother, Elizabeth Donnelly, looked after me. Grandma Lily was my mum by day before my mother resumed parental duties at night. During the day she worked in the old Irish Hospital Sweepstakes building in Ballsbridge (opposite the front entrance to the RDS) and was employed four nights a week by Bord na gCon, the Irish Greyhound Board, at their tracks in Harold's Cross and Shelbourne Park.

All this was primarily to aid my education. After making my First Communion in St Louis National School, my mother sent me to the educational institution next door, and to the Holy Ghost Fathers of St Mary's College, Rathmines. Most of my friends went to the vocational schools in Clogher Road and Sundrive Road. Aided by my mother, I too found work with Bord na gCon. This, along with painting and decorating during the day, and running summer camps, helped fund my third level education.

At this point I would like to pay a heartfelt tribute to my mother. She made enormous sacrifices for my benefit and I can never thank her enough. I cannot speak highly enough of the Holy Ghost Fathers in St Mary's as well. Attending that school provided me with some of the happiest days of my life growing up. It was the springboard to my future sporting careers. My affection for, and pride in, 'Mary's' continues to this day. I met my best friend, Denis Hooper, former principal of Glenstal Abbey, when I entered second class in the junior school. I am proud to say Brother Denis and I are as close now as we have ever been. If it's true that you can judge a man by his friends then I stand tall.

My mother played camogie, the women's equivalent of hurling, in her youth. My father would also take her along to as many soccer, rugby and boxing competitions around the city as he could. This interest would later rub off on me. There were so many sports on offer and I delved into most of them. I participated in soccer, cricket, rugby, tennis and athletics. Being a rugby school, Donnybrook was our theatre of dreams. When we played there for the juniors (JCT) or seniors (SCT) in front of family and friends, it was the realisation of our childhood ambition. I know my mother took immense pride and interest in those early Donnybrook games.

My interest in the academic side of education was zilch. If I was not playing sport then I was training. The only thing going on in my life back then was rugby in school and soccer outside. Studying at home in the evening played second fiddle to going outside for a kick-about. My street was similar in some ways to the fictional Albert Square on the set of BBC soap *EastEnders*. Unlike that square, which has a green park as its standout feature, the sight which greeted us each morning as we walked out our doors was a statue of Our Lady, coincidentally erected in the Marian year I was born, 1954. I say 'we' because this is where my friends and I kicked our footballs. The street was our Dalymount, our Milltown, our Wembley Stadium. Indeed, just a few years ago on the other side of town, Dublin Corporation erected a statue in honour of John Giles, who grew up honing his genius and skills in Ormond Square in the inner city. There is also a plaque commemorating our greatest footballer built into a wall across the street from his former home.

With all the sports on offer, something had to give. It was impossible to play and train in them all. At the time I was soccer-mad, but rugby was compulsory in 'Mary's' so it was meant to take precedence. However, it did not stop me playing both codes constantly. This was particularly so after England won the World Cup in 1966 when I was eleven going on twelve. It was also a great time for pop and rock. I was a child of the 1960s and they were magical years; innocent but magical. The Beatles, the 'Stones, Cat Stevens, Neil Young, Rod Stewart, Bob Dylan – they were all immense, but it was the television coverage of the World Cup and *Match of the Day* that grabbed my attention.

Television aerials were twitched and twisted in all directions to get the best black and white reception from either ITV or BBC. With respect to life beyond the Naas Road, for those living in 'Jackeen land' (Dublin), soccer ruled. Being able to watch great players such as Pelé, Beckenbauer, Eusebio, Moore and Charlton in your sitting room had an amazing effect. At school, on the pitch, in training, we all talked about these players and were in awe of them. So just imagine the thrill I got on my first rugby tour in 1975 when flying from JFK airport in New York to Trinidad and Tobago, and finding among my fellow travellers Pelé and Beckenbauer.

Some of us were infected by the soccer bug which took hold and would not let go. I was chief among them. No matter how rugby tried to pin me down, soccer was a passionate fire that could not be doused. I began with OLOR (Our Lady of the

Rosary) in the Rosary Field on Harold's Cross Road as an under twelve in the under-13E Dublin and District Schoolboys League. From U-13 to U-18, I played 'A' football for Rangers A.F.C. in Bushy Park. Along with St Kevin's Boys from Whitehall, we were the top clubs in the city. The Ellenfield-based club had rivals in Home Farm, Tolka Rovers and Villa United north of the Liffey, but on Dublin's southside our Rangers ruled.

Players like Pat Byrne, Gerry Ryan, Kevin Moran and Don Givens came through the Rangers ranks. Kevin later achieved infamy at Manchester United as the first player sent off in an FA Cup final, but what a dual footballer the Drimnagh Castle lad was. I played in a very good Rangers side which produced players who went on to play for top English clubs like Donal Murphy (Coventry City) and Tommy Maguire (Liverpool). Eddie Miller (Shamrock Rovers) and Sean Byrne (St Pat's) made it to League of Ireland level, while Tommy Kenny, Mick O'Toole and Shay Smith eked out football careers in the United States and Australia. It was certainly not a bad return for just one, albeit very talented, under-age team. Sadly Sean passed away much too early after suffering with MND in 2003.

Tony Guy was central to that team evolution. As our manager at Rangers through the various age grades, I have to thank him especially for helping in the development of my love of the game. Tony was a particularly close friend of John Giles growing up, and had the same football mindset. He did not just help in the physical aspect but, on the contrary, everything I learned about the game's philosophy was instilled into me by him. Tony drilled into me the importance of putting the emphasis on skill rather than merely booting the ball up field and pressuring from the front. Football was a game that had to be played to feet. When I was fifteen, he spent an entire evening trying to convince my mother to let me go over to north London for a trial with Arsenal. Bill Derby was their Dublin-based scout and a regular caller to my Priory Road door.

Another measure of the high level to which we were playing as schoolboys can be gauged by one of our big rivals who plied his trade with St Kevin's. Liam Brady was central to their brilliant team and became a good schoolboy friend. That side included outstanding underage players like Pat Daly, Terry Wyckham, Jimmy Dunne, Clive Beegan and Peter Ferrari, to name but a few. We played many times against each other and inevitably we met in the DDSL finals. It is hard to remember how many were won or lost. I think it was evenly split, but they won the big one at U-15, the Evans Cup. By the time we reached U-18 level, with Brady now in north London, we had passed them out.

In 1969, when I was fifteen, I set myself the target of making it to the Irish international underage squads. Back then there were two Republic of Ireland underage sides: one at U-15 (schoolboy) and the other U-18 (youth). To achieve this I had to come successfully through a trials process. The December trials were held in Glasnevin's Virginians Ground and subsequently Richmond Park. It may sound very immature now, and even vain, but one of the main reasons for my wanting to make it was to get my name in the papers. More to the point, I not only wished to see my name in the sports pages but I wanted my club name in brackets after it. One particular day, I remember rushing into a shop to see if my name was printed in the early editions of an evening newspaper. Sure enough there it was: 'Tony Ward (Rangers)'. I felt so proud. To my mind this was the ultimate proof that I had made it. Your name in the newspaper was not just a reward for having come through trials, it rubber-stamped everything. It almost classified you as being that little bit more 'special'. The innocence of it now!

I made my debut against Northern Ireland in an away game at Shamrock Park in Portadown. Liam Brady and I manned the left wing with Liam at inside left wearing number ten and me on the outside wearing the number eleven shirt. We drew 2–2. What I remember most about that day was how disappointed and angry Liam became afterwards. Tony O'Connell, the former Shamrock Rovers winger, was our manager and he rated each player out of ten, much as you see today in newspaper match reports. He gave Liam a 'four' which meant 'very poor'. In the aftermath of that analysis, whether coincidental or not, Liam was dropped from our next game, away against England at Sheffield United's Bramall Lane ground in March 1970. 'Chippy' had the last laugh as we were hammered 11–0.

There were valid excuses for the woeful performance. We endured a rough ferry crossing from Dublin and had just a few hours' catch-up sleep because we were delayed along the way by heavy snow storms. This resulted in the game being switched at the last minute from Hillsborough (Sheffield Wednesday's ground) to Bramall Lane. We did not arrive in the Steel City until around 3.30 p.m. with kick-off at 7.30. There were a couple of star players for England that night with Steve Powell going on to play for Derby County and Brian Hornsby ending up at Arsenal. My last cap that season was against Wales at Flower Lodge, Cork, where Liam was again omitted. We lost 2–1 and the match was dominated by a tiny Welsh player who would later go on to great things with various English clubs. Brian Flynn was also capped many times by Wales at senior level.

In September 1989 I bumped into Liam by chance at Leeds–Bradford Airport. I was returning home from playing an exhibition in the north of England while Liam was joining up with the Irish squad to play West Germany in Dublin, having played for West Ham at Boothferry Park, Hull, the same afternoon. In the event, manager Jack Charlton substituted Liam in that 1–1 draw and it turned out to be his last international appearance. We both had time to spare while waiting for our flight, and in the course of a great chat, a fascinating realisation dawned on both of us. Liam could not recollect much about some of his biggest and most famous moments. Neither could I. However, when discussing our schoolboy soccer days together, we remembered every incident in minute detail. We could recall many of the players we played with, and against, and we wondered what they went on to achieve and where they were. We remembered matches played and scores. It was mind-boggling really, but what amazed me was the fact that Liam still had that bone of contention about being dropped following the Northern Ireland game. But even more, he never forgave nor forgot Tony O'Connell for that 'four' rating.

I started to come to the attention of a number of scouts and influential people on the Dublin & District soccer circuit. The hawks were hovering. How I wish they had pounced. In 1970 Arsenal and Manchester United (Billy Behan was their Dublin-based chief scout) made approaches. Tony Guy still tried to convince my mother, but before things got out of hand she gave a very firm 'No'. I would not be allowed to leave for England on the ferry and that was final. Although I think I hated her for a short while after for denying me this chance, I did not fully understand or appreciate her wanting a degree of security for me. She wanted me to find a steady job or go on to third level education. I managed to do this during school holidays in my final two years (fifth and sixth year) when I found work with PMPA, who were involved in car insurance.

It was here that I met and worked with Eamonn Coghlan, who would later go on to become one of Ireland's all-time great athletes. Eamonn and I worked in an office in Wolfe Tone Street where we did not find the work very stimulating. Our day consisted of 'filing'. A phone call or message would come from someone in the office looking for a file on a client and their insurance or claims. Files had to be extracted from a room choc-full of them and then put back properly by the end of the day. It was boring work but it helped me save up to buy a Yamaha motorbike which my mother was not best pleased about. Perhaps the biggest thrill I had was when Irish singing legend Dickie Rock came to the office one day to renew the insurance on his Rolls-Royce.

Just a few years later I was glued to my television set as Eamonn competed in the 1,500 metres at the 1976 Olympic Games in Montreal. I was screaming for him as he went so close to winning the bronze, finishing just outside the medals in fourth position. We always knew he was talented. In fact, PMPA had an annual fête in Phoenix Park, but Eamonn was barred from participating in any of the races because of his ability. It was fantastic to see him finally win a deserved gold medal for Ireland in the 5,000 metres at the 1983 World Championships in Helsinki.

After completing my Leaving Certificate, my only ambition was to play soccer professionally. But all of my obsessions with training, playing sport and dreaming about trials impacted heavily upon my education. An academic I was not. My school-leaving qualifications enabled me to find standard clerical employment. I began working as an insurance clerk with the NEM (National Employers' Mutual) in South Leinster Street, but again the work was monotonous and not for me. Looking outside the office window to see students kicking a ball around in College Park depressed me. They were doing what I wanted to do, but I was stuck in an office from nine to five. I began to worry that I wouldn't find my true direction in life, on or off the pitch.

Then, out of the blue one day, divine intervention came my way courtesy of a man of the cloth. A priest who had hurt me in the past had managed to sow a seed in my soul. His name was Father David D'Arcy C.S.Sp. When I was first selected for the St Mary's U-13 team to play Willow Park, the preparatory school for Blackrock College, he was the coach. I was very small in height and build and I was picked out of position on the wing. I will never forget my opposite number that day. Joe Rekab was black and huge. I was tiny, so it was a real David versus Goliath affair on the wing. I got nowhere near him when half-heartedly trying to tackle him. In the event he ran in so many tries that I lost count. Father D'Arcy was not very happy with my performance. In fact he was livid. We called him 'Noddy' as he twitched and nodded quite a lot when he became excited or agitated. At the half-time break he cut into me with a remark I have never forgotten: 'Where is your party dress, Ward?'

He and I have become friends down the subsequent years, and he had a very formative influence on my career, but that jibe really hurt. It hurt me so much that it taught me a valuable lesson. To this day, I have never made a disparaging or hurtful remark to any pupil I have taught or coached. If I have nothing positive to say, I do not say anything. It is enough for my young players to know that I am disappointed post-match. It is always best to let the heat evaporate first. Then, when we get back to training the following day, we can iron out the problems or mistakes. I have always felt that I am a person who is much more tolerant of young people and youth culture.

In my final year at Mary's, we lost to High School in the Cup semi-final. John Robbie scored the winning try in the Wanderers' corner at Lansdowne and we were shattered.

Until then we had been unbeaten all season and were desperate to win the Cup. I failed to get into the Leinster schoolboy rugby team that year with Ian Burns (who passed away suddenly this year) picked ahead of me. Instead I had to be content with a place on the substitutes' bench with Robbie alongside.

I remember long lectures from Father Walter 'Wally' Kennedy on Fridays at school the day before Five Nations internationals. Even though he was addressing all the rugby players, he looked at me as he told us to 'watch how Gibson deals with problem situations'. From day one, Father Kennedy and Father D'Arcy saw me as an out-half and only on rare occasions up to JCT was I switched to the wing. Even though I made mistakes they had a lot of faith in me.

But Father D'Arcy kept saying something to me that had nothing to do with rugby. Before the penny dropped, his words had just been smothered away in a hazy and cloudy mind. Great advice was stifled in a stuffy South Leinster Street office. One day, from nowhere, his voice echoed through the thick grey misty matter in my head and helped me cut through the gloom and see quite clearly a path laid out in front of me with the words: 'Why don't you become a PE teacher?' I did not remain with NEM much longer. I applied to join a course at the National College of Physical Education in Limerick. I was successful. It would turn out to be the most important decision I made in my life. I would never look back.

CHAPTER 2

LIMERICK, MY LADY

Following my mother's refusal to allow me to attend soccer trials in England, a few years later I received a beautiful second prize. In 1973, not long out of school, Liam Tuohy asked me to sign for Shamrock Rovers. I did not have to think twice as I was a mad Rovers fan. In the late 1960s and early 1970s I went to most of their home games in Milltown. Back then the League of Ireland was huge and Rovers were the best team. I even travelled to away games and to towns like Drogheda and Dundalk. A few days after meeting 'the Rasher', as the legendary manager was known, and thinking over what he had to offer, I sat in the plush Burlington Hotel with Tony Guy and discussed terms with their chairman, Louis Kilcoyne. I felt like a king and so I signed as a part-time professional with 'The Hoops'. By putting on the famous green and white jersey, another major ambition of mine had been realised. It really was a dream come true. So, too, was my signing-on fee of £750! That was quite a lot of money back in the 1970s and a huge lump sum for a teenager like me. The money was enough to pay for my first year in college, which my mother could not afford.

After my time at St Mary's, where rugby was compulsory and soccer frowned upon, I was now operating the reverse scenario: soccer was first, ahead of rugby. Although I could have continued with my rugby on a sporadic basis I made the conscious decision from 1973–74 to give soccer my all. I did play one game that season for the St Mary's RFC U-19s in the McCorry Cup against UCD at Fortfield Road. We lost.

Soccer in those years was termed 'semi-professional' as the vast majority of players also had jobs on the side from which to make a living. I was now a semi-pro soccer player while also studying and playing rugby on the side. When I began my career with Rovers, I went straight into the first-team squad. Indeed, my first involvement was in a pre-season friendly against Glasgow Celtic who had a side still including some of the European Cup-winning Lisbon Lions from 1967. That was a huge thrill, but by the start of the following season, although still a teenager, I was pretty well-established in what could be best described as a transitional period at Milltown.

Playing for Shamrock Rovers will always be a huge highlight in my sporting career. Getting to know Liam Tuohy, a fantastic tactician who went on to manage Ireland, and just to be one of his players, was a privilege. But there was also another very special man I will never forget. The great Billy Lord really was 'Mr Milltown'. He was a very learned man and was rarely seen without a trademark fag in his mouth. On one occasion he said something to me which I have never forgotten, and I try to practise in my everyday life: 'Remember, Tony, we eat to live, not live to eat.'

In my first year at college in Limerick, I tried to continue playing with Rovers and I did so up to early 1975. However, away matches, which were played on a Sunday in far-flung grounds like Ballybofey or Kilcohan Park, made college life nigh on impossible. Very often I would make it back to the Plassey campus, at best, by midday on Monday. But my attendance at lectures suffered in the process. It was a recipe for disaster and something eventually had to give. My lecturer in Biomechanics and Anatomy was Tony Lanaway. He was British with a very strong English accent and he played with the famous Munster club, Garryowen. He was affectionately named Paddy Lanahoe, but naturally everyone in the first year addressed him as Mr Lanaway and he ruled with an iron fist. He gave rugby coaching sessions and must have felt that, as a soccer player, I might have something to offer. That is because Mr Lanaway had tipped off Garryowen and spoken to Shay Deering about me. Shay knew me from my days in St Mary's as I had been in the same class as his twin brothers Kevin and David.

The Garryowen team trained at the college two nights a week. One day I was approached by Shay, Mr Lanaway and Garryowen's captain that season, Des Quaid. They asked me to play the following weekend for the Garryowen second team against Birr. That was because Johnny Moroney, the regular Garryowen out-half, had broken his leg in the Munster League final which left the club a bit of a quandary going into the all-important Cup campaign. We had a typical student's party on the Saturday night so I was still in bed next morning when team manager Tommy O'Brien came to collect me for the game. Suffice to say that on this occasion I was not very well prepared. My one vivid memory of the game is of Paddy Lanahoe, who was in the second row that day, getting the ball in his hand and making a run. I ran alongside him looking for a pass and instinctively shouted at him: 'Mr Lanaway, Mr Lanaway' because I felt it was the natural, respectful way to address one of our lecturers. He was clearly so embarrassed that he almost stopped his run. Later he told me, in the most emphatic way, that I was to call him either 'Tony' or 'Paddy' on the field of play and around Dooradoyle, but certainly not 'Mr Lanaway'.

A few years later he returned to Birmingham where he lectured in PE. When I eventually went on to win my first cap for Ireland, one of the first congratulatory notes I received was from him. It read simply: 'Remember, Tony, girls love international out-halves' hips!' This kind gesture meant so much as he had been such an influence on me during his time at NCPE and Garryowen. He trained the club when I was in the first year and he said it would be a good experience for me to take some of the training sessions myself. I received modest money for overseeing those training sessions which, of course, was his real motive for involving me. That game against Birr turned out to be my only appearance below first-team level until I played my very last game in 1991 for the Greystones' second team.

It was an unusual path as I missed out on the normal apprenticeship most players serve before making it to the first team. This was thanks to my involvement in soccer. In the event, I hit twenty-nine points in a 58–4 win over Birr. On the strength of that I was selected on the senior side to play Wanderers at the home of Irish rugby, Lansdowne Road, the following week. The night before the game I played a full game for Rovers against Home Farm at Tolka Park. It could not continue like this.

The match against Wanderers was on at the same time as the Wales versus Ireland game in Cardiff. Therefore we only had a small scattering of spectators watching our efforts. At the same time the clubhouse was bulging. I loved the whole sense of occasion and afterwards I can recall our scrum-half Liam Hall getting up on the table and leading a singing session through the never-ending chorus of 'Any dream will do'. I remember that feeling of kinship to the point that I decided: 'This is the game for me.' That weekend signalled the beginning of the end for soccer as my first love and the start of my rugby career in earnest. However, I never gave up on soccer, even though rugby became my number one sport. Throughout my career I would always regret that the rugby and soccer seasons coincided. It meant that I could only really play soccer for a few months of the year, either before or after the rugby season. Had they run at different times I would definitely have combined both.

A week after the Wanderers game, I was selected for my first Munster Senior Cup game when I lined out for the Light Blues (Garryowen) against Sunday's Well in Cork. I had never previously heard of the 'Well' as Munster rugby was a new experience for me. I was only familiar with playing Leinster schools rugby. The passion and commitment of the players in Munster will always remain with me. It was unbelievable. In many ways it was a culture shock. There were boots and fists flying all over the place! I was shocked at the time, but I learned subsequently that this was typical Cup rugby down south. The referee was a Limerick-based 'Dub', Martin Walsh, and that helped my confidence and my play. He had a very strong Dublin accent and I like to think he took care of me that day.

In the semi-final we beat Old Crescent and the reward was a place in the final against Cork Constitution, who had already taken the League title a couple of months before. The match would live up to everything a Munster final should entail. It was tough and bruising. After half an hour 'Con', as they are known, took the lead through a try from Dave Meagher. But crucially for us it was not converted. Just before half-time, I kicked a penalty from the left touchline, and a few minutes into the second half I landed another. Surprisingly, that is how it finished because, despite Barry McGann shaving the posts with an attempted drop goal at the Well end of Musgrave Park, Garryowen held out to win 6–4.

In my three Cup encounters during that 1974–75 season I tallied twenty-three points, but much more important statistics were achieved that day. For starters, it was the first time since 1940 that a Limerick team had won the Cup away in Cork. It was also the first time we had beaten Cork Con since 1932. Furthermore, Garryowen were now the kingpins in the south as it was the first time since 1920 that we had won the Cup in successive seasons. We only lost two games all year and one of those was a friendly. In that respect, I will always be deeply grateful to my club team-mates. When I played my first game with them I only received my opportunity because John Moroney, who had been a great personality and dominant figure in the club, was cut down with a career-ending leg injury. Playing alongside guys like Larry Moloney, Seamus Dennison, Liam Hall, Des Quaid, Frank Hogan, Shay Deering and all the others could only inspire great confidence in any player. Quite simply, that team was probably the greatest Garryowen team of all time. I came into a side comprising players with outstanding ability and it was impossible not to learn from them. For instance, to have Liam Hall as your scrum-half was a wonderful bonus. I was blessed. Back then, many at the club and in Limerick rated him as the best scrum-half in Ireland. He was peerless at relieving the pressure on his out-half as he had a precise pass. He was also very fast on the break, and boy could he boss his pack.

Then there was the highly experienced Seamus Dennison. He gave me so much confidence by insisting that as out-half it was my duty to always call the shots. Initially I tended to turn to him to ask his opinion when I was in doubt. But he would forever drill into me that I was to make up my own mind. There was also great back-up for a relatively inexperienced player like myself. The traditions of the club had a lot to do with it, as well as the great players who were always available to listen and offer advice.

Shay Deering had a very special place in my heart. I first got to know 'The Deero' as a starry-eyed schoolboy at St Mary's in 1966. Shay was in the sixth year and was captain of the school's cup-winning side. As mentioned earlier, his twin brothers David and Kevin were in my first-year class when Deero, Johnny Moloney, Billy Hooper et al. won the cup. When we were in the sixth year I got word from the twins one day that their parents were away over Christmas. So they held a party at their home in Dundrum. Shay was in UCD at the time but he came in late that night and we managed to get him to sing 'My Brother Sylvest'. He was a man of many talents as he proved with his stirring rendition of that famous song. He won eight caps for Ireland between 1974 and 1978 and topped off a great career by captaining Ireland in his last game against the All Blacks, a match in which I am proud to say I was a part.

He won Leinster and Munster Cup medals and was as brave as a lion on the field and then off it when he battled terminal illness. In losing his battle for life, he displayed fighting qualities right to the end, which was only to be expected of a player's player. Whenever I have been asked down the years who was my number one, all-time hero in either sporting code, I have consistently stated it was, and is, Shay Deering. Even now, whenever I hear the song 'Wind Beneath My Wings', and specifically the line 'Did you ever know that you're my hero?', the late and great Seamus Deering springs immediately to mind.

A couple of days after our Munster Cup win a funny thing happened. I was queuing for coffee in the college canteen when I heard a voice behind me inquiring: 'What have you been up to in my absence?' It was the Dublin Gaelic footballer Brian Mullins, who was a very popular figure in our college back then. He had been away in the United States on the victorious All-Stars Tour after helping Dublin win the All-Ireland title. Our chat continued and then it transpired that on his flight home he had noticed my picture in a newspaper. He then quipped: 'How the fuck did you win the *Irish Independent* Sport Star of the Week award after only ever playing three games!' We laughed loudly, and even louder when he retorted: 'Jesus Christ, you had not even started playing rugby with Garryowen before I left for America, and then I come back a couple of weeks later and you are a big star!'

Apart from being a great and legendary footballer, Brian had a big interest in rugby and he went on to play for Dublin rugby club Clontarf. He also won a McCorry Cup medal with Black-rock and was a good cricketer, too. He is now Director of Sport at UCD. There was a real 'who's who' of great Gaelic footballers around the college back then. There were great Kerry players like Pat Spillane, Ogie Moran, Mick Spillane and Jimmy Deni-han, as well as Brian Talty and Johnny Tobin of Galway, and another Dub, Fran Ryder, to name but a few. Gaelic football is a sport I would love to have played. I regret I did not get the opportunity. If I had arrived in Limerick with less of a sports portfolio to my name I probably would have tried. But I was steeped in rugby and playing for Shamrock Rovers.

I really did not appreciate at the time the huge significance and effect that our Cup win had on the club and with the general public. Years later I realised that winning this competition is the ambition of every single rugby player in that proud prov-ince. A certain Ronan John Ross O'Gara never managed to taste Senior Cup success in his time with Cork Constitution as well as in his sole season at University College Cork. He was in good company when you think of some of the great players who never won it. People like Tom Clifford, Jim Buckley and Phil O'Callaghan never won it, either. Then you begin to appreciate the importance of it. It was all new to me, and even today players from outside the province cannot appreciate the passion Munster rugby still arouses.

The Munster supporters are so passionate and fanatical as we know from their recent successes. After helping Garryowen to the semi-final win over Old Crescent, Limerick City showed its pride and I was amazed by what I saw. I remember taking a turn off William Street and a couple of Corporation workers who were surveying the road at the back of the Round House pub shouted at me: 'All the best in the Cup final, Wardy.' As I was almost a complete unknown in the city, and a newcomer at the club, I found the experience very moving, but also very surreal and strange. This would rarely, if ever, have happened in Dublin. Similarly, there was an extension being constructed at the college and many of the workers knew so much about rugby and what was happening. They all stopped to wish me luck in games and to ask how I was. I also recall O'Shaughnessy's Florists near the Franciscan church with a full window display of flowers in Garryowen's white and blue. This was replicated almost everywhere with colours pinned to the masts in shops like Nestors and O'Mahony's. Again, and I speak from experience of both places and people, Dublin folk would find this strange and may think I exaggerate somewhat. But this is the way of things in that daft, but beautiful, rugby-mad city of Limerick.

A month after our victory, we were playing in the Centenary Club Championship at Thomond Park. I managed nineteen points (two tries, four conversions and a drop goal) in our 35–14 win over Galwegians. Against Leinster champions St

Mary's in the final, I kicked our points in a 9–9 draw. But Mary's took the Bateman Cup after extra time on the basis of having scored the only try of the match. Current IRFU treasurer and former Ireland captain Tom Grace scored their winner against us that day.

Going back to Brian Mullins's quips about me getting into the Garryowen side so quickly, I feel there were several reasons for that. The first and most obvious was that I had played rugby in Dublin from a very young age. Soccer helped my rugby immensely, my footwork especially. I always had a natural jink which became a trademark of mine during my rugby career. Unquestionably though, the very good facilities and personnel provided by Thomond College (former NCPE and now UL), was the real reason. It provided an unequalled environment for a sports person. There was top advice on training and coaching, videotape facilities and, in short, everything was available to me.

There were also some outstanding lecturers who were of invaluable help and assistance. One of the best was P.J. Smyth, who was perhaps the biggest influence in my time there. I know one of my student house mates, Eddie O'Sullivan, feels exactly the same. On my very first day at the college, I was in the queue for registration and an ID card. Also in the queue was P.J. and it turned out to be his first day lecturing. It says a lot about the common bond the oval ball can generate between people that we began talking about all things rugby. We became firm friends from day one. In the course of our conversation I learned that he was a former captain of Bective. P.J. had a great passion for the game and was a fitness fanatic. His own rugby knowledge is immense and his analysis of the game – and of our performances – was very sharp. I benefited so much from his expertise in PE. Things like how your body functions, what you can expect and demand of it, how to develop special skills and how to train for particular sports and particular occasions.

He placed a great emphasis on 'specificity'. That is learning to play in a specific way for a specific occasion. For instance, training and playing on a mucky pitch was of little advantage when it came to playing on a smooth surface like Lansdowne Road. Consequently, to prepare for those games I trained on a smooth surface in college. I also did a lot of my running with ball in hand. It is simply not good enough to develop speed and stamina without a ball. You have to get used to carrying that ball. This consideration would also apply to 'hurlers'. They should not train without timber in their hands even when they are just doing sprint exercises.

This concept was not just confined to Limerick. I remember when Doctor Tony O'Neill was in charge of training at Shamrock Rovers, we did all our training with the ball. I also learned how to plan and carry out all my training in advance of a game. In the week before a big match I would do a lot of hard, physical training. But this would be followed by honing my sharpness and practising kicking a lot. Then after the actual match, P.J. would discuss my performance with me in depth. His analysis was so astute. This was particularly important since most of the comments I received post-match were generally congratulatory from supporters. That was very nice but in the grand scheme of things not very helpful. Often I knew instinctively after a match what mistakes I had made or what I failed to do right. That is when it was crucial for someone else to come in and confirm that for me, which P.J. did.

In conditioning terms I will never forget his 300-metre runs and cross-field sprints behind the goal line, followed by short breaks which never seemed long enough. I was also lucky in that I trained two nights a week with the Limerick soccer team

(Mondays and Wednesdays) and two nights with Garryowen (Tuesdays and Thursdays). On Fridays, before the match on Saturday, I would work solely on my kicking. Even on Sunday there was no rest. I often had a squad session then, which meant that in the entire season I togged out almost every day.

I know we were amateur compared to today's ultra-professional set-ups, but in terms of attitude and commitment we were every bit the same if not more professional. P.J., in his capacity as a lecturer in psychology, also worked on the attitudinal side of my game. This was of great benefit to me at international level. Before a big game we went through a negative mental rehearsal which meant that, in my mind, I considered everything that could possibly go wrong. I would get into such a mental state beforehand that I was actually used to real-time mistakes and failure when the match was in progress. The benefit was that if I made an error early on in the game, it would not affect me. One sign of a great or world-class player is that they do not allow any negativity or mistakes to impact on the rest of their game. A good example is the goal-kicker who isolates goal-kicking to just that.

Another aspect largely overlooked in rugby is the importance of two-footed players. They always say that to be able to use both your feet in soccer is an invaluable asset. Well, I became reasonably adept with both feet through playing soccer and this was of enormous benefit when it came to playing with the oval ball. All players favour a particular leg and I prefer kicking with my right. But my left helped me out of many tight corners as well. Indeed one of my most memorable drop goals came off the left peg for the Lions against the Springboks in the first Test in Newlands in 1980.

Playing soccer from an early age in kick-abouts in the street helped my rugby goal-kicking. Incidentally I always hated the tag 'goalscoring machine'. It was as though I was incapable of doing anything else in rugby. The thing about goal-kicking is that it really influences the rest of your game. The more successful you are at kicking for goal on the day, the more it gives you a general confidence-boost. Conversely, if you are having a bad day at the office and your kicking is a little off, it can have a detrimental effect on the rest of your game. As in most sports, confidence breeds confidence.

Many players view the Inter-Provincial Championships or Inter-Pros as a stepping stone to the national team. But the vast majority of Munster players felt very proud just to wear the red, if nothing else. It was an end in itself. Often when representing Garryowen in Munster senior games you would be dealing with opposing supporters and players who could be very nasty and hostile towards you. But the very same people would cheer unconditionally when you represented Munster! I cherish those memories. I recall a League game against Young Munster in Greenfields. It was very early on in the game when I heard a shout go up from the crowd: 'Get the film star.' The comment just typified the fiery passion of the Munster supporters. That very raw passion has endured to this day, by way of the province's awe-inspiring and huge travelling support right across Europe.

So everything I learned in college from lecturers, and the invaluable advice and fitness practices drilled into me by the coaches at Garryowen, gave me a great grounding. I was blessed and it would stand me in good stead for the future.

CHAPTER 3

'SLASH DONKEY – SLASH CART'

I really had to pinch myself when I was called into the Munster side to face the touring Australians on 13 January 1976. Everything was happening so fast. It seemed like only yesterday I had been sitting in a small Dublin office feeling disillusioned because I had no idea what direction my life or career was taking. The sudden transformation was surreal.

Here I was in third level education down in Limerick, busy with a second year of assignments and exams, playing for Garryowen and now about to put on the famous red shirt of Munster worn by so many legends before me. For instance, I would be lining out with a Munster side who contained one survivor from the team who beat Australia in 1967. Tighthead prop Phil O'Callaghan was part of that illustrious side who were the first Irish province to beat one of the big touring nations. Another member of that team, Tom Kiernan, who had scored eight points in Munster's 11–8 win, was now our coach. He had made the ultimate decision to call me up after Barry McGann suffered a nasty thigh injury and failed a late fitness test.

When I ran on to the Musgrave Park pitch, I could not believe the atmosphere. My heart was in my mouth as I left the dressing room. It was a huge occasion against top-class international opposition and, of course, I was very nervous. But then the 'Munster roar' which greeted our appearance dispelled any negative thoughts or feelings. Our support was inspiring and we could not have responded better.

We began in great fashion. The Aussies were penalised from the first lineout and I made a sweet connection from close to the right touchline only two minutes in. I added a second penalty on twenty minutes and just before the break I nailed a drop goal from forty yards. That successful attempt came about thanks to Larry Moloney's great run down the right wing. However, all of our good work was cancelled out by the Australian full-back Paul MacLean who slotted over three penalties. With both sides tied at 9–9 in the thirty-fourth minute of the second half, Australia scored a try through Paul Weatherstone, which MacLean converted. It was very tough on us, not least because we were convinced there had been a forward pass in the build-up.

Then, when all seemed lost, Shay Deering scored a try for us five minutes into injury time. The crowd went berserk and there was a temporary pitch invasion. This hindered my concentration somewhat as I had a conversion attempt to draw the game. When everything settled down, all eyes were focused on me. The huge roar was now replaced by a stone cold silence. I could feel my body freeze up with the mountain of pressure forced down on my shoulders by a passionate crowd. I could catch glimpses of the mustard-coloured jerseys of Aussie players in front of me and I knew they were praying for me to miss. In moments like those you wish that your eardrums could be muffled, that your vision can just have a square with very wide white posts, that everything will be just the same as it was in the few minutes before. But sport, as life, is never that easy. Obstacles abound. Here I was – a novice with no experience at this level – suddenly cast into the spotlight of having the final say. But if you give anyone this chance, they will not turn away. We have a clan to die for.

In normal circumstances the kick would not have been difficult. On any practice day I would land nine out of ten between the posts. It was ten metres to the right on the twenty-five-metre line. On this occasion, my kick was hooked and it tailed wide.

Even after that miss we could have snatched victory. The English referee Peter Hughes played on into the fifty-second minute of the half. Some say he felt guilty about allowing the controversial Australian try. We kept throwing everything at them and with one last-gasp attack, Ginger McLoughlin burst forward, but his overhead pass to Pat Whelan was obviously forward. The ref blew up and it was over. We lost 15–13. It was a cruel end to what had been a stirring performance. Players from both sides patted me on the back to commiserate afterwards, but I was crestfallen. It took me quite a few days to get over it, but time heals.

I have two other memories from my first Munster game. The non-Cork players stayed at the Silver Springs Hotel, and because I was in digs and in college the hotel and the food seemed out of this world. It was sheer bliss compared to the canteen back in Castletroy. The other memory was the crowd. When I landed that drop goal the roar was so loud that even now I can still hear it. Of course, I would play in front of many bigger crowds in subsequent years, but because it was my first experience of the big time, it was something I will never forget. It was so raw, so pure, so special.

There was little time to feel sorry for myself, though. It was back to studying, and back to training and playing. But I also knew I could not continue travelling to Dublin every weekend. So I asked Shamrock Rovers to place me on the transfer list. They did just that and their asking price was £500! They were chancing their arm. No transfer ever materialised. It was after all semi-professional and as long as I was able to keep everyone happy then that seemed to suffice. Occasionally I would help out Rovers, and the new manager at Glenmalure, Sean Thomas, was extremely accommodating in that regard.

My first match with Munster may have ended in bitter disappointment, but by the end of my first year I could feel very satisfied. I ended up beating all previous Munster scoring records and accumulating 227 points. The second season began in similar fashion when I scored twenty-seven points in a 46–9 win for Garryowen over UCC in the Mardyke. The tally included three tries and surpassed the twenty-six points Barry McGann scored for Munster against Cheshire in 1971.

That thumping win was all the more remarkable as it was played during the weekend of the October Bank Holiday when I was not in the best shape. My preparations were not ideal after I went to a Halloween party in Dublin the night before. Having had a pint or two more that I should, I was none too sharp when lining out the next day. In the first minute UCC scored a try when Danny Buckley ran the length of the field. I remember thinking: 'This is going to be a nightmare.' Then, for some unknown reason, I went on to have an inspired match. I could do no wrong. To score three tries was particularly satisfying. Anyone who had seen me the night before would not have believed it.

That was one of the very last occasions when I let my professionalism slip. I vowed never to get into that state again.

Despite my stirring performance there was no moral. I knew full well that alcohol and late nights were detrimental and counter-productive to top performance. I could not drink too much. It was as simple as that. When I found myself in situations at celebratory events or get-togethers where alcohol was being consumed, I would get a hangover while I was drinking, not just afterwards. It was my body's way of telling me that alcohol was a no-no. So I nipped it in the bud quite quickly. That is not to say that I do not drink. I love a drink. But I emphasise 'a' drink and there is nothing quite like a cold pint or glass of wine to quench the thirst.

My form was good and regrettably I deposed Barry McGann from the Munster team. One might have thought I would be delighted to be selected almost automatically, but it gave me no pleasure whatsoever to see B.J. dropped. Following an indifferent display from McGann in the opening inter-provincial against Leinster in Dublin, he was left out and I was called up for the second game in Cork against Connacht. I was one of seven changes, two of them positional. Irrespective of whether we met at training or before games, Barry was always available to give me advice and he often sought me out to do just that. I will always be grateful for his invaluable insight into rugby and sport in general.

Another Leesider I would mention is Des Barry. He was Munster's head coach during my second season there. He was a very tough coach but a thorough gentleman. Sadly he is no longer with us. But I can still hear his rallying cry to all of us in the Munster dressing room before we went out on the pitch for almost every game: 'Slash Donkey – Slash Cart!'

We beat Connacht 13–6 and I had a fairly good game. I kicked one long-range penalty and I was proving troublesome for Connacht to deal with all around the pitch. I opened the scoring with a fifty-yard penalty and closed the scoring by converting Greg Barrett's try. The reason I mention that game, and the significance of it, is that my display caught the attention of selectors. It was rumoured that I was at the head of the queue for the out-half position for the upcoming Ireland B international away to France. A short while later came confirmation via a telegram from the IRFU in Dublin. Dated 29 November 1976, and sent to 'A.J.P. Ward Esquire' at my mother's home in Priory Road, Harold's Cross, Dublin 6, it read:

Dear Sir,

I have pleasure in advising you that you have been selected to play for Ireland 'B' v France 'B' at Dijon on Saturday, 4 December 1976 and shall be glad to receive your acceptance by return post.

If following acceptance you find that through injury or illness there is the slightest doubt about your fitness kindly advise Secretary by phone without delay.

Your jersey will be supplied and must be returned immediately at end of the game.

Headquarters: Hotel Geneve, Dijon.

The I.R.F.U. provides transportation and provides hotel expenses covering meals only. (Gratuities, telegrams, phone calls, etc of a personal nature must not be charged to the I.R.F.U.)

Please see that your passport is in order and bring your dinner jacket.

Each travelling player or reserve should provide himself with training togs, clean white shorts, towels and soap and see that boots are in good playable condition.

Yours truly,

R. Fitzgerald (Treasurer and Secretary)

On Saturday, 4 December 1976, I pulled on the green jersey of Ireland for the first time. All right, it was not a full international, and I did not receive a cap, but nevertheless I was so proud, especially with all the messages, letters and telegrams of congratulations. In the event, my first international turned into a bit of a nightmare. We were comprehensively beaten 16–3. I scored our penalty from close-in after fifteen minutes.

Leading up to the game, I received a number of good luck messages which was a new experience for me. It was really quite astonishing the amount of correspondence I received all through my playing years. The vast majority came from the Garryowen and Greystones clubs with whom I played the bulk of my career. Messages throughout my playing days were not just confined to my winning honours with Munster, Leinster, Ireland or the Lions but for achievements of any distinction. With regard to milestones I achieved with Munster or Ireland, I lost count of the number of 'official' presentations Garryowen acknowledged and made to me over the years. While my playing time at Templeville was all too brief, priests and teachers at St Mary's school sent on so many messages of goodwill that meant as much then as they still do now. St Mary's Rugby Club awarded me honorary life membership in the club's centenary year in 2000. I am enormously proud of this and the honour was mainly due to the endeavours of Paul Dean in his year as president. He was aided and abetted by the inimitable Dermot 'D' O'Brien.

I learned a big lesson that day in Dijon about the warm-up for a big game. Roly Meates was the coach and Robbie McGrath the captain and naturally it was their job to psyche us up. Forwards need to be high on adrenaline and fully pumped as they are involved in physical confrontation right from the kick-off. The requirements of the backs, however, are of a much finer quality. They can become tetchy if too wound up or overly tense. We went through a really tough and intense warm-up before going out for the official team photograph. Bear in mind rugby teams only prepared in the dressing room back then. When we came back in from the Dijon chill, the coaches did their best to get us all worked up again. This meant that when we went back on the pitch to start we had already experienced the extremes of hot and cold. It was a sobering lesson very early in my career. Today's professional generation of fine-tuned athletes experience no such problems. From a personal viewpoint, this was a very uncomfortable scenario. I vowed that I would never become party to such a situation again. Of course, I participated in warm-ups in future years like the rest of the players. But never again in such a frenzied way as Dijon.

A week after the French loss, I lined out for the last of the inter-provincial matches when Munster faced Ulster in Limerick. The press billed the game as being between two out-halves pitting their wits against each other. On the Ulster side was the wily Mike Gibson and they trumpeted me as the jinking young pretender from Munster. In the event, it was a tough and brutal encounter. It boiled over on several occasions and ended in controversy when, late in the game, the referee sent off our hooker, the Irish international, Pat Whelan. It was a very harsh decision and also very unfortunate for us because the scores were locked 24–24 at the time. It was reported that Pat was sent off for an 'off-the-ball incident', but I think this hid the real reason. Many people felt that it was payback time for Pat for an incident in an earlier game which went unpunished.

That incident took away the gloss from what was a glowing, sparkling game. There were many vintage performances. The old fox Gibson did not disappoint. He scored twenty points and I also hit twenty by way of six penalties and a conversion. When everybody was talking about the two of us taking centre stage, it was actually another back who was the unlikely hero that day. The sending-off duly put us on the back foot and we conceded a penalty. Frank Wilson, who had not previously taken a penalty as Gibson and I slotted them over tit-for-tat, won the game 27–24 for Ulster by kicking the deciding penalty from close to halfway. I was disappointed, but not as much as I was a few days later.

Munster dropped me for their next game against Cardiff. It was a bolt from the blue and I will admit that I was shocked beyond belief. I suppose nobody should take anything for granted – least of all a young rookie like me – but I had scored twenty points and played reasonably well. I cannot recall too many players scoring so many points in a game and then being dropped. The selection committee who picked the team included Noel Murphy. It was the first of many axings I would experience under him.

Moss Finn of UCC was the man who replaced me. It gave me no pleasure whatsoever that Munster were thumped by over fifty points by Cardiff. On the contrary, I felt sad and angry at such a loss. Nobody actually picked up a phone or sought me out face to face to tell me I had been dropped. The first I knew of it was when I read about it in a newspaper. No social media back then! It was a sign of things to come. After I was dropped, a lot of players cried off the panel through injuries and whatnot and they actually asked me to travel. My exams were coming up so I had a legitimate excuse to refuse, but compared to now travel arrangements were less than ideal. The itinerary involved a long coach journey from Munster to the ferry port, the ferry crossing which could be rough enough, then a coach from the ferry terminal to Cardiff. There was little or no time to relax ahead of the match.

That season had begun on a high for me. I was included in Garryowen's exciting and exotic two-week tour to Trinidad, Tobago and Barbados. The club were so good to me. They footed my bills and paid my expenses because being at college money was at a premium. We flew to New York and then on to Trinidad and we had another big surprise awaiting us at JFK Airport. At the time the Americans were trying to start up a professional soccer league and were pumping millions of dollars into its foundation. New York Cosmos became their first big glamour club with World Cup winners like Carlos Alberto and Pelé of Brazil. To our pleasant surprise, they were sitting along-side us on the flight to Port of Spain. Pelé was unbelievable and his graciousness was extraordinary. He had his photo taken with each of us individually and signed autographs for every-one. When Pelé got up out of his seat to go to the toilet, Shay Deering quipped in his best Dublin brogue, amid much laugh-ter: 'Jaysus, Pelé actually goes to the jacks!'

Looking and marvelling at Pelé on that trip taught me another lesson for life. Here was one of the greatest soccer play-ers and sports icons the world had ever known, yet he had so much time for every single person who approached him on that flight. The sight of him accommodating everyone served me well throughout my career. I received thousands and thousands of letters and autograph requests and I have always tried to oblige every person who requested something from me.

After returning from our trip abroad, Munster recalled me to the team who faced Leinster in the opening inter-provincial of the season. We won 15–10 which was a bit of a shock as Lein-ster were favourites. It was no surprise when they drew first blood with a try from John Moloney after twenty minutes. I managed to break clear and set up a try for Gerry 'Ginger' McLoughlin, and a short time later found Donal Spring on my shoulder for another. By half-time we led 12–4 and never really had a moment's worry thereafter. That victorious Munster team contained seven Limerick men. In our next match we faced Connacht. Again we won, but the 10–6 scoreline underlined that it was a very tight encounter. It was actually played in dreadful conditions with a wicked wind, so it was no surprise that it was error-strewn. My own performance was equally poor. I failed to convert a Billy Cronin try and struggled to make any sort of impact on the game. As a result, I remember thinking that if any selectors were watching then they would be none too impressed.

Even so, I was called up again for the Ireland B team to face Scotland at Murrayfield. That turned out to be one of the coldest days I ever experienced. So cold in fact, that many race meetings and soccer games across Britain and Ireland were called off. The game was originally scheduled to be played in Ayr, but the ground there was frozen. It was quickly switched to Murrayfield which had undersoil heating to keep the frost and snow at bay. Scotland's up-and-coming half-backs, John Rutherford and Roy Laidlaw, were not at their best. By contrast, Colin Patterson and I managed to get our act together and played pretty well, and Patterson scored the only try of the game. I failed with the conversion but did tag on a penalty which was crucial as we ran out 7–3 winners.

RTE televised the game 'live' as there was no other sport to show. The reason I mention RTE here is that I believe the decision to air the game had a very significant impact on the careers of many of the players involved who went on to win many caps for their respective countries. No fewer than ten of that shadow side went on to wear green at the highest level. I believe the exposure they received that day was crucial.

Amazingly, Scotland's points came from our mistake in the

opening minute and we were 3–0 down soon after kicking off. That was a bit of a shambles, but skipper Ciaran Fitzgerald was typically inspirational. He clenched his fists and gritted his teeth in that inimitable way of his and led by example. Even at such an embryonic stage in our representative careers the best leader I played under – in any code – was already making an impression on me.

Later, it transpired I was one of the players to benefit from that television coverage when I was selected to play my first full international for my country. When I look back now, it was phenomenal really. From a personal perspective everything coincided with my move to Limerick and my progression through the years of third level education at college. It had been quite a meteoric rise for me.

CHAPTER 4

IRELAND'S FIRST RUGBY SUPERSTAR

Sometimes I wonder what would have happened had I not taken the decision to leave that boring office job in Dublin when I did. It was quite noticeable that each year in college brought about another remarkable step up the ladder for me. In my first year I surprised Brian Mullins by getting into the Garryowen team and winning a national newspaper's 'Sport Star of the Week' award – having only played three games. The second year I was playing for Munster. A trip to Dijon for my first Ireland B cap came in my third year. In my fourth year I reached up and touched the stars.

I was over the moon when informed that I would be winning my first cap for Ireland. It was against Scotland on 21 January 1978. My inclusion came because of a number of changes and new blood being brought into the squad. There were four new caps: centre Paul McNaughton, myself as out-half, wing forward John O'Driscoll and second row Donal Spring. Like me, McNaughton had played League of Ireland soccer. He played with Shelbourne and was also an Irish amateur international.

There was one Ulster man on the team: centre Alistair McKibben. Later, a fifth new cap was added when Mick Fitzpatrick was brought into the front row after Ned Byrne sustained a badly damaged knee.

I never thought the feelings I experienced when helping Garryowen beat Cork Con, or Munster almost draw with the Wallabies, could be matched. But when I ran out in the green jersey of Ireland the sensation was out of this world. (And that was after I had almost puked up in the dressing room!) 'Sensational' caps it in a nutshell. Moreover, it was like something out of those boys' soccer annuals; it really was *Roy of the Rovers* stuff.

On the morning of the game I went for a walk with Ireland captain John Moloney. While we strolled in St Stephen's Green we tried to take our minds off the game and talk about everything bar rugby. As with 'Deero', Johnny was a natural born leader and a hero of mine from my schooldays in St Mary's. We had a good relationship on and off the field which is a pretty good starting point between scrum-half and out-half. At that time, I was back in Dublin doing my teacher practice at Ballyfermot Vocational School. Although I played with Garryowen at weekends, I had been training with Mary's in Templeville, so I worked out with Johnny a couple of nights a week. In the hours before the Scottish match we were too nervous to talk about the game and what might lie ahead. It was his first game as captain, and my first run-out at the highest level, so there was an awful lot at stake for both of us.

I was nervous before any big game. Throughout my career I found my sleep broken the night before. The Shelbourne Hotel in Dublin was our team base and there was a lot of tension in the air. Things were not made any easier when meeting rugby fans. It was even worse if you happened to bump into past and present internationals. But worst of all was if you encountered members of the opposing team in the hotel foyer. Nervous tension was generally a part of your make-up, so in that respect things were fairly normal until I left the team bus to walk towards the old Lansdowne Rugby Club dressing room. It was situated under the uncovered stand at the Havelock Square end of the old ground. Seeing a few well-known faces made me realise how big this was. I saw BBC Rugby presenters Bill McLaren and Nigel Starmer-Smith doing their pre-match stuff with their camera crews. Then there was all the top brass from rugby administration within the IRFU and SRU At that point it really hit me just how huge an occasion this was.

When I entered the dressing room and looked around I found that I was sharing it with players who were household names. The green jerseys were passed around and outside I could hear a brass band playing on the pitch. The sound of the piper was chilling. You could hear the drone of the crowd rise to a colossal din above the dressing room. It bellowed up and down with the opening and closing of the door as people came and went. All of this stirred the butterflies in my stomach. They were hopping mad, continually flying up and down in the confined space. It was as if an invisible hand had shoved a giant wooden spoon down my neck and was slowly stirring ... and stirring ... and stirring until a feeling of nausea began to envelop me. Johnny and Noel Murphy were barking out orders and suddenly I felt very warm. My heart was pounding and my head was trying to accommodate everything at the same time. I was not physically sick but I came mighty close.

In time I went on to play with some of the game's megastars who really did vomit before matches. The late, great Welsh centre Ray Gravell was a typical case in point. For Grav it was an integral part of his normal preparation. Like any human being, I became embarrassed and did my best to try and hide it. Mike Gibson noticed and reassured me. He told me that no matter how many times I would play at the top level for Ireland, I would always feel this way. His words were a huge comfort and were very reassuring. Moments later, after a final huddle, we hit cold air as we ran out into the most amazing atmosphere.

It was like nothing I had experienced before. There I was at Lansdowne Road making my Ireland Five Nations debut. To my dying day I will always remember that moment. It is so clear in my mind. As I ran on to the Lansdowne pitch, an explosion of noise came from everywhere. The only thing in my mind at that precise moment was a feeling of not wanting to let anyone down. Before the game, Barry McGann sent me a note saying how lucky I was to win my first cap at home just as he had. He explained how the difference between home and away is enormous. I thought I understood what he meant, but I only really knew what he was saying when I was met with that wall of noise. I was also very fortunate that I had a temperament ideally suited to the big occasions. Once on the field of play, I received a massive injection of confidence from nowhere. All the nerves, butterflies and feelings of nausea quickly vanished.

The Irish side who took to the field that day was: Tony Ensor, Tom Grace, Paul McNaughton, Alistair McKibben, Freddie McLennan, Tony Ward, John Moloney (captain), Phil Orr, Pat Whelan, Mick Fitzpatrick, Moss Keane, Donal Spring, John O'Driscoll, Willie Duggan and Fergus Slattery.

Once I put up a decent up-and-under early on, I felt fine. The pace was a bit sharper than I had been used to. But in all honesty I was a little surprised that I made the transition to international level so easily. We played with the advantage of the wind in the opening half, but found ourselves 6–3 down after forty minutes. The Scottish captain Douglas Morgan kicked two penalties and I landed one from around thirty metres.

Then, with my fourth kick, I hit the ball sweetly and the crowd roared to tell me that it was on its way between the sticks. It was 6–6 at the break. John O'Driscoll went off injured soon after and was replaced by Stewart McKinney who made an immediate impact. Stewarty was only on the pitch two minutes when he scored a magnificent try close to where we had run on nearly an hour before. It was Ireland's first try at Lansdowne Road since the Australian game in 1976.

The Scots, though, would not give up without a fight and they were laying siege to our line. Phil Orr had enough of all that and took off on one of his trademark, bull-like runs. He made a break out of our own half to the accompaniment of thunderous roars and urgings of our crowd. Other Irish forwards followed and piled in, but the referee gave a 'put in' to the Scots. However, from the scrum, Fergus Slattery turned over possession and this led to McKinney going over for a try. I converted and we were 12–6 in front.

The Irish performance was typified by big Willie Duggan. Willie hurt his shoulder badly and was being helped from the field. Then he saw Ginger McLoughlin – a prop – getting ready to replace him. Willie was having none of it. He shrugged off his injury and ran back into the heat of battle. Despite his handicap, he turned in a heroic performance that day. A few minutes later Tony Ensor was hurt and had to come off. He was replaced by Larry Moloney. But despite all our bravery, the Scots were still hanging on. Morgan kicked another penalty for Scotland in the seventy-fifth minute to make it 12–9 and it was anybody's game. Hearts were in mouths and fingers were chewed to the bone for the last few minutes.

The tension became unbearable when the referee added on a whopping ten minutes of injury time. Then disaster struck. Scotland were awarded another penalty just ten metres from our goal line, but fifteen metres in from the touchline. It looked like it would be the last action of the afternoon. It was a tight angle and by no means easy, but we all expected Morgan to slot it over for a draw. To our astonishment – and a huge gasp went up from the crowd when they saw what was happening – the Scots turned down the penalty and opted to run the ball. We defended to a man. We held out to win, but I still cannot believe what the Scots did. A draw was there for the taking, but they opted to gamble and ended up with nothing.

The late and great Jack Kyle, considered one of the best fly-halves of all time, was at that game. He really enjoyed what he saw and afterwards was quoted in the press as saying: 'I think Ireland's out-half Tony Ward had a splendid match. It was a great debut for him and I would not be despondent about Irish rugby after that performance.' I was chuffed.

I kept my place in the Ireland team for the away game in France four weeks later. The match was played on a rock-hard pitch in conditions which were more suited to an ice rink. We were very reluctant to play the game as it was far too dangerous. The risk of further injury on top of an already depleted squad was too great. Welsh referee Cenydd Thomas also considered the surface unsafe, but the French Federation insisted the game be played. France ended up beating us by the narrowest of margins, but it was another stirring and very proud performance. All things considered the French were worth their win, but their performance was by no means impressive.

Emmett O'Rafferty was due to make his debut but had to cry off just four hours before kick-off after sustaining a calf muscle injury. He was never capped again. We were severely handicapped with just one lock so Harry Steele – a back-rower – was called into the second row. John O'Driscoll had to be contacted in London and was brought in as cover. All of this put extra pressure on Willie Duggan in the lineout as he had to compete at the tail with the man mountain that was the legendary Jean-Pierre Bastiat. Willie competed magnificently and had another heroic game. Tony Ensor had probably his finest game in an Irish shirt. He was masterful all day and so brave under high kicks. I doubt his positional play and defensive kicking were ever better.

As ever, John Moloney led by example with his defensive play and clearances, and I played up to speed, too. We trailed 10–6 at half-time with me nailing two penalties. My third penalty ten minutes into the second half reduced the deficit further to 10–9. That was as close as we got. In fact it proved to be the only score in the second period as the French camped in our half for the last twenty minutes. Every man was a man that day and we defended as if our lives depended on it. We fought them off and repelled everything they could throw at us. Referee Thomas was looking at his watch when we almost stole it at the death. Then, to the astonishment of the French, and after enduring so much of the half with our backs to the wall, we went on the attack. The screaming and anguish of the French crowd in the Parc des Princes had to be heard to be believed. We were up and at them and twenty-five metres from their line, well within drop-kicking range. The situation was so frenetic that I do not exaggerate one bit when I tell you now that nobody heard the final whistle. Although we lost, we were so resilient and we won many new friends that day.

A warm communal bath in the dressing room after the game was never so welcome. It was sheer bliss after the coldness and the fatigue from our gallant efforts. We were still relaxing and enjoying the soothing water when our skipper John Moloney came in. He had completed his official duties, including giving his reaction to the media at the press conference, which explained why he was late arriving back. What a performance he gave that day. My abiding memory is of both his legs covered in blood from dive-passing on the granite-like surface. John was such a whole-hearted and honest player, and as a result his knees were red raw and badly bruised from contact with the pitch. That was just another reason why the game should never have been played. I will always remember the sheer agony on his face, and his groans of discomfort, as he eased his tired and tortured torso into the warm water.

On the plus side, our performance augured well for the game with all-conquering Wales a fortnight later. The Welsh were going for their third Triple Crown in a row. This meant another very difficult game in prospect despite the fact we had home advantage. I recall a torturous moment the night before the game. Both sides were staying in the Shelbourne Hotel, which is a practice that has changed since then as the last thing you want is to be bumping into the opposition, or their supporters, in the front lobby. For that reason I used to make my way to the lift at the back of the hotel. On this occasion, when the elevator door slid back, there were Gareth Edwards, Phil Bennett, J.P.R. Williams, Ray Gravell and J.J. Williams all standing looking out at me. I was horrified. I was not sure if they knew who I was since I had only played two full internationals to that point. There was no way I could turn my back and retreat so I squeezed inside with them. I kept my head down and did not look at any of them. There was an awkward and loaded silence which was only broken when I went to push the button a few minutes later to exit. That is when Gareth Edwards said, and I can still hear his lilting Welsh accent: 'See you tomorrow, Tone!' The door had shut before I could offer a polite answer, but I remember two thoughts coming into my head: 'Wow – Gareth Edwards knows my name!' and 'If only I had my autograph book with me'. Mind you, I made up for it later. At the post-match dinner, I got the match programme autographed and I still have it. As with Leeds in football, to me the Welsh epitomise everything great about rugby and if ever a team defined greatness it was that one.

Another gutsy Irish performance, another admirable failure, was the net result of our efforts. Midway through the first half we trailed 13–3 with all the Welsh scores coming from Steve Fenwick with three penalties and a try. With Derek Quinnell and Alun Martin controlling the lineouts we seemed set for a hammering. But I slotted another penalty which spurred us. Keane and Duggan began to dominate the lineout, and in the mauls and rucks we began to hold our own. Then a controversial incident arrived right on half-time. Mike Gibson was winning a record sixty-fourth cap when he was felled by J.P.R. Williams in a late tackle following a chip ahead. But the referee failed to give a penalty try. J.P.R was booed every time he touched the ball subsequently. Early in the second half I dropped a goal which gave us a strong scent of victory. For a while we were frothing at the mouth and in a frenzied state in pursuit of any possible way to win. This intensified when Moloney crossed for a try which levelled the scores. Even though the angle was tight and difficult, I was disappointed to miss the conversion after all the team's hard work. Our try only served to spur on the Welsh even more and for the remainder of the game we had to revert to a valiant defensive display. Fenwick kicked a penalty and that was effectively that. His insurance kick actually served him well. His reputation and standing were firmly established after that game and he was no longer seen as a mere support to Williams, Bennett and Edwards. He was a class player. A minute from the end I reduced the arrears once more when a penalty brought us back to within four points of them, 20–16. Alas it was too little too late and time ran out. But, most deservedly, the win enabled Wales to rack up a hat-trick of Triple Crowns in the process.

In our last championship game, against England at Twickenham, we lost again. I kicked our points – two penalties and a drop goal – in a 15–9 defeat. My points total equalled the Five Nations record of thirty-eight, which was held jointly by Phil Bennett and Roger Hosen at the time. We put on our worst team performance of the campaign in that final game. The only exciting moment came in the second half when a streaker did his stuff!

CHAPTER 5

1978: IMMORTALITY

Tuesday, 31 October 1978. Halloween. It was the day when one of the most famous moments not just in Irish rugby was delivered, but in Irish sporting history. How privileged and proud I feel to have been a part of it. I lined out with a band of brothers against a merciless outfit of grim reapers clad in black. Everyone expected us to be slaughtered. The printed press, broadcast media and every pundit prophesised doom and destruction. There is no sensationalism here. It is true. Very few, if any, gave Munster a chance of beating the mighty All Blacks. All the experts back then were falling over themselves to laud the latest in a long line of power houses from the southern hemisphere. They were running out of superlatives to describe how good they were.

And they were truly awesome. On their tour of Ireland and England, New Zealand laid waste to every team who strayed into their path. Middlesex had been annihilated, so what hope was there for us? After all, we had been hammered by Middlesex on our woeful summer tour. The 'Blacks' had gone through the best of the English and Welsh sides with ease. In contrast, we flopped on a tour of London. The media hype had even infiltrated our squad with a lot of slagging and banter going on behind the scenes. It was hard to know if this was a good or bad thing. I recall on Thursday at club training in Templeville, before heading to Limerick on the Saturday, former Leinster winger Noel Kenny, in friendly banter, offered outrageous odds on Munster even showing up! Shay Deering was having none of it and blasted back: 'OK, Noel, put your money where your mouth is. I'll bet you £20 we beat them.' Noel agreed to the wager. I am not sure if it was bravado or sheer confidence that encouraged 'Deero' to make that punt. I suspect it was more pride in his Munster jersey than anything else. Not that Noel was bothered if he lost because it would mean Munster had won.

Munster's coach was Tom Kiernan. He had an iron will and a steely-eyed determination which transmitted itself to the players. So much so that they were willing to die for him and the red jersey against the All Blacks. In sport there are certain individuals who elicit that response and Kiernan was one of them. He was our Brian Cody, our Davy Fitzgerald, our Anthony Daly rolled into one.

The day before the game was Bank Holiday Monday. A few thousand people turned up to watch the last All Black training session at Crescent College, Dooradoyle, whereas only a scattering of people watched Munster go through their final warm-up at St Munchin's College on the other side of the city in Corbally. The prevailing view was that New Zealand would polish off their tour with another convincing win. It was amazing the way everyone was talking and viewing the game. It was almost as if Munster were expected to roll over for them.

On the Monday afternoon we went on an excursion to Lough Derg. Before you think we had gone mad and embarked on a pilgrimage to seek guidance through prayer, it was not that Lough Derg. We went out boating on Lough Derg in Kilaloe, near the Tipperary–Clare border. It was organised by Bill McCormack and his cruising company. Bill actually hailed from New Zealand but was now a local resident. It must have looked a very strange sight to the locals. Three boats full of beefy Munster rugby players descending upon a quiet rural lake – and we were anything but quiet. As they say, 'the craic was mighty'. When we arrived back at our base at Jury's (now the Strand Hotel) on the Ennis Road, nobody was as wet from head to toe as T.J. Kiernan. I can still see him with a bucket of water in one hand and an oar in the other. He larked around with the youngest members of the side, and helped organise the whole day with ammunition and artillery: buckets, hoses, the whole shebang.

But something happened that afternoon. It may have seemed such a simple and unexciting outing, bordering on lunacy, but it bonded us all into a tight group. We were like blood brothers as we built up a very strong and common aim: to beat New Zealand. T.J. had insisted all along that we could win. Later that evening we watched videos of their previous games on the tour. In particular, we looked at how they trounced the London Division. London were a better side than Middlesex who, in turn, had destroyed us a few weeks earlier. But for the life of me, I could not get a handle on the principle. Watching videos is not the sort of thing to be doing. In no way does it instil any confidence in you. Whether it was with Munster or Ireland I never enjoyed watching videos in advance of important games. I always preferred to concentrate on our own game rather than worrying about the opposition. Amateur times, amateur values, I guess, but for me ignorance was bliss. Kiernan stressed how he wanted to see how good the Kiwis were going backwards. So the logical plan was for me to turn them around and reverse the pressure when putting the ball in behind them.

The crowd crammed into Thomond Park. New Zealand performed their pre-match haka. Perhaps they thought we were fearful staring at them, but I like to think we were looking with pride in our eyes to the glorious backdrop of the Clare Hills. We provided the usual welcome for overseas visitors to our pitch by way of a standard 'garryowen'. The crowd were up for it, and so were we. More to the point – from Ginger at loose head to Springer wearing number eight – our pack was charged and angry. All they needed was the carrot. That role was mine. Seamus Dennison broke the opposition's attack with his predetermined tackle on Stu Wilson in a game-defining moment. 'Shay' was probably the smallest and lightest man on the pitch. But with that tackle he set the tone. It united crowd and players as one. The umbilical cord between terrace and pitch was connected as tightly as it had ever been. When we saw that happen, we realised the extent to which we were *all* prepared to go. We would fight to the bitter end for each other.

To the letter of the Kiernan law, handed down to me before the game, I chipped delicately over the top of All Black heads in the eleventh minute. It was risky. The bounce could have gone either way, but Jimmy Bowen judged it beautifully, gathered at full tilt and made a sharp and incisive run. As he was felled, he fed Christy Cantillon who crossed the Promised Land at the Ballynanty end. The lush green grass right next to the white posts had been firmly stamped in red: try! Clenched fists, screaming, wild faces, mad and angry delight – how dare you doubt us. We are Munster. This is *our* patch. It is a field we cherish, and like 'Bull McCabe' we have had blood on our hands scratching rocks from rugged earth. We will die here.

The great roars from the crowd could be heard for miles. As they surged forward to bellow their approval, the decibels got louder. It must have frightened the life out of our foe. The 'invincibles' were rattled. We were all in the zone and singing from the same hymn sheet. I kicked the conversion with ease, 6–0. New Zealand now knew they were in a war zone. We could sense their unease. They did not know what had hit them. They were losing their trademark composure and were penalised in the seventeenth minute for indiscriminate use of the boot. My resulting penalty attempt (surprisingly the only one for either side in the entire game) fell short. However, the pressure was building and unbelievably my effort was knocked on by Brian McKechnie. From our scrum, Donal Canniffe teed it up and this time I made no mistake. My drop goal made it 9–0. Minutes later Welsh referee Coris Thomas blew for half-time.

We gathered in a passionate but euphoric huddle in front of the main stand. In those days rugby teams did not leave the pitch. Less than fifty metres away we knew what was being said among the opposition. Donal Canniffe left us in no doubt as to what they were discussing. New Zealand's pride had to be restored and they would throw everything at us from the restart. We would have to meet that inevitable frenzy head on. They duly battered us in the opening minutes after the break. The siege of Limerick took on a whole new meaning. In contrast to the first half, where we had a right go on the offensive, we found ourselves defending for our lives. The pressure exerted by the All Blacks was enormous. We stood tall. We stood strong. The men from the southern hemisphere were met with crunching defensive tackles the like of which they had never known before from an Irish team. Seamus Dennison, Greg Barrett and Colm Tucker were nothing short of heroic. But how long could it last?

As the minutes ticked by and the hearts and minds of the crowd began to feel for us, they echoed their emotions in one collective and loud lilting chant: 'MUNNN-STERRRRRR . . . MUNNN-STERRRRRR . . . MUNNN-STERRRRRR'. We all felt twelve feet tall. It lifted us and spurred us on. More than that, it raised the hairs on the back of my neck as I am sure it did for the rest of the team. I then helped alleviate the pressure by dropping another goal, this time from a Tucker pass, and ultimately we held out to win. Final score: 12–0.

We became the first team from Ireland to inflict defeat on the All Blacks. We were ecstatic. Everyone went berserk. Even now, words cannot adequately describe the immense importance and significance of that game. They say that actions speak louder than words and perhaps one moment afterwards sums up perfectly what I am trying to say. To beat a team who were God-like figures was a huge achievement. It brought everybody together and to their senses. Even though we left the pitch in such a state of unbelievable bliss, the crowd stayed on. Not only that, but they demanded that we come back out on to the pitch. It was the only time I was central to a sporting event culminating in mature adults openly crying. To be able to say you were there was, and is, great, but being at the heart of the action was even greater again. The official attendance was given out as 12,000, but to this day hundreds of thousands still claim to have been there!

Russ Thomas, the All Blacks coach, paid a very generous tribute to us after the game, but New Zealand manager Jack Gleeson described our defensive work as 'kamikaze tackling'. There was a sad postscript to the victory when our captain, Donal Canniffe, later received the tragic news that his father had dropped dead. Dan Canniffe collapsed and died in Cork while listening to the game. At the post-match dinner in the

Limerick Inn, a minute's silence was observed in memory of Donal's father. Vice-captain Pat Whelan stood in for our absent leader, who had obviously returned to be with his grieving family.

Later, a surprise telegram was read to us. It was sent by one of Munster's most famous sons, the legendary film actor Richard Harris. A former Crescent schoolboy, Richard played rugby in the province as a young man and to a fairly high standard. His words went something like this: 'I'm away on set in South Africa and I just want you to know how thrilled I am and that every newspaper out here has reported your magnificent achievement. I have been on the dry now for ten months but I cannot think of a better excuse to have a drop. I rang Richard Burton [the Welsh actor who was married to Elizabeth Taylor] and he was also delighted. But I felt there was a tinge of jealousy in his voice!' Dickie Harris's brother in law, the Berkley Court-based Jack Donnelly, was his constant source of information and communication on all things rugby back then. To hear those words just summed up the worldwide stir we created.

That was one of the greatest days of my life. It was also, and without any doubt, the highlight of my rugby career. I talked about this with a great many people over the years, but especially so with the great Moss Keane. Unlike me, Moss would later go on to be an integral part of the Ireland Triple Crown-winning team in 1982. He was also capped by the British and Irish Lions. But he, too, agreed with me: Munster's 12–0 win in 1978 was the undoubted high point of his career.

CHAPTER 6

MY BROTHERS IN ARMS

Before I leave that epic match against the All Blacks, here are my thoughts and tributes to each of the Munster bravehearts I fought with that day. Time moves on and we have already lost three (Mossie, Colm and replacement full-back Micky O'Sullivan), but I love and miss them all. I am sure that when the last images flicker in my mind's eye, they will be there beside me again. For the present, and as I sit here in Finnegan's pub in Dalkey sipping coffee, a smile breaks out on my face. My eyes light up again just thinking about that team. It is something I never tire of talking about. There is no point in my poring over their performances in that game as every man stood tall and was counted. All of them played exceptionally well. It had to be that way. So instead I will give my take on each individual's career. From what I know, I will also try and relate what these players went on to achieve in their lives and where they are today.

LARRY MOLONEY
Without any doubt whatsoever the most talented attacking full-back I ever played with. I will not say Larry was lazy as sin, he was

just as laidback as they come. Getting him to train was near impossible. His physique was like that of a greyhound: he never put on any weight. It stood to him greatly. When he hit a line he just had this incredible burst of speed. Larry was a very gifted full-back who, in my opinion, never went remotely close to fulfilling his potential. It was just his attitude. As I said, he was too laidback. He took his rugby seriously, but he did so on his terms.

He became a banker with AIB in Limerick and then in the Midlands.

MOSS FINN

A great out-half and one of my favourite people on planet Earth, so I am going to be a little biased here. He will always be remembered for linking up with Ollie Campbell to score two tries against Wales in 1982 that helped Ireland win the Triple Crown. Mossy was my rival when we came up through the ranks with our clubs in Munster because we were both out-halves. In fairness to Munster, their selectors saw the merit in picking and playing us both to maximise our potential. Unlike Ireland.

He had incredible pace for a big man and he was very strong. Talking about Larry, Mossy was of a completely different build and physique altogether. Again, he was very under-rated and could have been even better because he did not quite fulfil his potential, again like Larry. Perhaps he did a little bit more than Larry, but not to the full limit of his potential.

Mossy runs a very famous sports shop called Finn's Corner in Cork City which has been there for years. Top man.

SEAMUS DENNISON

Seamus was hugely influential on my career. He gave me lots of advice on and off the pitch; on it, he always told me to use my initiative and make up my own mind. What I liked about Seamus – and Paul McNaughton was similar – was that he liked to give it a lash. His reputation has been built on that one crunching tackle that stopped the on-rushing All Black Stu Wilson in his tracks. That was quite unfair really because Seamus was much more than that. People get totally the wrong impression of him because of that one tackle and Seamus is very uncomfortable with it. The great thing about that tackle was the 'timing'.

Seamus was a brilliant attacking player. He played on the wing for Ireland and in sevens where he got to the final at Murrayfield in 1974. Talking about the physiques of the three mentioned so far, they were all so different: Larry as lean as a whippet; Mossy big, sturdy and strong; Seamus tiny, scrawny. He was so small he simply would not live in the modern game.

He has long been a teacher based in Roscrea.

GREG BARRETT

Greg was a very strong, hard-running but intelligent centre. And very under-rated. I suppose that was because he was a late starter and did not make the breakthrough into representative rugby until late in his career. He always had to wait in the queue behind others to win a starting position, but when his chance finally came along he nailed it.

The combination of Barrett and Dennison worked and they got on very well. Greg was totally different to Seamus in that he was a harder and stronger runner, particularly adept at taking it up route one to the gain line. Seamus, on the other hand, was the better, natural attacker with his vision and timing.

Greg was a future Munster President in the making and is still involved in finance.

JIMMY BOWEN

'Boweny' will always be remembered for his weaving burst from the chip which set up the try for Christy Cantillon that effectively beat the All Blacks. He came out of Pres in Cork and in that team there were three outstanding schoolboys: Moss Finn, Jimmy Bowen and a powerful prop, and equally talented swimmer, called Brian Clifford. Jimmy and Moss went on to play for Ireland, but Brian did not make it to that level. Jimmy was a very good prop for Cork Con. Jimmy's wife Kaye actually went on to become the first female president of an Irish rugby club in Trinity College, Dublin. Based in the capital for many years, Jimmy played for Lansdowne and St Mary's to telling effect.

Today, like Greg Barrett, Jimmy is still involved in finance.

DONAL CANNIFFE (CAPTAIN)

One of my favourite players because in my own position as an out-half I lived for quick ball. The one way the game has never changed is in the speed and accuracy of pass. From that perspective we live and die by our scrum-half and his delivery to us. When you have scrum-halves like John Robbie, Colin Patterson, John Moloney, Robbie McGrath, Tony Doyle, Liam Hall and Donal Canniffe, you are blessed. Donal was also quite unusual in that he was very tall for his position. That said, so too is Conor Murray now. Donal had long arms that were like huge slings and levers. When he passed the ball it was more than just a pass – it was like a bullet. It was slung out and seemed to travel in the air forever like a rapidly turning torpedo. I liked to find space and to have a cut at the opposition. Donal was heaven to play with. More than that, he was a great tactician – and I mean a really great reader of the game. They were his two finest attributes.

Donal has spent a lifetime in insurance.

GERRY McLOUGHLIN

Like most rugby people, I have a wry smile when I hear mention or think of 'Ginger', or 'Locky' as he was and is affectionately known. He was a unique prop and a dyed-in-the-wool Limerick man. He was hewn from the same granite as Tom Clifford. He was also as tough as nails, a real red Popeye. His uniqueness lies in the fact he could play on either side of the scrum. Being so adept at this would mean that in modern currency today the guy would be a millionaire. He is always central to the conversation whenever we meet. He is such a jovial character and brings out the fun in all of us. We all view him the same.

He is like Atlas, who bore the Earth on his shoulders. We see Ginger in the light of Ginger perhaps seeing himself as 'the man who beat the All Blacks'. It is a bit like the famous try that Ireland scored at Twickenham many years ago, or in 1982 when a huge push went over the line for the try that won the Triple Crown. Well, not quite in Ginger's eyes – he viewed it all as him dragging the guys over the line! I laugh heartily just saying this, but honestly this is the way we all view Ginger. I laugh so much because over the years it has become more and more like that. We could all be at a reunion or some function and sure enough Ginger will be there spinning his line to someone about 'how we "really" beat the All Blacks'. We suspect it is said in jest, but to be honest we're not sure!

A former teacher, still working part-time, Ginger served as Mayor of Limerick a while back, having branched into politics. He and his daughter are both politicians in Limerick where he once ran a pub called, appropriately enough, The Triple Crown.

PAT WHELAN

'Pa', as he is known, is now on the International Rugby Board, helping to run the game. He always had that administrative streak. We both go back to the very start, coming up through the ranks together in Munster. His wife, Deirdre, is the daughter of Paddy Reid, who is one of the few members of the 1948 Irish Grand Slam and 1949 Triple Crown-winning team still alive today. That was the team who made Jack Kyle a household name. Paddy also played Rugby League and his wife was president of the Irish Ladies Hockey Union, so it is a family steeped in sport. Pa and his wife are lifelong friends of mine.

On the field of play, Pat was ruthless, single-minded and always worked really hard at his game. He could also put himself about. Perhaps his biggest quality was his influence on all of us in the dressing room as he barked out instructions. He was inspirational. The best comparison I can draw is with Ciaran Fitzgerald. For me they both pressed the right buttons – Pa while I was with Munster, and Fitzy when I played for Ireland.

LES WHITE

Les was quite unusual in that Munster cast their net to London Irish to include him in the team. From that point of view he is often 'the forgotten man' of our group. I mean that in the nicest way possible in that when people are asked to name the 1978 Munster team, Les is the one very few can recall. That is only because he was playing and living in England where he still resides. It is therefore understandable that people miss out his name. The rest of us were all playing week in and week out in Munster and Leinster so it is easy to remember our names.

Les was a latecomer into that team where he fixed a gaping hole. He was and is a very nice guy, but boy was he tough. Technically he was superb in the scrum and that was where we needed to be strongest in order to beat the Kiwis. If you look back at the video, you will see that our scrum was rock solid and that was largely down to Les.

MOSS KEANE (RIP)

Sadly, big Mossy is no longer with us. He will always be remembered for two things: his headband and the ball tucked under his arm as he steamed forward, Phil Orr-like. Three words sum him up: Larger Than Life. People might find this strange but I liken him to Paul McGrath. I saw Paul on television recently and he is now so articulate as a media operator. This was something he was very definitely not in the past. He shied away and never talked much. Moss was the same. He was the life and soul of the party when in the pub, telling stories and singing songs. That was Moss. But if you put a microphone in front of him, or put him out front, he became uncomfortable and almost withdrawn.

Another thing I find amazing was that he was never a captain at representative level. In all the times I played with him I never recall him wearing the armband. That was strange when you considered his stature and his experience. I go back to the larger-than-life personality, the ball and the headband. Lansdowne Road would erupt when he played, and for the rest of us this proved inspirational. He ignited the crowd.

We got on great together and had a long and lasting friendship. Our marriages actually took place the day after each other: he married Anne, I married Maura. He was the original gentle giant and a true friend. I miss him greatly.

It is interesting that Ginger and Moss played on the 1982 Triple Crown-winning team. I did not. But all three of us have gone on record as stating that, even after various successes with Ireland and the Lions, the Munster win in 1978 was the highlight of our careers.

BRENDAN FOLEY

Brendan is father of current Munster coach Anthony 'Axel' Foley and another one of my favourite people. He was always modesty personified. Actually, whenever I see Anthony being interviewed now, before or after a Munster game, I see Brendan. Anthony often throws his eyes back as he is uncomfortable with being interviewed in the public spotlight. He gets that from his dad. I will not say Brendan was a gentle giant as he could put himself about, but he was and is a really nice man. His daughter Rosie is a former ladies international and a most informed commentator on the female game.

Brendan was the original workhorse. The term 'boiler house' for second rows was almost invented with the elder Foley in mind. For father, read son. Brendan stoked the engine and fires in that boiler room. He was in there with sweat pumping, doing the really dirty stuff. He was anything but a fancy, dancing Tony Ward; he was the complete opposite. When I was dropping a goal, he was the one getting his head kicked off down at the bottom of the ruck.

Along with wife Sheila – an absolute angel – they once ran a pub in the Ballina–Killaloe area before Brendan branched into the coach hire business. He was not a bad soccer goalkeeper, too.

COLM TUCKER (RIP)

Colm is one of the three who have sadly passed away, and that is scary. I was a guest at a recent reunion of the 1972 Irish team and every one of them was there, yet three members of the 1978 Munster team are no longer with us.

Colm was a huge man for a back-row forward. It is amazing to think that he only received three caps for Ireland, yet he won as many with the Lions when he was out in South Africa with me in 1980. The best I have ever seen, bar nobody, at a skill which is not often mentioned today – dribbling the ball at feet which he learned from being a talented soccer player in his younger days. He was renowned for that facet of his game because it stood out. In other words, in the scrum, when the ball trickled out, instead of someone latching on to it and booting it down field, Colm would start to dribble it as the scrum shifted sideways. I was often there at his side. It was great running along behind, but when immediately opposite in the number ten or number twelve channel, it was not the prettiest sight. He was like the conductor orchestrating his group in that scenario. Like Ginger and Brendan/Anthony Foley, Colm was a true-blue Shannon and the 'heart of the parish'. Much like Deirdre Whelan, Colm's wife Ger (Hartery) was steeped in rugby and sport, specifically through Thomond Rugby Club.

He was taken away much too young.

CHRISTY CANTILLON

Another great friend of mine and I laugh to myself when I think of Christy and 'sledging'. This is a big issue with the GAA at the moment. Christy was the original 'sledger' on the rugby field and I say that in the most down to earth way. I recall many times when I was about to take a kick, he was one of three players who always mouthed at me. His words were to the effect: 'You're going to fuck this up, Wardy', or 'You'll miss this one'. Two others notorious for sledging were Charlie Quinn and, believe it or not, Fergus Slattery. Mind you, Ciaran Fitz could do it a bit, too. But Christy was the original of the species.

Christy had a fantastic engine, comparable with Roy Keane as a footballer going from box to box. In fact, whenever I used to see Keane, I would always be reminded of Christy Cantillon.

He ran all day without tiring. That was his great asset. Christy never won an Ireland cap. There are always a few guys who you feel were desperately unlucky not to have been capped and he was very definitely one of them. He was part of the Ireland tour of Australia in 1978, but he did not get a Test game. That said, he will forever be immortalised as the man who scored the try in Munster's famous win over the All Blacks.

If I am not mistaken he works in insurance and his family also own Little Island Golf Club in Cork.

DONAL SPRING

A brother of former Labour leader and Ireland international Dick Spring, Donal had a very sharp rugby intellect and was a fantastic reader of the game. He was also one of the most natural leaders on the field. When Donal Canniffe was captain, Springer was one of his first lieutenants. He went to school in that great rugby dynasty, Cistercian College, Roscrea, and then on to Trinity College and Lansdowne. He also went to play in France for a while. But he never quite fulfilled his great potential. For sure injuries did not help. A very direct parallel would have been Anthony Foley. When Foley the younger first came on the scene at St Munchin's, everyone said he would be a fantastic player and he lived up to that. They said the same about Donal, but to my mind he didn't quite make it. This is probably borne out by the fact he only won seven caps for Ireland. He competed with Willie Duggan for the number eight position and was picked ahead of the Kilkenny man for the Australian tour. But injuries hindered his progress all along the way.

Springer was a solicitor with a very successful practice based in Dublin.

*

They are all heroes to me and they instil a great sense of pride. Even more so, they are family. A band of brothers who stood up and protected our lands and our traditions from any who doubted us. Each gravestone need not look for any etched word, or words, but one – Immortal.

ENDURANCE

I get up out of bed not knowing whether I have slept or dreamt. Perhaps I lay in a sort of semi-conscious state throughout the night. Thinking. Always thinking. These thoughts are driving me mad as I am still confused. Me being me, I need to get all the angles on this.

It is a new day. I will search the web and ring people and try to find out as much as I can about prostate cancer. I will co-operate with my doctors and specialists and, as if listening to Deering, Dennison or Canniffe, their words will be my command.

I am ready for the biggest game of my life – literally. Who wrote 'It's Only a Game' – was it Dunphy? Who said the game 'is not a matter of life or death – it is much, much more important than that' – definitely Shankly. Well this prostate challenge is my biggest game.

You think not? You laugh? You think I trivialise it? It *is* a game. It is a game of war. It will not be a battle; it will be a long war. This opponent wants to beat the living daylights out of me and into deathly darkness. I have to floor it with an uppercut, but even then I know that will not suffice. It will keep coming at me. I will have to blast and bomb it into disintegration until nothing is left. That means but one thing: the other dreaded 'C' word. 'Chemotherapy'. I will ask my doctor about this.

On Tuesday, 3 April 2012, I was admitted to the Beacon Hospital for four days where they did every test imaginable, including CAT scans, DEXA scans, MRI scans and, of course, the dreaded biopsy. Doctor Hubert Gallagher, who had played with me in the same Greystones and Leinster teams in times past, was my consultant.

Chemotherapy is a course of treatment that strikes fear. It makes you physically sick and one notorious side-effect for some is that body hair falls out. So if I am honest I expected Doctor Hubie to tell me that would be the treatment I would require. He began by telling me my PSA readings were sky high. From my limited research – courtesy of my girls – I was already aware of this fact. The situation was serious but I was also extremely fortunate. He described my prostate as being like an orange. As the tumour developed inside my body, and as I moved about, the juice seeped through the orange peel. These overflows were cancerous. It was aggressive and extremely virulent, but I was lucky in that none of it had spread to my other vital organs.

This, and the ability of my bones to take radiation, was key. The word 'Chemo' was not mentioned and I was damned if I was taking the conversation there. 'Brutal' is not too strong a term to describe the essential treatment, but it would leave me in awe of what the human body can withstand. But nothing could prepare me for the test which caused me the worst discomfort of the preparatory work and treatment process. A biopsy is a sample of tissue taken from the body in order to examine it more closely and I guess by extension to determine the most appropriate course of action.

It was without doubt the most excruciatingly painful medical experience I have ever been through. Pulled hamstrings, torn ligaments, dislocated shoulders were run of the mill sporting injuries. This was entirely different. I had my biopsy. Three years on and even the mere mention of it instils a feeling of pain. If you are squeamish look away now or tighten your seatbelts. I was in such discomfort I could have blasted off the operating theatre and splattered against the ceiling.

For want of better words or medical explanations, this is where they do raw and 'live extractions' from your prostate. When I say 'live' I mean with localised anaesthetic; when I say 'extractions' I mean scraping and inserting sharp devices into my very soul. I am led to believe that this is a subject of contention and controversy between medical people – whether, in such procedures, a patient should be given a general anaesthetic or a local anaesthetic. I was given the latter.

Having spoken to many people since, the general consensus is of a painful experience best forgotten. I spoke to some who breezed through it without noticing, so it is very much a case of different strokes for different folks as it affects people in different ways. I have heard that taking a scraping of bone can be excruciating, well this must be in the same league. The procedure took place on Good Friday and never could a day have been better chosen. This was my Calvary. As long as I live I will never forget that day. What made it even worse from a mental standpoint was that my agony was oblivious to the medics. I think they had to insert somewhere in the region of twelve rods into my prostate.

Your dignity departs early because there, standing beside me, was the doctor and a couple of nurses assisting. I know that for them it was run of the mill, just another patient. They have seen it all before, but it felt so embarrassing for me. After the third or fourth rod I became familiar with the rhythm. So when the doctor did something and said something, then the nurse handed him something, I knew the routine when the pain was going to hit hardest.

In another attempt to describe the pain I will leave the ladies out of this so they can just imagine the following. It is something akin to a very strong hand clutching your balls as tight as possible for five to six seconds. As much as you want to scream there is no let-up. You just want it to end. I would not wish it on my worst enemy. The knocks and bruises taken on the rugby pitch and the pain of injuries come nowhere near what I had to endure in that Easter week of 2012.

It seemed like an eternity as they slowly inserted rods into my rear end. Just think about a very thin metal knitting needle or better still – a gleaming envelope opener – and think about it piercing the skin of your nether regions and moving sharply in. When they finally finished, my bed was wheeled from the operating theatre to go back up to the ward on the fifth floor. There were others in beds waiting to go in. I just hoped and prayed they would not ask me how it was. Nobody said a word.

I looked and felt like death warmed up. My face said it all. I left hospital next day with the tests to determine the course of treatment now completed. It was all uphill. Against the wind. Playing into a blinding sun. But the fightback was underway.

After the biopsy, Doctor Hubie had a much clearer picture of the situation and so he knew the exact diagnosis and prognosis. On 24 April I returned for another very important procedure. Doctor Alina Mihai, a living genius in the Oncology Department of the Beacon, inserted a hormone implant into my upper arm just behind the bicep muscle. It was a Vantas implant and

I was told it would continue in place for the next three years of my life. It is akin to a contraceptive device for a female whereby a little bar is implanted under the skin. The difference here was that my implants were designed to kill the natural testosterone feeding the tumour.

A small medical incision of around one and a half inches was made under my arm just below the main muscle. I would have to live with this implant for the next three years. It may have seemed a nuisance, and in truth did have me feeling very sorry for myself, but in the bigger picture of recovery it was a very small price to pay. Quite simply, I had to live with it. The alternative did not bear thinking about.

CHAPTER 7

MANHANDLED ('SORT WARD OUT')

Shortly after our win over the All Blacks, I made a very important career move. I decided to forsake teaching and go into business. I teamed up with international colleague Pat Whelan and Garryowen FC administrator Frank Hogan to open a sports shop. It was situated in Thomas Street in Limerick and was officially opened on 2 December 1978 by my good friend John Giles. I decided to take the bull by the horns and go for it because had I not done so, I would only have regretted it later. There was a downside: everyone knew my whereabouts, my place of work, and in the coming years I would never know pressure on a rugby pitch, or in my rugby career, compared to the stress of running my own business.

Without wishing to sound conceited, so many people wanted to have a piece of me. It got to the stage that when I was in the shop I felt close to hiding away. People were constantly looking for me and many were a real nuisance. I do not mean the fans *per se* or the huge volume of mail I received. That in itself was time-consuming, but a nice sort of pressure, if not always work-related. Of course, the situation I found myself in was not helped by my name being up in lights across Limerick – literally. When my mother came down for the official opening, she stayed in Jury's Hotel. As she looked out of her room window one night, all she could see was a giant neon sign across the River Shannon with my name emblazoned on it. She got an awful shock.

Mind you, it was not as big a shock as I got when I first laid eyes on it. Frank and Pa had ordered this particular sign as they wanted to make sure the shop and the name were clearly visible from all parts of the city. They certainly were, but it was horrendous. My name was up in lights, as they say. I hated it and had it not been for my business partners having gone to considerable lengths to have it erected, I would have taken it down.

Some of the attention was quite embarrassing at the time and even more so now as I look back. One woman named her horse after me and registered it under the name 'Outside Half'. Her letter elaborated further: 'My horse is at present known to her friends as "Trotskie", but something tells me she has a crush on you! We were grooming her yesterday when she was in a bad mood. Then I said the words "Tony Ward" to her and ever so slowly she pricked up her ears and went all floppy.' It was cringeworthy stuff but appeared to go with the territory. I also received a letter from a girl informing me that she had named her dog after me. It was called 'Ward of Cooley'. People of all ages wrote for autographs. There were so many, but the Pelé lesson on that flight to Trinidad stuck. I responded to each and every one, but it was not at the click of the finger. In Ireland of the 1970s it was by snail mail.

On the pitch, Munster capped off a great season in perfect style. A few weeks after opening the Tony Ward Sport shop, we beat Leinster 12–3 to win a first grand slam of home provinces since 1968, a first Lansdowne Road win since 1972, and a first championship since 1973. I registered our points with a try, conversion and two penalties. That game was played on a Sunday and the previous day we all sat down in the team hotel to watch the All Blacks wind up their tour with a mouth-watering game against the Barbarians. New Zealand only managed to win the game with a very late drop-goal. But all of our players were on the edges of their seats. When the ball went over the bar, we all leapt up in unison clapping, screaming and roaring. There was a very good reason: the win meant that the All Blacks won seventeen out of their eighteen tour matches that year, so it only served to highlight our huge achievement in being the only side to beat them. We were the blot on their copybook.

My 1979 season with Ireland was ultimately disappointing and therefore, in a sense, forgettable. Personally it will be remembered for a series of controversial moments and a number of off-the-ball incidents involving me. Our first game was at home to France. After a heavy tackle ten minutes in, I was so concussed I did not know where I was. I had blurred vision but persevered through to the half-time break, and then went straight into the medical room with Doctor Mick Molloy for treatment. When I ran back on to the field, English referee Roger Quittenton had to chase me into the French half to tell me to rejoin my team at the other end. In my dazed state of confusion I had joined the wrong huddle.

With such head injuries today a player would play no further part. And that is as it should be. The game ended somewhat controversially when we were awarded an indirect free-kick around twenty yards from the posts at the Lansdowne Road end. I asked the ref if I could take the ball back a few more yards to give myself space for an attempted drop goal. I could see that the French players were lining up to charge it down and I was still quite groggy. But to my surprise the match official did not reply. He remained silent. It was only afterwards he told me the reason was that he could not influence my kick according to the laws of the game. He would be giving me an unfair advantage so it was my decision. In the event, the French rushed to charge my kick down. They succeeded and our winning chance was gone. It was galling. It got worse when post-match analysis showed categorically the French failing to retreat the requisite ten metres as I was about to tap the ball.

One of the few good things to take out of that game was the birth of a new star. Mike Gibson dominated the lineout and he was the launch pad for our attacks while also enabling me to use the touchline to set up field position from which to probe the French.

Controversy reigned again when we met Wales at Cardiff Arms Park in our next match. All I cared about was getting out there and doing my utmost. I was bursting out of my skin and relishing getting at the Welsh. But someone else could not wait to get their hands on me – literally. I could feel it as well. When I was out on the pitch waiting for the referee to signal the start I could feel there was an edge to this game. Something did not feel right. On my first night in the team hotel in Porthcawl I hardly slept a wink. Things were a bit better on Friday when Fergus Slattery took us all to the cinema. After that I went for a long walk on the beach alone to relax myself. We played brilliantly. Scoring twenty-one points was a record for an Irish side playing away in Wales. The problem was that we handed them so many points that they ended up winning 24–21. There was a catalogue of errors from both sides with the difference being that ours were punished more severely. I put over two close-range penalties in the first fifteen minutes to put us 6–0 up. It had been twelve years since our last win there so things were looking good.

However, from my point of view, I was not happy. Even though I played one of my best games for Ireland that day I really let the close attentions of Welsh forward Paul Ringer get to me. He declared himself out to 'get me' and he was shouting this and other things at me from the start of the game. It was not long before he was true to his word and gave me a right good smack off the ball. After the game, and amid my dejection, I confronted him to find out what it was all about. He just smiled and shrugged it off saying that it was all part of rugby. But there was more to come from him off the field.

Another thing that began to incense me was the slating certain Irish players were receiving from the press. They seemed to be showering me with adulation while almost using this as cover to have a go at others. It was terrible and way below the belt. One player unfairly shipping flack was Paul McNaughton. What bugged me even more was that it was misinformed. Macker was a real player's player and great to play beside. He gave me added confidence and did so much invaluable work, unseen from the press box.

Ringer joined the cohorts of the gutter press in an article he wrote following the game. He talked about an 'instruction' before kick-off to 'sort Ward out'. He was quoted as saying: 'The meaning was clear and I stuck to it. The trouble was he was so good that I could not lay a finger on him until late in the game. But I eventually flattened him off the ball and we went on to win. I got such a booting from the Irish forwards for doing it that I could not get out of bed for two days after. After I laid out Ward, he turned up late for our post-match dinner reception with a massively swollen eye.'

Ringer had a 'hard man' reputation. As we came out on the pitch to take up our positions for the anthems, he stamped on my ankle and then winked at me as he ran off. Rugby is a full-on sport and so is no more dangerous than any other contact code. If the referee gets on top early then things run smoothly. If not, then problems occur. I was angry at Ringer's antics but managed to hold my head. The best way to retaliate is by putting points on the board. That hurts.

Against England it was more of the same but we produced our most positive performance of the season. It was a match that had everything. The crowd and players were all wound up from the start. In my diaries from back then are some interesting observations:

Wednesday, 14 February
I escaped for an hour's kicking practice at the college and travelled up to Dublin in the evening. The roads were grand in Limerick, but not so good further up, and at Monasterevin in Kildare I skidded and aggravated an old wrist injury.

Thursday, 15 February
In the morning I recorded a TV interview with Thames Television where I did a piece talking about soccer star Liam Brady and he did a similar piece about me.

The build-up to the England game began with a team assembly at Dublin's Shelbourne Hotel at 12.30 p.m. for lunch. From this point on players are put under intolerable pressure from fans looking for match tickets. We receive two free tickets and an option to buy two more and after looking after friends or family, you don't have much left. [The situation changed for the better later with players receiving four stand tickets, a further option of purchasing six more stand tickets and twenty ground tickets. I'm not sure what the situation is for players in this professional age, but I suspect it is a lot more accommodating.] After lunch we travel by coach to Anglesea Road in Ballsbridge for a training session. If there is a newly capped player on board, he must perform the mandatory song. It was a hard training session after which Gerry McLoughlin and I went to St Vincent's Hospital for treatment. At 6 p.m. we had dinner after which we watched videos of our game with Wales and England's game with Scotland.

Friday, 16 February
Breakfast in bed and then off to Anglesea Road for a much quieter session. I was one of a few players called by RTE to do a piece for the evening news. Following lunch back at the Shelbourne came the bit I love – off for a spot of bowling in Stillorgan. I am absolutely useless at it but I still love the buzz of it. The best I could manage was thirty-seven pins out of two hundred and there was great laughter as big Moss Keane cleared everything out of sight and was the overall winner! Watched a film with the team and then I was in bed at 11 p.m. Thankfully, I slept well.

Saturday, 17 February (Match Day)
I really feel it on the day with plenty of butterflies in the tummy and a lump in the throat. I walk with Colin Patterson in St Stephen's Green. I have a lunch consisting of a few pieces of plaice and orange squash. The worst time is between 12.20 and 1.40 p.m. You are just hanging around and then it is the team talk. During the talk we received a great psychological boost as we watched Eamonn Coghlan's win in the US [where he was known as 'Chairman of the Boards'].

On the journey by coach to the ground, you see people from

your window walking on the sidewalk or coming out of pubs. They look up and give you a wave or thumbs up. The motorbike escort makes you feel a real VIP for the day.

The first thing you hear arriving at the ground is the wail of bagpipes out on the pitch. I go out with some players to test the condition of the pitch. I tog out at 2.05. The team photograph is taken at 2.20 and the warm-up begins around 2.30.

From 2.45 it is the fifteen players with Fergus Slattery and Pat Whelan giving their motivational speeches. Then the ref checks our studs and we are running out for the most fabulous moment of all. Once I am out there then finally all nerves are gone.

We won the game 12–7 which was all the more satisfying as the English employed thinly disguised intimidation tactics against me and others. In the opening minutes Tony Neary got his retaliation in early – as Ray Gravell would say – with a thundering late tackle. That challenge left me with a badly bruised right cheek. The Scottish referee Alan Hosie then warned Tony Bond when he followed up with a late charge. It was all part of the softening-up process, but as I said before, the best way to get back at opponents using less than honest tactics is to hurt them with points. I guess I succeeded as I registered eight points in that win.

Next up was Scotland in Edinburgh and from playing some of our best rugby against England, this was a forgettable performance. It was a very poor match played by two poor teams, though a strong swirling wind did not help. It finished in a draw, which was only the fourth in eighty-nine meetings. Two tries by Colin Patterson and a penalty from me were cancelled out by a try each from Andy Irvine and Keith Robertson with Irvine also adding a penalty.

We met Her Majesty Queen Elizabeth before the game. She shook hands and wished both sets of players well. I did not know what to say to her as I had forgotten the proper etiquette by which one addresses British royalty. So I settled for a basic 'Hello, nice to meet you'. Former President of Ireland Paddy Hillary greeted us regularly at Lansdowne Road and he was a man I got on very well with. He was from Clare and always had a little chat and extra smile for me, probably because of the Munster connection.

The thing I will never forget about that Scotland game actually happened off the pitch. I did a photo-shoot with an English tabloid newspaper and it transpired to be one of the biggest mistakes I made. It would have repercussions for me for the rest of my career. A newspaper photographer contacted me with a view to doing a photograph with a difference. I was so naïve and stupid not to see what was coming. The *Daily Mirror* then published a photograph of me on page three in swimming trunks. His exact words to me were that he wanted 'a beefcake photo' and in my foolishness I did not stop to think what it was all about or ask questions. Of course, those very words with regard to a tabloid should have put me on red alert.

That was part of my problem down through the years: I always tried where possible to accommodate everyone. The shot was taken in the swimming pool at Newpark Comprehensive in Blackrock where RTE was filming the sports celebrity series *Superstars*. The minute I saw the picture in the newspaper I wanted the ground to swallow me up. It had a devastating effect. This was particularly so since I am sensitive by nature and am also caring and respectful towards family, friends and people in general. When sports presenter Liam Nolan showed the photo during RTE's build-up to the game back in the Montrose studio, it added more fuel to a fire set to rage. This ensured that through the medium of television a greater majority of the public had seen the picture than would otherwise have been the case.

Colin Patterson mischievously pinned the page up in my room and however well intended that did nothing for my confidence. It meant I dreaded getting on the team bus as the lads would have a good laugh and give me a right ribbing over it. The chances of someone like Paul McNaughton letting you get away with something like that was zero. On the bus the atmosphere was strangely quiet and restrained. Nobody said a word to me about it. Later I learned that Noel Murphy went around to the lads individually and ordered them to keep their mouths shut. I am glad he did. The whole episode cast a huge shadow over my game that day. It only serves to show how you can be caught letting your guard down. It was a stupid mistake. In retrospect, it was entirely my fault and mine alone.

You live and learn and it was a highly embarrassing situation for me, my family and those close to me. Individuals within the IRFU and their head coach were furious about it. And rightly so. Murphy gave me a right rollicking. What I learned from that incident was that I was not going to be at everyone's beck and call. Saying 'no' to interviews and media requests became that little bit easier. Previously it was alien for me to say 'no', and unfortunately some took advantage of that.

Meanwhile some people in high places felt that I had become too big for my boots. In their view I was a prima donna. Of course, none of this was true. I was just the same as every other player in the side. Still, they say perception is everything and eventually I paid a very high price ... a price that would leave an indelible mark. In hindsight, it tore the heart and certainly the soul and confidence out of a career which was only in its infancy and developing.

CHAPTER 8

BADGERING, BAITING & BULLYING

My performances during the 1979 season earned me high praise and many awards. However, for reasons that still baffle me, the IRFU put the boot in. I was barred from accepting various awards as well as attending a number of functions. When I go through some of the incidents that were perpetrated against me it will seem almost inconceivable that this could happen. It would not register on the Union agenda today.

Before the dawning of the age of professionalism in the 1990s, 62 Lansdowne Road operated like a KGB machine. The name A.J.P. Ward was akin to a red rag to a bull. That was totally wrong and nothing short of scandalous. In daily life, every individual should have access to 'basic human rights'. Similarly, athletes participating in their sports become involved in ancillary activities, which is only natural. They are, or at least should be, perfectly entitled to do so. In modern times, examples of this would be promotions, marketing, education, charitable fundraising and so on. Financial gain through rugby fame was anathema to the authorities back then. They ruled with an iron fist. Today's ruling body is a different animal entirely. More than anything it is 'transparent'. That word had not been invented in my playing days.

During the 1979 Five Nations Championship I received the man of the match award for three of the four games we played. Colin Patterson won the other one. The IRFU had no objection to me accepting the first award. I received an inscribed clock presented by Paul McWeeney on behalf of the rugby writers. But what I cannot comprehend is why they refused to allow me to accept the other two.

Apart from those awards, *Rugby World* also organised a Golden Boot prize for the player of the year from each of the five countries participating. I won their award for Ireland in 1978 and 1979. Then, in 1979, I was also named European Player of the Year and there was no problem with me accepting an inscribed silver salver which was a perpetual trophy. But that same year when I was named Rugby Writers' Player of the Year, the IRFU for whatever reason were not happy. They stepped in and as a result the situation became farcical.

The awards were held at a lavish dinner at Lingfield race-course and some of the biggest names in rugby were present. They included stars such as Terry Holmes (Wales), Andy Irvine (Scotland) and Jean-Pierre Rives (France). However, before leaving for London I received an instruction from the IRFU that I was not to accept the award although I could attend the function. This angered me as I could see no logic to it. But I felt that I had no option but to do as they said. When my name was called out, I walked up to the podium shook hands with the MC, but I could not lift the trophy or cradle it in my arms. I could not even touch it. I just made a brief speech thanking all and sundry.

This award, and others which I could not accept, went to good causes. I remember that particular one went to Sunshine Homes who helped underprivileged children in the UK. There was one explanation for the IRFU's actions, but even then it was nonsensical. They shunned individual awards because they espoused rugby as a team game. Nobody believes in that concept more than me. But in all team sports you can never get away from the fact that individuals often dominate a game above others. That is why in all sports there are awards for man of the match, player of the year, player of the tournament, team of the year and so on. There always have been and there always will be. So the problems I had with the IRFU seemed to be unique. I guess I was the trailblazer, the jumped-up kid who had to be brought down a peg or two. But surely a player voted by rugby fans or rugby writers as their outstanding player of the year reflects well on the country for whom he plays as well as his team-mates. To argue otherwise would really mean that you must make a team consist of fifteen faceless individuals, then there would never be any individual recognition. Of course, that does not happen, but for some reason best known to some who sat around that Union table I was their *enfant terrible*.

It did not end there. In March 1979, having been asked to play for the Barbarians as I had been the previous year, I received yet another letter from the IRFU This time they asked me to turn down any invitation to play for the Barbarians that season. Your guess is as good mine as to why.

On 4 January 1980, I also received a letter from Wilson Hartnell O'Reilly which informed me that the IRFU had contacted them to say I would not be accepting a Sport Star of the Week award from the *Irish Independent*. It stated:

Dear Tony,

As you know, you were one of those chosen as Sport Star of the Week during the year. As you will see from the attached invitation, the presentation function has now been arranged.

However, I draw your attention to a letter received from the I.R.F.U. which would indicate that you would not be in a position to attend this function. I would appreciate if you could phone me on this.

Regards,

Ronnie Simpson

I ended up not going to receive the award. I meekly gave in. I was afraid of the consequences of what would happen if I ignored the letter. Put simply, I was an Irish international with an ongoing career which I wished to protect.

On 1 March 1980 another letter arrived from the IRFU about a match we had played against France a few weeks previously. It requested that I immediately pay back £1.92 owed to them:

Dear Tony,

Please let me have the sum of £1.92 being the sum of fifty per cent of phone calls charged to the room which you shared with John Robbie in the hotel in Paris.

An early reply would be appreciated so that match accounts can be finalised.

Yours sincerely,

Bob Fitzgerald

Secretary

The point I would make here is the mean-mindedness in the way they operated as a governing body. Before this, and following the

Ireland game against the All Blacks, I had one which demanded that I foot fifty per cent of my room bill with Colin Patterson. It really is too embarrassing to give the breakdown, but the total amounted to £2.66 which again included phone calls plus newspapers and milk! You could not make it up. Bear in mind, too, that as amateur sportsmen we were taking time off work *without compensation* to represent our country.

April Fools' Day 1982 brought another missive. Because of the date, I found it difficult to ascertain whether or not it was genuine, even though it was seemingly written in a serious tone.

Dear Tony,

Your involvement in various television and radio programmes during this year's internationals was discussed at a recent meeting.

The President Mr John Moore advised the Committee that you had communicated with him regarding your participation in various programmes including the current affairs programme Today Tonight.

Your communication with him involved the following:

(a)   to participate with Carwyn James in a BBC programme on coaching;

(b)   to commentate on TV or radio on the occasion of the Ireland versus Wales match;

(c)   to appear on the radio programme Talking Sport.

Mr Moore asked you to get Carwyn James to outline to us what was required.

Permission was not granted to you for (b) and as regards (c) it was pointed out to you by Mr Moore that it would be in your best interests not to do so at that time.

Furthermore, no permission was granted for you to appear on Today Tonight.

We would like to hear your response to these matters at your earliest convenience.

Yours sincerely,

Bob Fitzgerald

Secretary

Some three months later, on 7 July 1982, I wrote back (I feel embarrassed reading it now):

Bob,

Your letter was received and I must apologise as I have been very busy due to business commitments.

On the points you raise, it has never been my intention to contravene IRFU rules.

I must also stress that I did not participate in any interviews during Ireland versus Wales. I watched the game from the upper deck of the West Stand. I was asked to give a comment and this I did. After giving that comment I immediately went back to my seat in the stand.

I am therefore at a loss as to how anyone could think I was involved as a commentator.

With regard to Today Tonight, *I most certainly did contribute. But, on a current affairs show, I did not feel that I was in any contravention of IRFU regulations.*

However, I offer sincere apologies, if as it seems from your letter, that I should have sought permission for appearing.

I have always tried to do things right by the IRFU as evidenced by my approach to Mr Moore in advance.

In conclusion, I hope the Committee will accept my explanations on these matters and may I again apologise for not replying sooner.
  Yours sincerely,
  Tony Ward

On 14 February 1983, and again that date is something of an eye-catcher being that it is Valentine's Day, I received another request from them to explain myself. Perhaps they fell in love with the hassle they dished out or the replies and attention I was affording them. This one dealt with a CIE Marketing campaign whereby the transport company sought the services of various Irish sportsmen to sing the praises of their train services. I was one of four people chosen by them to participate in the four provinces and I agreed to help. The IRFU were very unhappy with my involvement in this. There were some high-profile hurlers and footballers involved in that radio campaign as well, but rest assured they received no such hassle from the powers-that-be at Croke Park at that time.

They wrote to me to inquire whether or not I had breached my amateur status. Not only that, but they also wrote to a Mr. Dargan, advertising manager for CIE in Middle Abbey Street, Dublin. Referring to the CIE adverts which were broadcast on RTE, Bob Fitzgerald also wanted me to furnish details of any money I may have received for participating in the campaign. He said I was to give details about my 'CIE contract'. I was given fourteen days to reply. So I wrote back to them explaining precisely the rationale behind the campaign. However, I omitted to mention anything about money to which they immediately replied asking about any payments or contracts. On 18 April I replied:

Dear Sir,

I refer to your letter of 21 March and I am rather surprised that further explanation is deemed necessary. However, in order to satisfy your Committee fully, I am explaining everything in the hope that I may be allowed to get on with running my business.

I have never had a contract with CIE nor do I presently have a contract with CIE.

Also, no agent has ever acted on my behalf nor do I have an agent, being an amateur sportsman.

I took part in the advertising campaign on behalf of Tony Ward Sport, which, as I've already explained, is made up of outlets in Limerick and Dublin.

As head of Tony Ward Sport, CIE paid me £100 which was to highlight the Limerick–Dublin rail link. This is nothing whatsoever to do with my rugby duties and responsibilities and has since been clarified by my legal advisor.

I do hope this will be the end of the matter. Quite frankly, I find it very strange and more than a little disconcerting that I am constantly being asked for explanations by you and your Committee. It seems that others are not being asked to explain similar matters to mine.

Yours faithfully,
Tony Ward

The matter came to a close on 27 April when the IRFU replied saying they were satisfied with my explanations. However, in a brief letter they reminded me about my responsibilities towards 'amateurism' as outlined by the International Rugby Board. It may have been the end of the episode for them but it was not over for me. A short while later a letter arrived from my solicitors seeking payment for their work on this case for me. CIE may have paid me £100 but it was quickly wiped out. The whole sad and sorry saga was to cost me financially. It left me out of pocket to the tune of just over £100 when I had to foot my legal bill for £203.28p. Smart business it was not.

More controversy arrived in 1987 when I was asked to participate in a coaching scheme by an organisation known as Rugbyclass. Their aim was to set up summer camps in Ireland and the UK coached by well-known rugby players from the four rugby home nations. Bill Beaumont was the coach in England, Andy Irvine in Scotland, Phil Bennett in Wales and I was asked to run the Irish camp, which would be based at Blackrock College, Dublin. Participants had to be aged between eight and eighteen with the fee very affordable. It sounded like a very good idea and I did not envisage any problems. Then the IRFU came at me again.

George Spotswood wrote to me asking that, in advance of their Committee meeting, he get the following information:

(i) for whom is the course intended;
(ii) who would be staffing the course;
(ii) what will it cost;
(iv) who is in overall charge of this organisation?

The new IRFU Secretary, Paddy Moss, then replied to me on 21 January 1987:

Dear Tony,
  I refer to your letter seeking permission to organise a coaching course in Blackrock College for August 1987.
  The Committee of the Union considered your request at a meeting and it disapproved of the fact that details of the

course had been circulated to schools when approval for the course had not been given by the Union.

It further noted that a brochure sent to schools, as well as newspaper advertisements using your name and photograph, are in contravention of Law 19 (2), a copy of which is enclosed for you.

The Committee asks that you give an immediate explanation as to why, as a current player, you allowed your name to be used in advertising a course which is being run as a commercial venture.

Yours sincerely,
G.P. Moss
Secretary

I replied to the new IRFU. Secretary in a spirit of final submission. With the new man in situ I decided that I did not want any more hassle. I drew a line in the sand, but the reality was they had won the war.

28 January
Dear Mr Moss,
I refer to your letter dated 21 January.
I wish to advise you that I had no idea my involvement in that course was in contravention of Law 19 (2).
I presumed, as PE is my full-time livelihood, that such a course would be regarded as part of my work in much the same way as summer sports camps are viewed.
As you have now pointed out to me that this is not the case, and as I do not wish to infringe my amateur status, I will therefore unreservedly withdraw my name from this course.
I will await your advice on how this should be done and will act upon that advice when received.

Paddy Moss then wrote to me saying that my letter was most co-operative. He also said that he contacted Rugbyclass and Simon Cohen asking that they desist from using my name for any future summer camps. It must be remembered at this juncture that all this nuisance correspondence came in the lead-up to the inaugural World Cup in Australia and New Zealand, a tournament and an Ireland squad which I dearly wanted to make. Paddy went on to advise me to contact Simon Cohen myself just to confirm this. In putting an end to the whole episode, he said that he would then issue a press statement. It read as follows:

PRESS STATEMENT

The Irish Rugby Football Union has today written to its four branches as well as to all schools and colleges affiliated to the Union. We have informed them that the Union disapproves of the proposal for a course for schoolboys to be held in Blackrock College in 1987 which has been organised by Rugbyclass Limited.

The course is being advertised as a Tony Ward School of Sport which is in contravention of the laws of the IRFU.

Tony Ward, on being advised of this, has withdrawn his name from the course.

The Union is not satisfied that this course would be run in conjunction with the laws and rules of the International Rugby Board relating to 'amateurism'.

It does not believe that a course run on a commercial basis is in the best interests of the game in Ireland. It has therefore advised its branches, schools and clubs not to participate in any way in this course or other course of a similar nature.

G.P. Moss

Secretary

The whole point in disclosing these correspondences is not just to show how it impacted on my daily life, but as evidence to show how a young athlete, in trying to make a decent career for himself, had to endure all of this cloak-and-dagger nonsense going on in the background. It went on for the best part of a decade, specifically targeting my off-field and business-related activities. I had become a major irritation to them. With regard to that particular governing body, there was only ever going to be one winner. And it sure as hell was not going to me. I lost and the damage was massive.

CHAPTER 9

IN THE SOUP WITH CAMPBELL

When your life revolves around rugby and suddenly you find yourself on the outside looking in, it is then you need support more than ever. That was my biggest gripe when I was ousted by a certain Seamus Oliver Campbell while preparing for the first Test in Surfers Paradise in June 1979. Had any one of the three-man jury who passed judgment – namely coach Noel Murphy, captain Fergus Slattery and manager Jack Coffey – had the gumption to explain to me why I was where I was at that point in my career, it would have made all the difference. The axe came down on me so quickly and, in the context of how the tour had gone to that point, unfairly. I was dropped from the Ireland team a number of times subsequently, but each and every one I saw it coming and I could prepare accordingly.

Australia 1979 caught me cold. What would have softened the blow significantly, and helped me move on, was a little bit of tact and sensitivity. What would it have taken for any of the three to have had the balls to explain where I was coming up short? Moreover, they could have told me what I needed to do to get back on track. But their punt was calculated. They had in Ollie Campbell a brilliant footballer who played to the maximum of his ability. A consummate playmaker and game-manager who steered us home in both Tests. I can state categorically that while the coach made a superficial effort to ease the hurt in the immediate aftermath, the captain and manager barely spoke to me for the remainder of that tour. By contrast the man who replaced me could not have been more sensitive or more attentive had the axe actually fallen on him.

The Campbell–Ward rivalry began in Donnybrook in the early 1970s. It was 1972 to be precise when Belvedere College and St Mary's came head to head. Our rivalry was honed on competitiveness, but out of mutual respect we became great friends. We have remained close friends ever since and there is hardly a month goes by when I don't hear from him. We have discussed everything about our careers – and our rivalry – which was a huge public talking point during that era. To put it in per-spective: it was almost a parallel of the recent O'Gara versus Sexton rivalry. The only difference was that Ollie and I inhabited the same rugby planet at pretty much the same time. On the other hand, Ronan O'Gara was in the latter stages of his great career when Johnny Sexton came along to take up the out-half reins. By contrast, there is a mere six months' age difference between Ollie and me.

While it all began on the schoolboy field of dreams at Don-nybrook, fast forward to 1979 when we were both named in the Irish squad for the tour of Australia. He was a relative novice in terms of Test exposure whereas I was pretty well established on the back of nine caps on the bounce. I guess as Five Nations Player of the Year it would not be stretching it to say I was the first-choice number ten heading out there. Or so

I thought. Perhaps there was an even split in that regard, but on the plane to Australia I never felt my position was in danger. Yes, Noel Murphy had dropped me in the past. And, yes, Murphy was now Ireland coach. But I was carrying all before me. Ollie would have to bide his time and wait. Only injury or a very poor performance could see him starting ahead of me.

Ollie's one and only previous Test appearance was against the Wallabies in Dublin in 1976, and on his own admission it had not been the happiest. He picked up a career-threatening injury shortly afterwards, but with typical courage and conviction worked his way back. Just making that squad for Australia was a fantastic achievement after he missed almost the entire season preceding. Ollie had sustained a nasty ligament tear so everything appeared to point to me having the responsibility for putting points on the board in the matches of consequence. I was not in the least blasé, but you could hardly have had two more contrasting situations setting out. So imagine my mild surprise when I was left out for our first game of the tour. Ollie was selected against Western Australia at Perry Lakes Stadium, Perth, on 20 May. I say mild because even though the newspapers were somewhat taken aback as well, it was felt that perhaps Ollie being short on game-time was being given an early tour run-out. He did well, too. He scored fourteen points as we won 39–3.

My disappointment did not last long. Three days later I was back in for our second match with a point to prove. I played to form. In attempting to show any doubters my full capabilities, I felt I sealed my place in the first Test with a record-breaking performance against Australian Capital Territory in the Manuka Oval, Canberra. We won 35–7 and I scored nineteen points, made up of a try, three penalties and three conversions.

My tally broke the previous record for an Irish tour game of seventeen points scored by Tom Kiernan against Queensland in 1967.

Just two games in and I felt I had done enough to be selected for the opening Test, and creating an Irish record added the gloss. That said, an incident with Jack Coffey left an indelible imprint on my mind. The manager came over to me in the dressing room before that game in Canberra. He was clearly not happy as he said: 'This is ridiculous. It is crazy – all this media stuff. I suggest you stay away from them.' This was not the Irish but the Australian media he was talking about. Sometimes you truly do despair and this was one such time. I bit my lip, but with his harsh words left a mark. This exchange, with a tour manager I was only just getting to know, certainly set me thinking. Coffey was almost like the messenger boy who sowed seeds of doubt in my mind. Those doubts, which every rugby player has, were always there. They are natural. But you erase them when attempting to be positive in order to survive. In retrospect Jack Coffey was reinforcing that Noel Murphy was no fan of mine.

So many thoughts started to enter my mind. Why did the manager react like that? Did Murphy put him up to it? Old images began to filter through of the coach on the sidelines at Dooradoyle or Temple Hill when my career first took off. 'The Soccer Player' was the term he constantly bellowed at me. All I ever heard from him, in mocking tones was 'Hey, soccer player this and that . . .' or 'Give it to the soccer player'. Even before we left for Australia I felt he was having verbal swipes at me at various squad sessions. He kept going on about the need for everybody to be there for the team and about team-work. There was no star system and no star. I may have many faults but getting ahead of myself is not one. He stressed that no player should think they were automatically in the starting team. I became very sensitive to what he was saying. No matter how hard I tried to banish these feelings, deep down they had rooted and I felt they were aimed in my direction. I reported the goings-on back to Frank Hogan, a father figure to me in Limerick. He told me to treat them with disdain, only in a lot more colourful language than that! In truth the constant harping on about the team aspect ate away at my confidence subconsciously. The vibes were not good. Even when we beat NSW 16–12 in Sydney, and I contributed two penalties and a conversion, I did not feel great. We led 16–0 in that game only to concede a couple of late tries. In the dressing room after the game the management banged on about those late scores, and once again I could not help but feel they were having a swipe at me.

So even though they said I would be rested for our fourth match, the last one before the first Test, with Ollie selected in my place, those sickly feelings in the pit of my stomach kept resurfacing. I was not happy with the situation which was developing. Of course, I was well aware that we had a big squad and, with four games and only three days between each one, the players had to be rotated. Then Ollie hit all eighteen points in our 18–15 win over Queensland at Ballymore, Brisbane. Some in the media suggested that we would both make the Test side, and that Ireland might be a more potent force if that materialised. It was put forward that Ollie play at centre with me in my usual out-half slot.

That was not to be as my doomsday scenario came true. I was dropped for the first Test against Australia. It created something of a sensation and here are some of the newspaper block headlines following the management triumvirate's white smoke:

WARD OUT – IT'S THE LATEST OF IRISH JOKES

IRISH DROP 'SOLO' STAR WARD

WHY WARD WAS DROPPED – THE ASTONISHING PRICE OF STARDOM

WHAT'S WRONG WITH WARD?

NO IRISH JOKE – WARD 'IS' OUT!

I remember now how I felt then as the bottom fell out of my world. I was nauseous. Now everything seemed crystal clear and made sense: Coffey having a go at me; Murphy's team references; Slattery's lack of communication. I also had a feeling that something was not right on the coach journey to Southport School immediately before training and the team announcement for the Ballymore Test. P.C. (Whelan) whispered to me: 'Prepare yourself.' I was rattled and dumbstruck. Although I had suspected as much in the weeks and days before, the reality of being dropped still caught me cold. My head was all over the place, so when I got off the coach I said deliberately in a loud voice: 'Congrats, Ollie – you're in.' Murphy heard this and had words with me. While I yearned for a bit of sensitive treatment, an arm around the shoulder, the last thing I needed was a verbal dressing-down.

The worst-case scenario had come to pass. I needed to confide in someone. After dinner on the evening I was dropped, Moss Keane and Pat Whelan brought me up to their room to escape and talk things out. But Murphy twigged that, too. His antenna was on red alert. Without any warning, the chief buck cat walked in a few minutes later and said to me: 'Come on, Tone – we'll go for a walk.' We went out and there was an uneasy silence between us as we strolled. But there was method to this madness. There was no talk about why he dropped me. There was no consolation for me or words of encouragement. Then he took me into a cinema. I was still feeling shocked and numbed by everything. All I can remember was that the film was about the Vietnamese War from an Australian perspective, but I was taking in nothing. Suddenly, well before the end, Murphy said: 'This is rubbish – let's get out of here.' I have no doubts what his *modus operandi* was. He was trying to get me away from the others. He wanted to try and stem any talk behind his back about me being dropped. He did not want any trouble in the camp. Understandable, but calculated. I interpreted it then as I do now. Tactically it was what it was.

We remained on in the Crest Hotel in Brisbane for the first Test against Australia on 3 June. Campbell was on fire. He played brilliantly in Ireland's 27–12 win, scoring fifteen points from four penalties and a drop goal. Everybody was ecstatic. I did my level best, too. But I can empathise with Brian O'Driscoll, when he was dropped in somewhat similar circumstances for the final 2013 Lions Test in Australia. 'All for one and one for all'? Do not believe it for one second! When the dust settled we had beaten Australia and were unbeaten in five games. As much as I was hurting inside, I put on a brave and united front for the rest of the lads. It was as genuine as I could make it. Have I been to reunions of that history-making 1979 side since? That hardly needs answering.

I was recalled to the side for our next match against New South Wales Country in Orange. I did not want to become the fall guy in a side that might have its unbeaten record ruined. This was all about the collective, but given the circumstances ahead of the second Test, I had a major point to prove. In truth, though, final team selection was already chiselled in stone. And rightly so. On Tuesday, 5 June we had a team meeting at 1 p.m. I could hardly look at the selectors. It was a tense time. In my diary I wrote the words: 'Very nervous'. We left for the Wade Park ground in Orange at 2 p.m. ahead of the 3 p.m. kick-off. We thrashed the opposition 28–7. I contributed twelve points and was reasonably happy with my performance, given the circumstances. It mattered not as I knew the crunch game for those looking to make a mark would be on the Saturday in our seventh and final match before the second Test finale at the Sydney Cricket Ground.

By that stage, several players were carrying knocks and others had cried off injured. This meant that against Sydney – New South Wales in disguise – the selectors played both Campbell and me. He was at full-back while I was wearing number ten and entrusted with the kicking duties. But I took that with a pinch of salt. We lost our unbeaten record despite holding a 9–0 lead and going in at half-time 12–3 up. Ciaran Fitzgerald scored a try for us after only three minutes and I converted. After adding two further penalties, it looked very much like we were set for another win. Sydney came at us like men possessed in the second period. It was a backs-to-the-wall job and we ended up scoreless in the second half. The tour had finally caught up with us in our penultimate game.

With all the changes I suppose we were bound to slip. Having said that, you have to give full credit to Sydney, who had learned from New South Wales' defeat in the earlier game. They saw blood and went for it. They had in their team some of the finest rugby players the game down under has seen with Tony Melrose, Laurie Monaghan and the legendary Mark Ella particularly outstanding.

While the media had speculated earlier that Ollie and I could be accommodated in the same team, the selectors were having none of it. Why should they? If it is not broke why fix it? If only that rationale had applied at other times on that tour. The triumvirate held the aces. They had gambled at Ballymore and won. The end justified the means. Not for me, but it certainly did for them. I guess you stand or fall by results and they did. I was trampled underfoot. But however downtrodden I felt the high moral ground was now theirs. That they were right to field the same team for the second Test goes without saying, and for one player in particular I was especially pleased. Former Mary's school-mate Rodney O'Donnell came of age on that tour, so much so that he was selected for the Lions the following year. As for me, I was a wounded animal hurting deeply.

We remained in Sydney for the rest of the week in Rushcutters Bay and returned to the SCG the following Saturday for the second Test. It was a poor game, but we won and Ollie was again the star man. In a 9–3 win, he slotted all our points and was made man of the tour. He thoroughly deserved it. In particularly trying circumstances, he had a role to play and he did it to perfection. He accumulated sixty points, which was an Irish tour record.

In everything that was said and written I will never concede that it was right to drop me. Subsequently, yes, but not then. Critics will say that Ollie's performances proved the selectors right, and as the fall guy who am I to argue with that? I would be lying if I said that it was not being dropped that hurt most. But the way it was done and everything that followed also hurt badly. I was never a star in my own mind, but as one Irish journalist wrote at the time: 'This star didn't fall – he was dragged down.'

I continued to play at the highest level for the best part of a decade up to 1988, but I was never the same confident player again. Ollie Campbell is a dear friend and his ability to step up to the mark was never in question. He was brilliant in his field, world-class. But my gripe was, and always will be, with the way things were done. This was Liam Brady's 'four rating out of ten' and my 'Willow Park party-dress moment' rolled into one. I may have been mature in years, but I was every bit as vulnerable nonetheless. No matter what heights we reach in whatever walk of life, we are all human and on that tour the human touch was missing. The powers-that-be had taken a gamble and won.

To their credit – and God knows they do not receive much praise for their work – the press knew this as well. Some of the most experienced and respected journalists out there on tour were central to the action and calling it as it was. They wanted to know why I had been silenced and told not to talk to them about my reaction to being dropped. Bear in mind they were staying in the same hotels as us throughout the tour. Before this we had all been allowed to mingle and speak freely. A number had highlighted this sudden U-turn. 'Why gag Ward now?' was typical of the type of eye-catching story filed by those on the spot.

Journalists Bob Messenger, Ned van Esbeck, Dermot Russell, George Ace and Colm Smith were all united as one. Colm Smith was particularly on the ball. He quoted manager Coffey as saying, 'It's not the end of a star', but Smithy retorted in his piece: 'I wonder. Quite clearly Ward was not happy when I saw him and he is not taking it well. A star has not fallen – he has been dragged down. Despite Coffey's assertions that the rest of the party are fine with it, there is uneasiness in the camp that is not healthy.' And when the decision to drop me was first announced, he wrote: 'What worries me about this decision is that it came as no surprise to me. Before we left Ireland I had heard rumours he was going to be dropped and in the past week the vibes were such that I knew he would be passed over. It is becoming increasingly dangerous to be a star in Irish rugby.' Back home eminent Irish rugby writer Mitchell Cogley pitched in: 'I have often wondered in the past that something strange seems to happen to normally rational thinking people when they become selectors and this particular decision fits right into the crazy pattern.'

All these years later, when I look back at that time, I see it as both a crossroads and downturn in my career. I bumped into former Lansdowne and Ireland selector Ray Carroll upon my return home. He reassured me that despite the tour success – as in the outcome justifying the route taken – the same decision would not have been made by an IRFU selection committee on home soil. It might have seemed innocuous, but, given his stature and moving into a new season, that comment meant a lot.

What Murphy, Slattery and Coffey did on that tour was to tear the heart and soul out of my game. My confidence was shattered and mine, much like Ronan O'Gara, David Humphreys and modern-day players of that ilk, was a game built on confidence. It is true that many great moments followed, and I stuck at it, but the damage was done. The jumped-up star was levelled. Even now in 2015 people still ask me why. I tell them that in all honesty I do not know, but I concede that my public persona did not help. Certain people felt I should be brought down to size and I was.

In a revealing and joint interview with me for the *Evening Herald* in July 1991, about the tour that made the man, and the man that made the tour, Ollie Campbell said: 'I was nearly as mesmerised as you at what happened. You have to remember that I had missed almost the entire preceding season through a serious ligament injury. Indeed I only returned from injury in a Leinster Cup game just before we departed for Australia. I had fully expected that Micky Quinn would be the number two out-half after you. So being part of the squad was the furthest thing from my mind that summer. In fact, I will make this point to illustrate my surprise at being called up. It was fully twenty-four hours after the squad was announced that I learned of my selection. If I thought I was in with a shout I would have listened to radio reports or gone out to get the newspapers. I did not. I was elated at the huge surprise of being included and the prospect of going out there to play made it all the sweeter.'

I replied: 'I have to say that was the one axing that I did not see coming. I should have, what with the *Daily Mirror's* "beefcake photo", but I did not. I have to say also that it was the one axing of my entire career which was not justified. Subsequent ones where you came in for me were, but certainly not that one.' Ollie concurred. 'I agree totally,' he said. 'I, too, never in a million years thought it would happen.'

A player works his way up the ladder, earns his stripes and then the others who come along have to wait their turn. That wait will usually only end when the premier guy is injured or endures a very poor period of form. I know I am not being in any way conceited when I say I was in the form of my life. So much for that long-established and much quoted myth of 'the Irish team being harder to get off than to get on'! Similarly, Ian Madigan, Paddy Jackson and others must now fall in behind Johnny Sexton. There is no way, barring a serious drop in form, that Sexton would be axed today. But now we live in a transparent age with transparent values underscored by transparent selection.

With everything taken into account, factors other than rugby entered into the decision-making process. On the subject of the

IRFU and selection, I have to stress that none of this reflects on the present governing body and how it goes about its business. In CEO Philip Browne they are blessed with a man of exceptional leadership and moral authority.

Noel Murphy and I developed a peculiar relationship over the many years that followed. Contrary to what many people would have expected in the circumstances, any bitterness has long since evaporated. Indeed, when word of my recent illness leaked out, three of the earliest calls of support that I received were from Leeside: Noel Murphy, Donal Lenihan and Moss Finn. I have no respect for what he and his fellow jurors did. But whenever we meet now, Murphy's greeting is warm and sincere. Today I can forgive, but I can never – and will never – forget. It is actually incumbent upon all of us never to forget. It is why I tell this story. I sincerely hope no young player or sporting talent of the future will be treated in such a career-shattering way. The way a young out-half took a noon flight to Australia from London on 14 May 1979, but never came back.

CHAPTER 10

LION IN AFRICA

Noel Murphy tried to reconcile our differences. One day, not long after we returned from Australia, he pulled up outside the Thomas Street sports shop. He wanted to talk. So, to find some privacy, we went outside to his car for what I guess he interpreted as a serious discussion. It was almost surreal. He asked, and advised, that I put behind me what had happened on the Australian tour. In his view we could have a fresh start. He also asked me not to be tempted into any rash decisions by listening to League offers from the UK.

In the furore surrounding the Australian tour I was considering every option when I arrived home. I had thought about leaving Union and moving to Rugby League. At that stage, although I had been named 1979 player of the year upon my return, my head was all over the place. For more than a fleeting moment I could have been tempted by League. Two years before, John Giles had approached me to meet him in Milltown to discuss signing for Shamrock Rovers on a full-time basis. We met but it was never a runner. He accepted that Rugby Union, along with my teaching degree, was then my chosen path.

Sensing I was unhappy post-Australia he came back to me. The chairman of a League club, and a close legal friend since his days at Leeds, had approached him to see if I might be interested in talking.

In my mind everything and anything was possible. There were also reports in various newspapers linking me with a move to Blackpool Borough. Apparently the seaside club from the lower division of Rugby League had offered £70,000 for me. At the time it was rare for top Union players to make the switch. Garryowen's Paddy Reid and the brilliant City of Derry and Ireland number eight Ken Goodall were the highest-profile Irish players to make the switch of codes. Ten years after my dilemma, Jonathan Davies of Wales blazed the trail. In a sense Davies created a much more enlightened attitude to what was until then close to sporting sacrilege in Union circles. It was an unadulterated snobbery all too typical of the amateur game back then. In effect, those who 'moved north' were ostracised within Union circles. It was a state of affairs actively driven by administrators, and specifically by those in the so-called four Home Unions.

Did Noel Murphy's gesture in coming to talk reassure me? No, although it was closer to the arm around the shoulder I had craved, or to anything I had experienced in Australia just a matter of weeks before. In my still confused mind it was much too little and far too late. I just wanted the politics and the messing-about to stop. I still loved the game and the only thing I wanted to do was continue playing to the best of my ability. Whatever lay behind the motive I thanked him for making the effort and we moved on.

Not long after his visit, Murphy was rewarded for his exploits Down Under. Having won seven out of eight games, including both Tests against Australia, he was put in charge of the 1980

Lions tour of South Africa. It was an honour and a recognition well earned. Despite his best efforts to make up with me, there was little likelihood of my name being announced in his British & Irish Lions squad. Ollie Campbell was the guaranteed out-half runner after his outstanding form in Australia and subsequently. There were also other out-halves from Wales (Gareth Davies) and Scotland (John Rutherford) who were well in contention. Sure enough, when the squad was announced, Campbell and Davies were the two number tens. Did it bother me? No, because it was justified. You know when you are in the running for selection, and for the original Lions squad in 1980 I was not. What transpired in Brisbane almost twelve months before was at the other end of that 'prepare yourself' spectrum.

But there was a glimmer of hope. Ollie's injury from two years before was beginning to play up. As he flew to South Africa with the tour party, he had a nagging hamstring problem and sat out the first two games. The Lions hit the ground running by winning fairly comfortably 28–16 against Eastern Province and 28–6 against an invitation team. Then Gareth Davies picked up a bad injury. The bush telegraph was hopping.

I got to hear about it fairly quickly. So many people told me that I would be flown out as an emergency replacement. I did not allow myself to get excited, but my heart did begin to beat a little faster. They had no recognised place-kicker available. Some journalists started ringing me, both from South Africa and closer to home, to say that I would soon be packing my bags. If I was called up there was every chance I would fill the out-half and goal-kicking void for the first Test which was fast approaching. My time in the lecture theatre with P.J. Smyth and Dave Weldrick was well spent as I dipped as deeply into psychology and mental preparation as I could go. Even at that distance I had to run through the permutations over and over again in my head. Campbell and Davies were both crocked: one man's injury is another man's opportunity, and boy was I up for it. The gods seemed to be giving me the nod. I waited for the official call.

Were the gods signalling their intent to have me back in my beloved position in the Promised Land? Was the Red Sea, ruled by the one who had hurled 'the soccer player' jibes, furling back its colossal waves? Those ferocious waves had smothered me, stifled me, swamped me, drenched me in tears. Now, at last, a parting of unbelievable and Biblical proportions appeared to be ushering me through. But I could not allow myself to be swept along by the tide of goodwill from the public. Not for a moment could I check to see that my passport was in date as some journalists had asked. There had to be official confirmation.

The suspense was unbearable. I knew I could rely on Syd (Millar) and Bill (Beaumont) as manager and captain respectfully for their full and unconditional support. The omens were good. Former Lions captain and IRFU administrator Ronnie Dawson had phoned to put me on red alert. That call meant the world. Ollie was being rested and given every chance to recover. He was now back for the third game against Natal. The Lions won 21–15 with Campbell kicking two penalties and a conversion. But injuries were piling up and the route to Cape Town and the opening Test was anything but clear. In the next training session, Ollie's hamstring injury flared up again. Time was running out and it was now less than two weeks to the first Test.

What made the situation even more acute was the knowledge that the Springboks were blessed with one of the world's greatest kickers in Naas Botha. The rumours did the rounds again: Tony Ward had to be called into the squad. Journalists kept putting the question of my involvement to the Lions management team at their daily press conferences. But the men in charge resolutely refused to comment. Eventually, though, under intense pressure and massive media scrutiny, they admitted having to wait on word from Union headquarters in London about replacements. A farcical situation was developing. While they were procrastinating, the Irish newspapers declared that not only had I been chosen to fly out but my travel arrangements had already been booked.

Eventually the manager and coach rang independently from South Africa to say that I was to travel out immediately. It was the news for which I had been waiting. But if I'm honest I still had mixed feelings speaking to Murphy. I was still sore after Australia and the Thomas Street rendezvous the previous August had done little to alleviate that feeling. Rightly or wrongly I suspected the motive. But those concerns soon dispersed and were replaced by an immense feeling of pride and joy. I was going to be a Lion, every player's dream.

I flew to London to catch a connecting flight to Jan Smuts Airport in Johannesburg. There was no business or first-class travel in those days, but the former South African captain and prominent business man Jan Pickard happened to be on that overnight flight and hearing of my presence arranged for a row of seats to be freed up so I might put my head down. It was a gesture much appreciated at the time and since. Sitting next to me on that flight was a rock and roll group called Des Henley and the Fumbles. They were Bill Haley's backing band and later one of the group arranged for me to pick up tickets to see them in concert in Johannesburg. After the show, John Robbie and I had a few drinks with Des and another band member, Ace, in the Landdrost Hotel in downtown Jo'burg. The insight into rock and roll was fascinating.

But something had been lost on almost everybody in the huge fuss created around me replacing the injured players: I lacked fifteen-a-side match practice big time. It was almost two months since I had last played a full-on match with Garryowen. That was when we lost to Shannon in the first round of the Munster Cup. However, I had been playing sevens in the UK, Paris and Amsterdam at a high level so was in good nick physically. But at the back of my mind it was still an obvious worry. The heat and humidity, as well as the altitude of the high veldt, would also be something else to endure and overcome.

Moving through the arrivals hall and out the exit doors of the airport, along with Syd Millar who had come to meet me, I was confronted by a large scrum of around thirty or more photographers and reporters. I was soon made aware that I was headline news. Arriving at base camp following a connecting flight to Bloemfontein, there to meet me with that look in his eye was Noel Murphy. I was on red alert from the outset. He took me aside for another private word. This time he had major concerns about the media. According to him, they were making it look as though there were major problems between the two of us so we had to do our best to try and get along. I had just arrived. It was some introduction. Here I was in South Africa and he wanted to bring up Australia all over again. Once more he said that we had to put it behind us. Welcome to South Africa, Tony. Did you have a comfortable flight? How is your fitness and kicking?

On 27 May, just over a week after I got the hint about being called out to South Africa, I was straight into action. After lunch at 1 p.m., I boarded the team bus for the ground. The match against another invitation XV was at 3.30 and all day I was extremely nervous. I was always tense before matches, but this was different. After everything that had happened, as well as all the questions and doubts in my mind, the day of reckoning arrived. Everything had happened so quickly, which in itself only added to the tension. Perhaps it was a little too fast and too rushed. It was against my nature to prepare for a match in this way. This was all new territory for me, geographically and psychologically, and with the heat, most definitely physically.

Although we were playing at sea level in Stellenbosch, the home of Mr South African Rugby, Doctor Danie Craven, it was still very, very hot. You felt you were playing in an environment starved of oxygen. The nervous tension remained in me right through the game. I do not know why. On the evidence at my disposal, I can say that my season was over and I had not practised kicking a ball at goal for the best part of two months. All the other factors I just mentioned come into play, not helped perhaps by jet lag.

My performance was woeful. The struggle I experienced transmitted to my general play. Out of nine attempts I only converted three. Some specialist goal-kicker! Furthermore, the injuries which plagued the camp claimed another victim when I received a bang on the thigh and suffered a haematoma or dead leg. We won 15–6, but of six first-half kicks I only put over one, which was a conversion of John Carleton's try. I suppose one mitigating excuse was that many of the kicks were long-range. But it was not good enough, not by any standard.

An order came from the sideline that centre Clive Woodward was to take over the kicking duties. But when Clive completely fluffed his first attempt, the responsibility reverted to me. Thankfully I grew into the game after the break and I landed two more penalties from two attempts. Much more significantly I struck the ball cleanly and I felt back in the groove. My handling, line-kicking and general play was much better and far more confident.

There was also a very serious incident during the game which could have resulted in a fatality. The heat was such that prop Fran Cotton had to be assisted off the field clutching his chest. His face was contorted in pain and it was discovered that he suffered a minor heart attack. Fran was sent back to England for treatment and recovery. There is no doubt we were jinxed in the injury department during that tour, and the severe limitations to the squad were probably the reason I earned my place in the team for the opening Test. There was certainly no way I would have made it into any international side the way I played in my warm-up match.

The big game was to be played on Saturday, 31 May. Despite everything that had happened, it had been some turn-around from being dropped in Australia exactly a year before. Ollie Campbell gave me great support in the days before the Test. He came to watch me practise my kicking, which is something we did quite a bit on tour during our careers. It was great having him there. His presence brought a sense of support and camaraderie, and away from all the rubbish written about us we were always good friends.

Also accompanying us was our liaison officer Choet Visser, who was a successful businessman from Bloemfontein. He looked after us on the practice pitch and in every other possible way. He was so far ahead of his time in the way in which he put our welfare first. His home was full of the most amazing rugby memorabilia from all over the world. I have never seen anything like it. It really was a museum to rugby. Choet was an amazing character and an out-and-out gentleman. It is important for kickers to get in practice on the eve of a big game, preferably in the stadium in which you will be playing. Now it is standard practice, but not so back then. For Choet, however, no obstacle was insurmountable: Newlands it was.

On 28 May the knock on my knee swelled up even more and I had to go and see the physiotherapist, Mrs Pilkington, in down-town Cape Town at 4 p.m. Next day I had to be up early to go and see her again at 9.30 a.m. When I went to training after seeing her, I could not kick the ball at all. I had lunch and spent the afternoon in my hotel room waiting until I could go and see her again at 4 p.m. There was a certain amount of pressure building up in my mind at this stage.

On 30 May, two days after my knee swelled and a day before the Test, I went to have lunch with Ollie and Phil Orr. Then we went out to train and I exacerbated the injury by tearing the fibres in my thigh. I was straight back to the physio again. It was not until 7.30 p.m. that I left, and that was only because we had a team meeting back in the hotel to finalise things for the game, otherwise I could still have been there at midnight! It was decided that no decision would be made about my fitness until the next morning. It must be recalled at this juncture that the added stress was as a result of the immense pressure on the entire squad and backroom staff. Remember: I was the only kicker.

Next morning, at 9.30, I was back at Mrs Pilkington's practice. She must have been sick of the sight of me, but in reality it was her job. However, I suppose she must have been feeling a certain amount of pressure herself to try and get me right for the match. She did the best she could and when I returned to the hotel it was decided after a lunchtime meeting that I would be risked in the game. I would play with strapping and I would also be given as much painkilling medication as was possible.

The team arrived at the ground at 2.30 p.m., and right up until 3.20, just ten minutes before kick-off, they worked on me. I was immediately whisked away, spy-versus-spy-style, to the medical room where I received a heavy dose of cortisone into the belly of the thigh. I didn't see the rest of the team until we went on the pitch for kick-off. We lost the match, but I had a better than average outing in the circumstances. I had no warm-up and my most vivid memory was all the treatment I received from the medics. In the bed in the cubicle beside me, also cloaked in supposed secrecy, was the massive Springbok lock Louis Moolman. And when I say massive I mean *massive*! He, too, was getting a jab.

We led 9–0, but endured a disastrous fifteen-minute period before half-time when we conceded three tries. My right leg was heavily bandaged as I kicked those three first-half penalties. In the second period I also kicked a drop goal off my left foot and two further penalties to tie the scores at 22–22. My personal tally of eighteen points was a scoring record for a single British Lions match up to that point. It beat the previous record of Tom Kiernan, which stood at seventeen points. But a late South African try broke our fierce and courageous resolve. We lost 26–22.

The newspapers highlighted our bravery and because of my goal-kicking return I was also singled out for mention. The *Sunday Cape Times* came up with an eye-catching line: 'The baggy-trousered general was simply magnificent'. I wasn't, but morally I was brave to a fault as there is no way I should have played given the nature of the injury. The headline probably referred to my heavily bandaged right leg which had the effect of making my shorts look baggy. My record stood for thirteen years before Scotland's Gavin Hastings equalled it in 1993, followed by Johnny Wilkinson in 2001. But the Irishman, Englishman and Scotsman were upstaged by a Welshman: Stephen Jones scored twenty points in the Lions' 28–25 loss to South Africa in 2009. Another Welshman went on to eclipse that and holds the current record: Leigh Halfpenny put twenty-one points on the board in July 2013 when the Lions routed the Wallabies 41–16. The magnificent Halfpenny scored five penalties and three conversions.

Mind you, there is no comparison between kicking then and now. In my time we had to kick a hand-stitched leather ball, not like the user-friendly, aerodynamic balls of today. When it rained the leather sucked in the water and it became like a bar of soap, and a very heavy bar of soap at that. We did not even have the luxury of sand to make our kicking tee – not even on the desert-like high veldt – never mind the ultra-techno kicking tees of the modern day. Getting the ball to stand still, particularly on a windy day, with a heel-made tee, was an achievement in itself. Different times, different challenges, I guess.

My kicking out of hand had been a bit wayward and I paid the price. Between the damage done through playing with an injured thigh and rehabbing, allied to Ollie's return to fitness, it was a fortnight before I would wear the Four Nations' shirt again. That was against the Junior Springboks in Jo'burg. While I admit that my tactical kicking was loose on occasion, the kick-chase and first-up tackling also left a lot to be desired. I knew I had underperformed and the consequence of being overlooked for the next game was easily handled. What had transpired in Australia twelve months before had not been so readily accepted.

In the second Test played in Bloemfontein on 14 June, the Boks again chalked up twenty-six points to the Lions' nineteen. That put them 2–0 ahead with two Tests to go, so we were playing catch-up. I had an outside chance of making it back for the third Test and had a run-out in a match against the South African Barbarians in Durban. A crowd of 40,000 turned up for the game in Kings Park. The legendary

Argentine Hugo Porta played opposite me and didn't disappoint. I was paired with John Robbie and we combined well. His passing and general reading was superb. I managed seventeen points, including my one and only try on the tour. We led 19–6 at half-time and my second-half try contributed to an eventual 25–14 win.

My performance, though, was not enough to win a place in the side for the third Test. Ollie, to his immense credit, scored twenty-two points against Western Province a few days later, and he was rightly picked for the Port Elizabeth Test the following Saturday. I was again named as a substitute, but I was in for a huge shock . . . self-induced, I might add. When I opened my bag in the dressing room to tog out, to my horror I found that I had left my boots behind at the hotel. It was bizarre and had never happened to me before or after. I was mortified. On top of everything else, and especially my less-than-ideal relationship with the selectors, this was a nightmare. My heart was jumping out of my chest. Then in the opening minute as the replacements were making our way up to our designated position in the main stand, Ollie received a smack in the face and had blood pouring from the wound.

My heart was pounding even more as I was given the nod to warm up and get ready to replace him. It was panic stations. John Robbie had managed to grab a ball-boy before togging out to find a pair of size nines, which were far too big for me. I would not have been able to play in them. To add to that, the studs were moulded and the pitch was waterlogged, so in such conditions a disastrous situation was in the making. It would be akin to an ice-skater having to perform in high heels. As I stood there on the sideline waiting for Ollie who was receiving treatment, I was thinking: 'This can't possibly be happening.' I wanted the ground to swallow me up. Fortunately for me Ollie was able to play on. But I vowed there and then never to go through that again.

South Africa won by the narrow margin of 12–10. The fall-guy on the tour was a certain Clive Woodward, and in Port Elizabeth he was accused – wrongly – of losing us the third Test. I have always felt sorry for Woody, who was arguably our best attacking back on that 1980 trek. For sure, he lost concentration when tapping the ball into touch and the South Africans took a quick throw to score what proved to be the winning try. It was a pivotal moment, and in the process secured the series for the Springboks, but to suggest the winning and losing of that tour came down to Sir Clive is as unfair as it is untrue.

Now, though, the only thing we had left to play for in the fourth and final Test was our pride. I was hoping to end my South African tour by making the team for the dead rubber in Pretoria. But I was actually very fortunate to be around at all. Between the Bloemfontein and Port Elizabeth Tests I experienced one of the most frightening moments of my life. John O'Driscoll, a great colleague and warrior on the pitch, saved my life when I came close to drowning. On a mid-tour break we were relaxing at the Umhlanga Rocks Indian Ocean resort near Durban. I went for a swim but was washed out to sea by what is known as the Northern Natal Coast Undercurrent. I am not a strong swimmer anyway but this underwater rip was mighty. I was shouting and gesticulating for help as I drifted out towards the shark nets. The current was strong and I was struggling. Thankfully, J. O'D was a very strong swimmer and he jumped in after me. So, too, did a lifeguard and between them I was pulled back in to safety. This was *Bondi Rescue* with knobs on. When I was pulled from the sea I was exhausted. Never had my energies been sapped in such a way on the field of play. I really thought I was going to die. Afterwards, Jim Renwick nicknamed me 'Flipper', but I don't think my team-mate understood how serious it had been.

We finally received a well-deserved, and long-overdue reward in the final Test with a 17–13 victory at Loftus Versfeld. But despite the Test results, morale in the camp was good. As in 1974, the midweek side, or 'dirt trekkers' as they were more affectionately known, remained unbeaten for only the second time in Lions' touring history.

So that was the story of my 1980 Lions adventure. I played in the first Test, having been brought out as an emergency replacement, and I broke a record that had stood since Tom Kiernan in 1968. The top Lions scorers were Ollie with sixty points from seven appearances, Clive Woodward on fifty-three points from eleven appearances and me with forty-eight points from five. Of the eighteen matches played, we lost three, but crucially they were all Tests, and that for any Lions tour is the bottom line. As we returned home via London, Colin Patterson sat next to me on several spare seats provided for him on the flight. His badly injured knee cruciate, suffered against Griqualand West in Kimberley, marked an end to his playing career, and I guess summed up the entire tour for us. I recall some big soccer names joined a few of us rugby boys in a sports debate of sorts on the flight. Dave Sexton, Steve Heighway and Viv Anderson were returning from a stint of coaching in South Africa. Coaching versus natural ability was just one of the topics discussed. It was a big downer when I returned home to normal living. After the hype, excitement, five-star luxury and red-carpet treatment wherever we went, I felt as if I had come back down to earth with a bang.

That was the rugby. But there was another, altogether different and much darker side to touring South Africa. From the

My mother was my rock and made so many sacrifices for me. I am indebted to her.

St. Louis Rathmines 1961

Taking my First Holy Communion at St Louis Primary School, Rathmines, Dublin 1961.

I am crouching on the far left and in the same schoolboy side as the great Liam Brady (third from left), ahead of a match in Portadown.

I am seated far left in the immortal Munster team that still remain the only Irish side ever to have beaten the mighty All Blacks.

My debut for Munster versus Australia in January 1976, which we narrowly lost 13–15.

Displaying nerves before my first ever Ireland Final Trial for the Whites (Probables) at Lansdowne Road, December 1978.

I am hidden behind Moss Keane's left ear (in centre) with try scorer Christy Cantillon (left) and Les White (right), after helping Munster beat the All Blacks in 1978.

My first Ireland cap versus Scotland, January 1978.

Breaking the line against France in our Five Nations encounter at Lansdowne Road, which ended in a 9–9 draw in 1979.

With Colin Patterson, having just been presented with the 'Man of the Match' award at a training session following the French game.

With the Lions, 1980. John Robbie, Dai Richards and myself posing in front of Table Mountain.

Friendly versus Spurs
at Thomond Park,
August 1981.

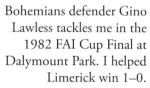

The flagship sports
shop in Limerick.

Bohemians defender Gino
Lawless tackles me in the
1982 FAI Cup Final at
Dalymount Park. I helped
Limerick win 1–0.

Guesting for Irish American football team on the day of the Super Bowl final.

The iconic moment when I came off the bench for Ollie Campbell to huge roars at Lansdowne Road – the one and only time I came on as a replacement.

Wearing a Southampton shirt at their old stadium, The Dell, after helping Limerick to a 1–1 draw in the 1981 UEFA Cup (Europa).

Kicking for touch at Twickenham with Philly Orr in the background.

Left to right: Moss Keane, Willie Duggan, myself and Tony Doyle during our 12–9 defeat to England at Twickenham in the 1984 Five Nations. I scored all our points.

My return to the national team in 1986, my first match for Ireland in two years. I think the overall score of losing 10–9 hurt less than tackling Gavin Hastings!

Ollie Campbell and me at a fundraising tag rugby event in Donnybrook for Aoife Beary (a Berkeley balcony collapse victim), July 2015.

My three daughters congratulate me at an Alumni Awards Dinner in the University of Limerick. From left to right, Nikki, Ali and Lynn.

Following my diagnosis, I was very pleased to get involved in the Men's Health campaign to promote their work.

Men's Health Week 2015
Creating Culture Change
Monday 15th - Sunday 21st June 2015

IT'S TIME FOR A NEW SCRIPT

Visit www.mhfi.org to find out more

On the steps at St Gerard's just ahead of going public with news of my cancer battle, September 2014.

time I walked through the arrivals area of Jan Smuts Airport I had made it my business to scratch below the surface of this rugby-daft country. I did – and it hurt. The reality of sport and life in South Africa was all too clear. I vowed never again to return as a player or coach as long as apartheid existed in that otherwise magnificent nation.

CHAPTER 11

APARTHEID

Having passed through Customs, I received my first real taste of South African life when I arrived at the baggage area in Jan Smuts Airport, Johannesburg, in May 1980. The signs glared out at me: 'Black Only Toilets' and 'White Only Toilets'. Somehow it put my own problems into context. South Africa had serious issues and real problems. I had read about apartheid, and seen images and examples of it on television, but here was the reality in front of my very eyes.

The following day, ahead of the Orange Free State game in Bloemfontein, I visited a black township outside Bloemfontein with Colin Patterson. It was Colin's idea, not mine. After all, it was my first full day in the country. But the things I saw broke my heart. It was like a different world. The impact was immediate and in retrospect, although I was only a replacement, it was probably not the best way to prepare for a game emotionally.

We drove around slowly in the back of the car. Colin was snapping photographs from his camera. There was a reason for this: we were too afraid to get out. The houses were made of aluminium and tin. It reminded me of the galvanised roofing on farm sheds back home. But these were tiny homes. There were thousands and thousands of them everywhere which collectively made up a 'shanty town'. They were crammed together and it was impossible to imagine how people could inhabit them. The majority of them looked no bigger than an 'outhouse', which, in western parlance, was the old-style toilet built outside the main dwelling. Speaking of toilets, they used a barrel. Another thing that struck me was the number of cars. There were old bangers everywhere. Under South African law blacks could not own their own house so they bought cars to use as extra beds.

I was deeply moved by what I saw. At a later stage in the tour, the day after the third Test, in fact, I tried to visit New Brighton Township just outside Port Elizabeth. I was with Bill Beaumont and a number of the press corps. However, the authorities had been tipped off – by whom I have no idea –and they refused us entry on the basis of civil unrest, or 'internal riots' as they termed it. In truth, they were not happy. Our earlier visits had caught the attention of the media. The reports did not make good reading, so the powers-that-be were forced into making a stand against a repeat.

There was a huge international media presence for the third Test so all eleven entrances to the township were sealed off. Armed police were taken there in a convoy of Land Rovers and their excuse was indeed 'that a riot had broken out'. This was untrue as the place was so quiet. Instead, we were invited by Cheeky Watson to visit his home. It made for an extraordinary experience with an extraordinary family. The Watsons were not liberal but a family with great Christian faith in justice. Along with brother Valance and Crusaders player Mike Ryan, Cheeky had joined the local, non-racial Kwaru rugby club. However, in South Africa at the time, things were never that simple. In order to train or play they needed permits to go into townships. Conversely, the black players needed permits to leave. Even so, by 1979 Kwaru had developed into a top-quality, highly-rated side.

Cheeky is the father of recent Springbok back-row player Luke Watson, but back then he was an outstanding rugby prospect himself. Four years earlier, in 1976, Springbok coach and selector Ian Kirkpatrick had told the aspiring winger that he was prepared to give him written guarantees that he would make the following year's South African tour to France. But there was a condition attached: he had to stop playing for Kwaru. The then twenty-year-old refused to compromise. He thereby become the first, and to the best of my knowledge, only player in South African rugby history to turn down the revered Springbok blazer on moral grounds.

Of course, Cheeky's decision, with brother Ronnie's support, went down like a lead balloon with the authorities. The repressive machine of the ruling regime went into overdrive. Their life became hell with the roadblock that morning in New Brighton just one tiny manifestation. The stories, ranging from house-burning to stabbings and robberies of the Watson clan, are too many and too detailed to list now. Suffice to say that for the best part of two decades the family was nearly destitute and went through hell. Listening to Cheeky and hearing what he was saying that June day had a profound influence on this aspiring young Lion. But like the would-be Springbok, I was more than capable of seeing for myself and making up my own mind. And that I did. As a postscript, and to show how far South Africa has progressed since apartheid was dismantled, Cheeky Watson is now the president of the Eastern Province Rugby Union.

Another thing which surprised us greatly was the widespread attitude of non-whites towards the Lions. They wanted us to win. We found this amazing as they were South Africans. Yet everywhere we went they implored us: 'Go man – beat the Boks.' A visit to a Bloemfontein golf course on the day after the second Test made for another indelible experience. Along with John Robbie, Clive Woodward and Paul Dodge we decided we would have an Ireland versus England golf classic. It was as much to banish the memories of the previous day's defeat as anything. When we arrived a large group of black youngsters surrounded us shouting, 'Masta, Masta' in their quest to become our caddies for the day. I wanted the ground to swallow me up. I was never anybody's 'Master'. I resented it even if it was standard practice and compulsory dialogue in the apartheid country. I took two young lads aside and introduced them to the golfers they would caddy for. 'This is John and this is Clive, this is Paul and I'm Tony,' I said. They were puzzled to the point of confusion, which in retrospect wasn't fair on my part. So, during the round, the youngsters did not call us by any name at all.

At least, minus the 'Masta' and a useless golfer to boot, I was much more at ease as Ireland slaughtered England. I wish. Later we learned the boys were only allowed to play golf once a week and that was at the crack of dawn on a Monday morning. They were paid a few rand for caddying but they had to fork out much more than that for the privilege of playing each week. Tipping was forbidden but needless to say we were very generous to our helpers. They were ecstatic with the small amount we gave them. It left them feeling like they had just won the lottery and become millionaires. These shocking inequalities were everywhere.

Despite all the superficiality and five-star treatment, as

politically important guests of the nation, hatred was never far below the surface. Even the slightest scratching and it emerged. A couple of incidents come to mind. The first was at Cape Town University (UCT) where I went to get in some kicking practice with Ollie Campbell on the morning before the Newlands Test. The word obviously got around the campus and a large crowd of mixed-race students gathered. They began to holler a tirade of abuse in our direction. They called us racists and told us, in no uncertain terms, to go home. We had to abandon the kicking session and quite literally run for cover.

Similarly, on the morning of the first Test, there was a South African soccer team staying in the same hotel at the foot of Table Mountain. They, too, made their antagonistic feelings known when mingling around the hotel foyer. While nowhere near as abusive as the students in UCT the previous day, the message was the same: 'You should not be here.' What registered was the multi-racial aspect to the soccer side with those most vocal being European or white.

Another time, in Bloemfontein, a group of us were coming down for breakfast. A chambermaid, who was struggling and weighed down with a tray of glasses, entered our lift. The hotel manager, who saw her getting in, ran over and roared at her in Afrikaans. She was told to get out and go by the stairs. You could have cut the silence in that lift with a knife. We were mortified. It was another deeply troubling reminder of everyday, run-of-the-mill apartheid.

The more places and people we visited, the more a conflict of interest grew in our minds. After the second Test, we were in the presence of a group of wealthy women who talked about 'the black problem'. As a human being I felt ashamed listening to them. Among other things they boasted about the number of servants they had. The most disturbing aspect was that it seemed so normal to them. It was as if they knew no different and that their views were inbred in them. It was sickening to realise that in their thinking, blacks were no better than animals. It was mind-numbing.

Doctor Roger Young, a former Irish scrum-half and long-term Western Province resident, took me to visit a handicapped children's home in Cape Town. John Robbie, Bill Beaumont and journalists Ned van Esbeck and Sean Diffley came with us. It was not unlike the former Harcourt Street Children's Hospital in Dublin or Our Lady's Hospital for Sick Children in Crumlin. To see children with terrible illnesses was one thing, but one of the saddest sights I ever saw was in that hospital. It impacted on me more than anything else on the tour. Accommodation was segregated. Having met us rugby tourists, these severely handicapped kids were returned to rooms and wards clearly labelled according to skin colour: 'Black Children', 'White Children', 'Coloured Children'. While these youngsters knew no different, the principle of a government standing over this clearly standard practice left me ashen-faced.

However, there were also many wonderful moments on that South African tour. One was meeting and befriending the legendary out-half Errol Tobias, who lined out opposite me for the Proteas on my Lions debut in Stellenbosch. He became the first black or coloured player to represent the Springboks and accumulated six caps between 1981 and 1984.

Even so, I will never forget the children's hospital. That experience has stayed with me and will remain with me forever. It was as much as I could take. As in any conflict of interest, my mind was made up for good right there and then. When I left in June 1980 I vowed never to return as long as apartheid was still in force. The following year I was invited to join the Ireland tour of South Africa. There was no decision to be made. In all I was invited back on three more occasions as a player. I refused each time. As a matter of conscience, and as much as I loved the game and representing my country, it was a no-brainer.

It bought me back to my days in college when I did a paper on 'sport and politics and their interaction'. The trouble was that in South Africa, specifically to the Dutch Afrikaner, they were one and the same. Not for a minute did I think that my stand would help overturn apartheid. But small steps such as people like me questioning the role of rugby and its connection with the outside world, might just provide a little food for thought. So if my refusing to go to South Africa made a small bit of difference to the point that an Afrikaner would ask himself the question 'why', then it could only be a good thing. Put simply, they had to ask themselves some serious questions. They had to toe the line. They had to bring themselves up to the same level of human rights as the rest of the world.

I am an Irish citizen. I am proud of that. A South African, whether black or Afrikaner, should also have had that feeling and citizenship as well. I felt strongly that *all* players in South Africa should have the same opportunities to play rugby as everyone else. South Africa tried to pull the wool over the world's eyes. They maintained for decades that blacks and coloureds were not up to scratch and could not play to the highest levels. But it was Catch 22: how could non-whites reach international standard when they were denied equal opportunity? Wherever I played around the world, we all went for a drink afterwards. In South Africa a black, even if he managed to play, did not enjoy that basic right.

So I had no compunction about pulling out of Ireland's tour in 1981. There were others who put their heads above the parapet: Moss Keane, Donal Spring and Hugo MacNeill were the most prominent. To this day I admire Hugo for having the courage to do what he did. For Mossie, Fitzy and Springer, there were other factors at play. Not for a minute does it detract from their impact. But for Hugo, a young student making his way in the game, his decision on grounds of conscience was equivalent to Cheeky Watson's stand in South Africa. Hugo went on to become one of the all-time great full-backs, but his decision not to play rugby in South Africa showed his most courageous trait of all.

In 1987, along with Jim Glennon, I was invited to play with a South Sea Barbarians XV consisting mainly of Fijian players. The year before there had been a Kerry Packer-style attempt to recruit a squad from around the world and, while flattered to be included, my answer was still a firm and definitive no.

I was also picked to play for a World XV in Cardiff as part of Welsh Rugby's one-hundredth anniversary celebrations. But the anti-apartheid lobby pressurised me not to play as there were several South Africans playing in the invitation side. I did not want to be seen to be hypocritical so I acceded to their request. Later, though, I felt they overstepped the mark on that occasion. As the years went on, and with the dismantling of apartheid, naturally my views mellowed.

I have been back to South Africa a number of times in a journalistic capacity since. Total isolation was never the definitive answer, but added to the little solo runs along the way it surely helped. Not for one moment do I believe that Tony Ward's refusal to go to South Africa impacted on government policy. But my mind was in step with worldwide opinion at the time. There was a collective of countries, sporting bodies, businesses and political organisations who opposed the apartheid system and that opposition snowballed. I was just the tiniest cog in that wheel, but a cog I was. So, too, was Hugo.

By contrast, my former colleague John Robbie not only travelled on the 1981 tour but made a major career decision to do so. However, John spoke to *Rugby World* a few years later explaining his decision to quit his top job with Guinness over his decision to go to South Africa. This is a short extract from what he wrote in 1993: 'Isn't it the supreme irony that during the days of apartheid rule, rugby supported South Africa? Ireland travelled there in 1981 and England in 1984. Those decisions were misguided and potentially damaging for players, fans and ordinary people alike. Many of us realise that now and will forever have to carry the can of participation.' John eventually moved to South Africa to live and has been inspirational in bringing about change from within. I find it difficult to articulate the respect I have for the former High School, Trinity, Greystones, Leinster, Ireland and Lions scrum-half. Through the courage of his radio broadcasting, he is very much an unsung hero in the fight for civil rights if ever there was one. I firmly believed from 1981 onwards a real change would come about by depriving South Africa of their international exposure through rugby. It may well have been naïve, but it was the collective thinking back then.

The Irish anti-apartheid movement, and its chairman Kader Asmal, were in regular contact with me. I suppose I had a high profile worth exploiting and, with my full and unconditional support, they most certainly did enlist my help. This was one such letter:

IRISH ANTI-APARTHEID MOVEMENT
20 Beechpark Road
Foxrock
Dublin 18
3 November 1980

Dear Sir,
We understand the Irish Rugby Football Union is shortly to decide on whether or not to accept an invitation from the white-dominated South African Rugby Board to undertake a full tour of South Africa in 1981.

We are appalled that the I.R.F.U. is still, after the experiences of the Lions Tour, determined to continue its links with apartheid sport in South Africa.

We urge you to consider this matter seriously once again. Officials of non-racial sporting bodies in South Africa cannot get passports to put their case to the international community so we take up the cudgels on their behalf. Once again we emphasise our willingness, indeed our urgent desire, to meet the I.R.F.U. to put the case to them.

The 1981 tour is not a case of Irish participation along with others – it is Ireland alone. We hope that you and your club will do your utmost to persuade the I.R.F.U. not to go next year. If they do decide to go, we urge you not to accept a place on the team if it is offered.

Please let us know your views and if you would like to discuss the matter further, we should be happy to arrange a meeting in complete confidence and without prejudice.
Yours faithfully,
Kader Asmal
Chairman
For freedom in Southern Africa

So a relationship developed, and when Kader became Minister for Water in the newly formed, post-apartheid Rainbow government I had the pleasure of meeting up with him in Cape Town when on tour with Ireland in the late 1990s. It was a privilege shared.

In 1982, I received a telegram from the United Nations headquarters in New York inviting me to speak on rugby's attitude to apartheid. Somehow the message got lost in translation. As in, I mislaid it! It was only when I rediscovered it sometime later that I realised the magnitude of the invitation and the opportunity missed. I regretted that inexcusable oversight. But then another exciting, if different opportunity came my way a few years down the line. Along with Donal Spring and the Dunnes Stores workers, I was invited to meet Nelson Mandela in the old Berkeley Hotel when he was given the Freedom of Dublin in 1990. Needless to say it was one of the highlights of my life to meet Madiba.

It was an enormous honour as I headed into lunch with Springer. When Mr Mandela walked into the room you knew you were in the presence of someone very special. There is no exaggeration in saying that it felt as close to a spiritual experience as is possible when meeting another human being. He received a standing ovation. I do not know how long it went on for but it seemed an eternity. Needless to say meeting this extraordinary man never figured on my anti-apartheid agenda, but it lessened the honour and immense thrill not a single iota. Accompanying him was his wife Winnie, along with Dick Spring as Tánaiste and Labour party leader.

As well as receiving the freedom of the city, Mr Mandela was in Dublin to greet the remarkable Dunnes Stores workers who took their own high profile and infamous stand against apartheid. He thanked all and sundry as he shook our hands. I am glad I took my own stand. For the Dunnes workers, and myself, too, I guess we recognised that in life there are mysterious forces at work which sweep us along on a tide – a huge and massive tidal force that moves mountains of sands around the world. At the time we may sometimes wonder why we do it, why we get involved, why we put up with all the aggravation. Seeing South Africa today answers our questions emphatically. Each tiny grain of sand builds colossal dunes.

CHAPTER 12

KICKED OUT
OF TRIPLE CROWN

The nightmare I endured in Australia continued when the squad was announced for the opening game of the 1982 Five Nations season. I was again on the outside looking in. The decision to play both Ollie Campbell and me in four of the five games the previous season had been most welcome. Newspapers rejoiced, the public was happy and we both enjoyed the opportunity. It appeared neither of us was going to be dropped to make way for the other. Ironically, Ollie probably felt a weight coming down off his shoulders with my inclusion. In the opening game at home to France he had one of those bad days at the office, so my recall probably gave him an extra incentive to play well.

The selectors bore the brunt of the public backlash over my latest dropping. The great Gareth Edwards very kindly stated: 'We in Wales believe him to be a better tactical kicker than Ollie Campbell. Kicking plays a huge part in modern-day internationals so the fact that you have both Ward and Campbell in the side gives you a big advantage in the place-kicking area.'

However, against the Welsh, that proved to be anything but the case. We led 8–3 and both Ollie and I set up Ireland's two tries. Unfortunately, neither was converted, and that failure came back to haunt us. Perhaps psychologically we were both handing the kicking responsibility to the other. Or maybe the intense media and public scrutiny about who was the best kicker eventually took its toll. We both missed every kick we were entrusted with and Wales came back to win 9–8.

Aside from our kicking, our general play was good and both of us linked well to cause problems for the opposition. The revered Con Houlihan (RIP) intimated in his *Evening Press* column that it was almost like I had never been away when he wrote: 'Ward made the return of Jesse James seem about as dramatic as the coming home of a man who has just taken the dog for a stroll. He began kicking up-and-unders that had the Welsh backs hypnotised by a swooping hawk.'

By this stage I was totally fed up of the whole debate. I think it definitely took its toll on both of us in that game. If I missed a shot at goal then Ollie was the best kicker; if he missed then I was better. Personally I do not believe it is a good idea to have two recognised kickers in a side. It can instil a *laissez-faire* attitude in the build-up where, in terms of mental preparation, both kickers renege on their responsibility. One player, and one player only, should be nominated as kicker. Our woeful day against Wales was down to a lack of responsibility. Call it passing the buck, but neither of us had been given the role outright so we were not as focused on the job as we ought to have been. This meant there was a constant and intense pressure on us both. Perhaps with the 1981 season out of the way, and the debate now quietening down after I was brought back, 1982 would not only be a fresh start for the team, but for me as well.

Limerick felt like a breath of fresh air after the stifling, stuffy and suffocating atmosphere I was feeling in Dublin. Limerick was a lady who treated me well. I was loved and welcomed as one of her adopted children. As the line from the famous song says: 'Limerick, you're my lady, the one true love that I have ever known.' What was more, I was back playing soccer again.

Limerick United were League of Ireland champions in 1980. Later that year they were handed a plum draw when pitted against the mighty Spanish giants Real Madrid in the European Cup. It was a great pity I was not part of the team just then. But in 1981 I returned to the soccer scene. After qualifying for the Uefa Cup the following season as league runners-up, Limerick were again handed a mouth-watering tie. This time they faced English First Division side Southampton. Where circumstances allowed, I played for Garryowen on Saturdays and Limerick United on Sundays. There was little or no opposition to my schedule. Garryowen and Munster always left things up to me and, for once, the IRFU in Dublin, kept out of it.

When chairman and owner Pat Grace, along with team manager Eoin Hand, asked if I could play against Southampton, I could have bitten their hand off. It had nothing to do with any possibility of personal glory. I dearly loved Limerick and was only too delighted to pitch in with whatever help I could offer.

It was only my fourth game for them. I had played a few pre-season friendlies when the rugby season finished, so this was an opportunity too good to miss. I could not wait to pit my skills against some of the biggest names in the game. Even now, the players who plied their trade with Southampton at the time remain household names today. The terrier-like, ginger-haired midfielder Alan Ball was an England World Cup winner in 1966. The long, lanky Mick Channon was a club legend who played for England many times. Dave Watson was the England centre-half. Then there was Kevin Keegan, who was not only a real dynamo for England, he had also engraved himself as one of Liverpool's all-time greats. I would play against Keegan in both legs. It is funny to think about it now. A small and curly-haired legend of soccer against a small and curly-haired rugby player.

The Markets Field in Limerick was packed to its galvanised rooftops on Wednesday, 16 September 1981. An estimated one thousand fans travelled over by boat to shout on the English club. However, even though we were one of the best teams in Ireland, we never really had a hope against top-flight English opposition. The gulf in class was enormous and they duly ran out 3–0 winners. But we gave a fantastic showing on the night. The match report even made it on to the front page of the *Irish Independent* the next day. There was a photograph of my curly head, and under the headline '£8 million worth of talent too much for Limerick', the opening paragraph read: 'Limerick United, a team of one professional and ten part-time footballers – a salesman, a machinist, a sports shop owner, an electrician and a couple of company reps – last night took on £8 million-worth of talent from Southampton and only conceded defeat after a gallant display.' The article went on to say how we played very well in the early stages: 'Limerick gave a tremendous display of courageous football in the first half and they were most unlucky not to have scored the opening goal.'

For the record, David Armstrong scored the second of his two goals to finally finish us off in the seventy-ninth minute. Steve Moran scored their second in between Armstrong's double. With that twinkle in his eye, the Southampton manager Lawrie McMenemy said after the game: 'They certainly hit us with everything in that first half and Tony Ward buzzed around as if he was at Twickenham. I was half-expecting them to bring on local man Terry Wogan, but we got our goals at the right times.'

Pat Grace, the Limerick chairman and managing director of Kentucky Fried Chicken, was delighted with the 10,000-plus crowd. He later revealed that the £40,000 takings were the biggest ever for a League club in the Republic. And we still had the second leg to come at The Dell. We created chances in the home leg and were inspired by the huge crowd. We could not wait for the return and we had high hopes of bringing glory and pride to our supporters.

I had not been involved with Limerick the previous year when they played Real Madrid. That game was played at Lansdowne Road and only seven thousand turned up. Switching the game to Dublin caused uproar among the Limerick faithful. They were annoyed that the small compact nature of the Markets Field was not utilised to make Madrid feel nervous. The official reason given by the FAI for moving the game concerned their doubts about health and safety. Their biggest worry was the strong possibility that supporters would run on the pitch in Limerick. As a result, many fans boycotted the game in Dublin. They missed a fantastic and heroic performance from United. Limerick had a goal disallowed after twenty-five minutes, but then deservedly took the lead early in the second half. From a free-kick, Gerry Duggan headed the ball on to Des Kennedy, who poked home from six yards. The crowd went mad. Limerick United 1, Real Madrid 0. The winners of more European Cups than any other club were rocked. Alas poor Limerick, though. They were the victims of a dubious penalty decision with twenty minutes left. It was duly converted, and then came heartbreak when Madrid scored the winner in the eighty-fifth minute. At the Bernabeu, Limerick walked into a cauldron created by a 60,000 crowd. Not surprisingly they crumbled under the weight of home expectation. They lost 5–1, and 7–2 on aggregate, but scoring again showed their great character.

When I was approached the following year, one thing I made clear to Mr Grace from the outset was that I would not accept any payment whatsoever. Even though the IRFU scrutinised every single payment I received, this decision had nothing to do with them. Aside from the IRFU constantly banging on to me about rugby being an amateur sport, I firmly believed in my amateur status at a personal level. Moreover, I wanted to send a clear message to the Limerick United players and staff that my involvement was voluntary. It was purely for the love of the game, the city and the club.

I look back on the return match in Southampton with immense pride. It seems like only yesterday. A party of thirty players and officials flew from Shannon to London just after 4 p.m. on the Sunday beforehand. Our new signing, John Minnock, was ineligible to play but he was invited along so he could get to know the rest of the players and our style of play. Joe O'Mahony also travelled even though he would play no part due to injury. The rest of the travelling squad was: Kevin Fitzpatrick, Mick O'Donnell, Pat Nolan, Brendan Storan, Tony Meaney, Eoin Hand, John Walsh, Des Kennedy, Gary Hulmes, Al Finucane, Ger Duggan, Mick McDonnell, Johnny Walsh, Tommy Gaynor, Jimmy Nodwell and me. Tommy Gaynor would soon come to the attention of clubs and scouts across the Irish Sea. A few years after Brian Clough signed Roy Keane from Cobh for £5,000, he would also sign Tommy for his Nottingham Forest squad. In addition, the officials on board were: Dave Mahedy (coach), Willie O'Flaherty (masseur), chairman Pat Grace and his wife Anne, secretary Mick Bourke and

Master J. Bourke, vice-chairman Ambrose Malone, John O'Dwyer and promotions officer Michael 'the doc' Crowe. Two members of the Garda Síochána, namely Detective Sergeant Michael Browne and Detective Fachtna O'Donovan, came over as supporters. We were all booked into the Post House Hotel in Southampton.

We were keen to reward the fans back at home listening to the match on the radio as well as the four hundred lucky enough to travel. We had little hope of overturning the 3–0 deficit, but with nothing to lose we were confident of putting on another good display. The memories of Real Madrid were still fresh in the mind and Southampton, despite their well-known players, were certainly no Madrid.

When we walked out at The Dell in front of 15,000 fans expecting us to be brushed aside, we posed for an official team photo. Actually in the first leg in Limerick, only ten Southampton players lined up for the official match photograph. Among them were Kevin Keegan and the balding David Armstrong. In the photo you can see some of their players looking around for the missing player and a few others spoiling the picture. Team photos were a bone of contention for Southampton. Apparently, the players refused to be photographed at the Markets Field because they were not getting paid for the snap. This was no reflection on Limerick or Ireland. Unless the club were paid for a team photo then they would refuse to pose.

After both captains swapped club pennants, the game kicked off with the partisan crowd in a party mood. They fully expected a feast full of goals from their side. It was not hard to see why. Many Irish clubs in the 1960s, 1970s and 1980s were at the wrong end of massive hidings from English clubs. But we were Limerick. Wherever and whoever we played, we performed with a passion and a fight for ourselves and our supporters. And we gave Southampton one hell of a fright. Our 1–1 draw remains one of the great European nights in Irish soccer and one of the best performances by an Irish club on English soil. Tony Morris headed our goal and silenced their fans. It was too little too late as we lost 4–1 on aggregate, but it was a fantastic memory for the die-hard Limerick followers who can say they were there. Great credit must go to Eoin Hand who was player-manager of Limerick at the time. He was ably assisted by my closest friend since our college days, Dave Mahedy. Eoin actually played at the heart of the defence with thirty-seven-year-old veteran Al Finucane. He wasn't the oldest member of our team: goalkeeper Kevin Fitzpatrick was forty! While the rest of the Limerick United party flew home early the next afternoon, I travelled up to London with a few other guys. We wanted to stay on and see Arsenal play in the European Cup the following night at Highbury.

Garryowen and Munster were also providing me with terrific moments and I was riding on the crest of a wave with them. Garryowen were flying in the League when the touring Australians visited. Having scalped the All Blacks in 1978, Munster now had a global reputation to live up to. Australia would treat us with the respect we deserved and, with all eyes watching us, we would have to slash this ass and cart as well. There could be no let-up. We led 12–0 and went on to beat them easily 15–6. I scored eleven points from two penalties, a drop goal and a conversion. The Wallabies simply could not handle our crowd or the pressure, and their performance was littered with enforced errors. The legendary Mark Ella went on a long, mazy run late in the game to set up their consolation try. I was elated after the game. I was happy with my rugby and, through maturity and top-level experience, my game was developing nicely.

When Garryowen beat hot favourites UCC at Musgrave Park

to win the Munster League title for the first time since 1954, it was just the icing on the cake for me. After a good showing in the final trial, everything was rosy in the garden. Incidentally, in that now defunct trial between 'Possibles' and 'Probables', there were a couple of bad head injuries. Ollie Campbell was one casualty and Paul Dean clashed heads with me. He still bears the scar from that clash today. Then the bombshell arrived. I was dropped from the opening game of the 1982 Five Nations Championship. Not only that, but I was not even named among the replacements. Was I numb with shock? No, but bitterly disappointed, for sure.

After the squad announcement at the Shelbourne Hotel in the immediate aftermath of the final trial, Ollie came outside to ask if I was all right. Although I tried to hide the hurt, I found it difficult. Right there and then he apologised to me for the way I had been treated. It was totally unnecessary. I do not know if this sort of thing would happen in sport today, but again it only served to highlight the calibre of the man. There was no explanation given by the management about why I had been dropped. I was playing well, but it would be stretching it to say the decision was out of the blue, given what had gone before. But it was still baffling since I had been recalled the previous season. At that time, it was as close as I came to snapping.

I thought about things over and over in my mind that night and next day. I vowed to myself that I would never play for Ireland again. I was as good as my word. I did not attend the next training camp and the media were all over my absence. Coach Tom Kiernan told the media that a misunderstanding had taken place. We both knew this was not true, but I did not want to ruffle Tom's feathers or have any beef with him so I went along with it. But as far as I was concerned I was finished.

Whatever reason was in their devious minds it was not a good enough one to kick me out of the squad entirely. Having thought about it so much over the years, there are perhaps two things that bugged the hell out of the IRFU about me in 1981 and 1982. But that was their problem and had nothing to do with me. I just played rugby for my country and I played to the very best of my ability. The first reason was to do with my stance on apartheid. In late January 1981, I received a letter from the IRFU asking if I would be part of the forthcoming tour to South Africa. Forty-three other players received the letter as well, but I was one of the first to steadfastly refuse to be part of it. As I have already stated, my conscience affected me deeply after the 1980 tour and I said then I would never return. My relationship with the anti-apartheid movement in Dublin could therefore have been a source of embarrassment or indeed a threat to the IRFU. Despite all the worldwide contro-versy, Ireland and the IRFU were hell-bent on travelling and I could have been viewed as a negative influence on other players. I guess I could have been seen as a 'big name' undermining their authority.

The second reason, which perhaps added fuel to the fire, was me playing high-profile soccer. The IRFU had long viewed me as a sort of 'golden boy', 'a prima donna', 'a celebrity'. Certain elements within the IRFU obviously did not like this and wanted to cut me down to size. The newspapers were full of me playing for Limerick. While the IRFU were preoccupied with trying to get players to go to South Africa over the preceding months, I was preparing for big Uefa Cup games. There is no doubt that my activities with Limerick United were relegating a lot of the rugby coverage in the national press.

Indeed there was one very glaring and mysterious piece from John O'Shea, who was also the former head of GOAL, the Irish charity devoted to helping the poor. I don't know who was feeding him his information. But in a national newspaper on 15 September 1981, John wrote in his opening paragraph: 'Tony Ward will not be in the Limerick side which takes on South-ampton at the Markets Field tomorrow (5.45 p.m.).' John went on to quote me adding: 'Rugby commitments keep him away from Limerick's bid to advance in the Uefa Cup as he will be in Cashel attending a Munster training session. "Naturally I'm a bit disappointed I'll not be seeing the game," Ward stated.' This was most peculiar. All the other newspapers, as well as radio and television, knew and reported that I was playing. Munster had also given me permission to play without any problem at all. The next day John corrected himself. Under a banner head-line: 'Limerick decide to play Ward', he wrote: 'Ward was scheduled to attend a training session with Munster in Cashel but after consultation with the chairman of the selectors, his request to miss the stint was granted.'

Watching Ireland go on to win the Triple Crown without my involvement really hurt. Ollie Campbell was at the heart of everything that was good about that brilliant Ireland team. In an interview I gave to the *Evening Herald* on the eve of the Triple Crown decider with Scotland, I was asked to give my thoughts about my rivalry with Ollie. This finally gave me the opportunity to get the whole thing off my chest. I said: 'It has all been so stupid and unnecessary and I am personally sick to death of this so-called Ward versus Campbell issue. It takes much of the enjoyment out of the game. Ollie has been playing superbly since his return from a three-month break. He has had a remarkable season. Against England he had the best game I have ever seen him play. His covering and support play was phenomenal. He had the type of game I would love to play myself. Campbell will once again be the key man against

Scotland. Last season we lost four matches we could and possibly should have won. I'm therefore delighted to see things click into place. Munster's win against the All Blacks was no flash in the pan – Tommy Kiernan is a great coach and tactician. I also know from my days at St Mary's what a fabulous organiser Fitzy is.'

When the Triple Crown headlines faded, and rugby retired for the summer, my name was to be up in Limerick lights again.

CHAPTER 13

AN FAI CUP
WINNER'S MEDAL

The warmth and affection shown to me by the Limerick United fans during the 1982 FAI Cup campaign in March and April lifted me enormously. It was the antidote and tonic I needed for my rugby despair. My underlying and undying love for soccer had been reawakened in 1981 with Limerick United in the Uefa Cup. As a boy I was soccer mad and yet here I was as an established rugby international playing in some of soccer's biggest competitions at home and abroad. The same thing was happening to the city of Limerick. Normally a rugby-mad environment, the people had become transfixed by the soccer club. The buzz and excitement was growing and almost every-body wanted to experience being part of the big days. The city's enthusiasm for all things Munster and Garryowen was the thing which had made rugby my number one sport when I arrived. Now I was not sure any more. The trouble rugby was causing me had brought me to a crossroads.

I was dropped from Ireland's 1982 Triple Crown-winning squad without any explanation. There was little doubt in my mind that one very plausible reason was my high-profile soccer activities with Limerick United. However, and this must be emphasised, at no stage did anyone from the IRFU approach me and issue an ultimatum. Nobody said that I was to give up soccer and concentrate on my rugby career. Furthermore, neither Garryowen nor Munster saw any problem with me playing both codes. They knew full well that rugby was my number one commitment, and that where possible I could, and would, play for Limerick. When Garryowen reached the League final, Limerick were playing Bluebell United in the FAI Cup the same day. There was no way I would have missed that League final so I did not face Bluebell.

As it transpired, United won which meant I was able to play in the FAI Cup clash with Shelbourne in Tolka Park. We took an early lead against Shels, and I played my part providing the cross for the boss, Eoin Hand, to score. Unlike the modern frenetically fast game, the style of play in Irish soccer during those years was generally to keep what one had. So despite some marvellous one-touch football up to our goal, we retreated and tried to defend our lead for as long as possible. Shelbourne punished us. They laid siege to our goal and equalised when Paddy Joyce back-headed a Terry Daly free-kick into our net. Incidentally, Terry was a former team-mate of mine at Shamrock Rovers.

The half time break was most welcome, not least because our defenders and goalkeeper were enduring a torrid time. Even so, Kevin Fitzpatrick, Al Finucane and Pat Nolan put in outstanding displays under fierce pressure. We came out after the break with much more purpose and almost scored through Tommy Gaynor. Our classy young striker looped a header over the crossbar and past a gaping empty net. Finucane then paid the price for his heroic first-half efforts when he had to be taken off injured and was replaced by Ger Duggan. Just when the game seemed set for a replay, the gaffer was on the end of a speculative cross into a crowded box. I swung the ball over and it landed at the feet of Hand, who had the simplest of opportunities to score. He made no mistake and we went through to the next round with our last-gasp 2–1 win. But not before that great Shannon RFC man Kevin Fitz made a brilliant late save from Daly. I enjoyed the game tremendously and I was happy with my performance.

We still had a long way to go before reaching the final, but following the wins against Shelbourne and Bluebell, we were on a roll. During Limerick's quarter-final against Aer Lingus, the referee awarded us a penalty. Suddenly a murmur from the three thousand crowd turned into a loud chant of 'To–ny Ward, To–ny Ward, To–ny Ward ...' Some of my Limerick United colleagues had smiles on their faces as they looked at me. In normal circumstances I would not have taken the spot-kick as regular taker Gary Hulmes was playing. But bowing to the demands of the crowd, he backed away. Eoin Hand threw the ball over to me and suddenly I was hit by stage fright. Unlike rugby, where scoring was second nature, my brief in soccer was mainly to create opportunities for others. I did know my way to goal, but only intermittently when compared to rugby. I stepped up. The ball travelled wide of the post. I had missed. In the grand scheme of things it was a good job it didn't matter as we won the game 4–0. It seemed as though every time I touched the ball, or was about to receive a pass, our crowd came alive. Their affection towards me was infectious and there is no doubt their enthusiasm inspired and drove me on. Contrast that with how I was feeling playing rugby at that point in my career, particularly when wearing a green jersey. I felt like a stranger ignored.

Athlone Town came out of the hat in the semi-final with Dundalk and Bohemians pitted in the other tie. I had to miss the game against Athlone because rugby duties meant I had to play for Garryowen in an equally important Munster Cup game. However, Limerick's game went to a replay, so I got another chance to play in an FAI Cup semi-final. It turned out to be a very tight and cagey affair. This was understandable in the circumstances with a place in the final at stake. But I loved the challenge and was particularly satisfied to be involved in the game's only goal, scored by Tommy Gaynor. When the referee blew the final whistle everyone embraced and wild celebrations began. We were in the final at Dalymount Park, an iconic ground I loved.

Our opponents would be Bohemians who got the better of Dundalk in a topsy-turvy replay which could have gone either way. The winning goal was scored by young John Raynor, the seventeen-year-old who shot to fame with one of the goals which put the Republic of Ireland into the Uefa Youths Finals in Finland after a 2–0 win over Northern Ireland. Drama would await him in the FAI final.

Largely thanks to the fantastic Limerick support life was good and I was more than content. I was in good form and really enjoying my soccer. I could not wait to get on with the next game. To reach the FAI Cup final was a dream come true. I almost had to pinch myself. When I originally signed for Shamrock Rovers, the club I had supported all my life, I obviously knew there were huge opportunities to play in Europe as well as perhaps winning titles. Yet here I was in Limerick with very real opportunities of achieving all those dreams. As it happened I had been in Dalymount for both games in 1971 when Limerick last won the cup following a 3–0 win in the midweek replay against Drogheda. Hugh Hamilton, with two, and Dave

Barrett scored the goals. Kevin Fitzpatrick, Al Finucane and Joe O'Mahony, our three wisest men, all played in that game, along with the great Andy McEvoy.

The newspapers went to town on my soccer exploits. Every time I picked up a national daily, an evening newspaper or a provincial, there was a headline about me. The phone never stopped ringing with journalists inevitably posing questions about soccer and rugby. I remember one very good question put to me. Away from journalists constantly probing and searching for any potential clashes between the two codes and their governing bodies, I was asked to compare the stamina required for both games. There is no doubt in my mind that soccer then required much greater stamina and overall levels of fitness, save for those playing at the very highest level of international rugby. Right from kick-off, soccer was non-stop running, whether with or without the ball, whereas rugby was much more broken up. There were so many stoppages for scrums and lineouts, as well as penalties and conversions, so there were more opportunities to draw breath. Now the difference in pace and intensity between our four main sports, Gaelic football, hurling, rugby and soccer, are minimal. The standards reached by amateur hurlers and footballers beggar belief. Soccer is 'go-go-go' from the start which means teams do not get the invaluable stoppage time that their rugby counterparts do. Also, remember that despite modern and beneficial changes to the other codes, soccer is always at least ten minutes longer than rugby and twenty minutes more than football or hurling.

The sixty-first FAI Cup final in 1982 was the fifth in Limerick's history. We won it for the very first time in 1971 after losing to Shamrock Rovers in both 1965 and 1966. We had also lost our last Cup final appearance five years previously against

Dundalk. Ahead of the Sunday final, we travelled up from Limerick the day before and stayed in the Burlington Hotel. Next morning we all went to mass in a church not far from Lansdowne Road in Haddington Road. When we arrived in Dalymount Park just over an hour before the kick-off, our captain Joe O'Mahony was told that we had to toss up for the dressing rooms. We won the toss and as part of trying to get inside Bohemians' heads, we kicked them out of the home dressing room at their own ground! It was far from the ideal preparation for them to have to move to the unfamiliarity of the 'away' dressing room.

When the teams were announced, Bohs blended a mixture of youth and age in their side. Vastly experienced defenders Jacko McDonogh and Gino Lawless would be a tough unit to break for our strike force of Tommy Gaynor and Gary Hulmes. They were especially strong in the midfield boiler room with Noel King, Paul Doolin, Tommy Kelly and Mick Shelley. The crucial question was whether Jimmy Nodwell, Johnny Walsh, Eoin Hand and I could wrestle possession from them. Up front they had the vastly experienced and hugely skilful Jackie Jameson alongside the exciting Rocky O'Brien. So it was easy to see why they were viewed as one of the best teams in the country, and favourites to win.

Twelve thousand fans wrapped up well and huddled under cover in Dalymount Park as the game began in driving wind and rain. We played against these atrocious conditions in the first half. Therefore it was no surprise it remained scoreless on the half-hour. Bohs had more of the possession and created several good chances early on. Jimmy Nodwell had to clear off the line from one of their opportunities, so it was somewhat against the run of play when we had our first real chance. On the break, Pat Nolan moved the ball to Hulmes who passed to me. I pushed it through to Johnny Walsh who just had the goalkeeper to beat. But from nowhere Lawless came across and cut out the danger with a marvellous tackle. This was a warning for Bohs. A few minutes later we went on the attack again and won a corner. I smacked the ball over low and hard and it found Brendan Storan who shot towards goal. The ball threaded its way between several pairs of legs with Bohemians goalkeeper Dermot O'Neill looking on helplessly as the net rippled behind him. Goal! Limerick 1, Bohemians 0.

Scoring gave us a huge boost. We grew in confidence and applied so much pressure that we became dominant. Dave Connell prevented Bohs going in 2–0 down at the break when he produced a fine tackle to deny Gaynor. We also had several claims for penalties which were waved away. The pity was that we did not wrap up the game in that short spell before half-time. But we began the second half in exactly the same fashion. We were all over them. Another corner found the head of Eoin Hand. Fortunately for Bohemians his effort was cleared off the line and this seemed to shock the Dublin side into retaliation. In the miserable weather which they faced after the break, Bohs went very close to levelling, but Storan cleared the ball off the line. Despite the gloom, the final was producing its fair share of thrills and spills.

With twenty minutes left, yet another corner this time found Gaynor whose header came back off the upright. A few minutes later I decided to have a go, but my drive was parried around the post by O'Neill. Ten minutes from time young Raynor came on for Bohs as they tried to salvage the situation. He had a chance to score only to miss the ball completely. It ran through to his colleague Mick Shelley who hit the ball sweetly. But the goalbound effort struck our brave captain Joe O'Mahony in the neck – the 'Adam's apple' to be precise – and we survived that scare. He had to go off with slight concussion. In injury time, the luckless Raynor was taken off on a stretcher after a sickening clash of heads with Storan.

The final whistle sounded seconds later with the blue of Limerick triumphant. We jumped around ecstatically. It was a richly deserved win and it was particularly poignant for the three survivors from the 1971-winning side. Goalkeeper Kevin Fitzpatrick, now forty-one, stated before the game that he would retire to make way for his understudy John Power. Kevin gave an incredible twenty-two years' service to the club after joining in 1960. The two other stalwarts from 1971 must also be mentioned: Al Finucane is simply a Limerick legend, and alongside him O'Mahony saved the day by putting his head on the block in the dying minutes. Sadly Joe passed away early in 2013. Along with Tony Meaney, he is in that great football stadium in the sky. We miss both so badly.

On Monday, 3 May we returned to Limerick for a civic reception. The atmosphere and the crowds who turned out took the breath away. Arthur's Quay in the city was thronged with people of all ages as we made our way there on an open-top bus from Colbert Station. As I looked out from my position on the stand, all I could see were thousands and thousands of happy heads and bodies packed tightly like sardines. The victory bus and podium were like ships floating along on a royal blue sea. It was without doubt one of the greatest days of my life and one which I am so proud to have been involved in. Just as when we defeated the All Blacks in 1978, the people of Limerick and Munster showed their pride and passion that day. And as I looked down time and again at the little square black box containing my FAI Cup winner's medal, I took great satisfaction in becoming the first Irish rugby international to win soccer's FAI Cup. Paul McNaughton had gone close twice before when he was in the Shelbourne teams beaten by Cork Hibernians in 1973 and Home Farm in 1975.

After the heartache of missing the Triple Crown season, I ended up with my very own 'Double Crown' in 1982. The Munster Senior League with Garryowen and the FAI Cup were not to be sneezed at. I was quick to make this point to well-known broadcaster Jimmy Magee when he interviewed Ollie Campbell and me for an RTE Radio 1 Sunday sports pro-gramme later that year. I was most taken aback when Jimmy concluded the transmission with the words: 'Well, Ollie it's been a great year for you, but, Tony, you must think your season has been a bit of a nightmare.' In his own inimitable way he was winding me up. I would certainly never consider win-ning the Munster Senior League and the FAI Cup in the same season as a failure! In fairness, neither did he.

In 2007, the FAI invited us back to the RDS for the cup final between Cork City and Longford Town for the twenty-fifth anniversary of our memorable day. Boy, did that time lapse register. Then, on 6 June this year, I was invited to attend the League of Ireland Premier game between Limerick and Drogheda United with the rest of the 1982 squad. It was a very special occasion as it marked the return of Limerick to the Mar-kets Field ground, having moved out in 1984. President of Ireland Michael D. Higgins was among the other guests along with the likes of Minister for Finance Michael Noonan and Minister for Education Jan O'Sullivan. It was also great to see Eoin Hand and many of my former team-mates. We do have the opportunity to meet up every year at a golf day which is held in May and organised by Johnny Walsh.

President Higgins told me an interesting story. First off he revealed to me that he was born in Limerick. I never knew this as, like most people, I had always believed he hailed from

Galway because he spent his political life there. He is honorary president of Galway soccer club and has attended many of their games over the years. But he told me his first love was Limerick football. As a young man he used to go to the Markets Field on an old battered Honda 50 motorbike, burning up the Ennis Road on the way from his Clare home to the heart of soccer in the sports-daft city that is Limerick.

CHAPTER 14

THE RETURN

Like Kevin Fitzpatrick, I too revealed before the FAI Cup final that I would be quitting Limerick United. Unlike our veteran goalkeeper, who was retiring through age, my decision was purely a personal, career-motivated choice. I wanted to move back to Dublin for three main reasons: I was moving house after selling up in Limerick, I was opening a business and, because I was leaving Limerick, I would therefore leave Garryowen to rejoin my boyhood club St Mary's. As a matter of fact I almost joined Old Belvedere RFC before going back to Mary's. Paddy Madigan, of the famous licensed vintner group, was a great ally of mine and an IRFU committee man for more years than I care to remember. He was also a Belvederian die-hard who was trying to entice me to go and play for the Anglesea Road club.

Although I stated to the media on the eve of the FAI Cup final that I was leaving, I had second thoughts when we won. I guess the euphoria of the moment took control. In the celebrations after the game I was ecstatic, and with journalists looking for quotes I told them something to the effect of 'How can I leave now?' With Limerick United experiencing the greatest period in club's history it was only human nature to want to hang on and see if more success could come our way. We were, after all, a close-knit and extremely talented group of players. However, once the euphoria wore off, I reverted to my original decision. Limerick came knocking on my door periodically thereafter and I did find it hard to say no as I truly loved my time at the Markets Field.

By winning Irish soccer's premier cup competition, the club booked their ticket to the European Cup-Winners' Cup. Limerick were drawn to play the famous Dutch club AZ Alkmaar and they asked me to play. The first leg was at the Markets Field, but regrettably I could not play because of rugby commitments. I missed what turned out to be another fantastic European night. On the evening of 15 September 1982, veteran defender Pat Nolan sent the packed little ground ballistic when he put Limerick in front. However, Alkmaar equalised and left with a precious away goal from a 1–1 draw. I did not play in the return leg in Holland either. By that stage I was away with Munster on a tour of Romania. Alkmaar won 1–0 to go through 2–1 on aggregate. It was another valiant effort from the lads.

Pat Nolan's goal in the first leg meant he became the only Limerick player to score a goal in Europe at home. As an attacking full back he had few peers. He asked me to play in his testimonial match a month before that Cup-Winners' Cup tie. In August mighty Manchester United had come to Limerick with a real star-studded team and won 3–1. It was a fitting climax to Pat's glorious career. It also turned out to be my last game for Limerick. It was a nice way to go out, even for such a passionate fan of the other United from across the Pennines!

One enduring memory I have from that night was heading

off for a post-match drink at the Parkway Motel Bar with my great friend Dave Mahedy, as well as Manchester legends Kevin Moran, Bryan Robson and Ray Wilkins. We were hoping to have a quiet drink, but it transpired it was Leaving Certificate results night and, suffice to say, the Parkway was bedlam. Nonetheless we all had a great night.

A few months later, in November 1982, I made it known to the IRFU that I did not wish to be considered for the final Irish trial ahead of the 1983 Five Nations. I had had enough. The final straw came when I gave a lacklustre performance in the inter-provincial championship game for Munster against Ulster. My announcement took rugby folk by surprise, but it was pointless going into the trial in my state of mind. I made a big mistake in playing far too many games at the start of the season. I think I played something like fourteen games in September alone, including three for Munster in Romania. It coincided with me setting up the business in Dublin as well. Of course, being axed in 1982 had also left me feeling drained mentally. Between the physical and mental fatigue, I suppose it would not be stretching it too far to say I was suffering from a kind of post-traumatic stress disorder. Even though there were 'some' good and decent rugby men in charge of the national set-up, my suffering was a consequence of several people within the IRFU who had an agenda. And that agenda was me.

Ned Van Esbeck, an extraordinarily brilliant but scrupulously fair rugby writer for many decades with the *Irish Times*, and a great personal friend of mine for over forty years now, has also gone on record many times reiterating what I have just said. When he learned that I was writing my autobiography, he told me he would gladly allow me to quote him on several issues pertaining to my career. So with regard to the way I was treated by the IRFU, Ned wished to state the following: 'The IRFU encompasses many facets relating to the game all over Ireland and at all levels. From that perspective there are so many good people who do very good work for that organisation. However, there is no doubt in my mind – and there never has been – that Tony Ward was treated appallingly by certain elements within the IRFU Those certain elements were out to get him.'

After the Triple Crown triumph in 1982, Ireland shared the Five Nations Championship in 1983. When all seemed lost and there seemed no end to my agony in exile, out of the blue I was recalled to the squad for the final game against England. Ollie's injuries were troubling him again and the selectors felt they needed a contingency plan. With the game against England so important, it was felt that I should be on standby in case something untoward happened to him. In the event, Ollie weathered the storm, but he did have to come off injured in the dying minutes. I was sprung from the bench and I could hear this gigantic murmur rise from the Lansdowne crowd. It was most reassuring. Unlike today, replacement appearances were like hen's teeth back then. In unison, thousands of voices were whispering: 'Ward is coming on for Campbell' . . . 'Is that Ward coming on?' and so on.

When I shook hands with my long-term rival, a great roar went up. As I ran out on to the Lansdowne Road pitch, the decibel levels rose even higher. It raised the hairs on every part of my skin. The warmth and affection from the crowd touched me deeply. Right there and then I knew I held a special place in the hearts of Irish rugby fans and, yes, it did feel good. They were in my boat rowing with me. They could identify with the frustration and hurt I had endured in previous years. It was such a morale-boosting lift. I had vowed privately to fight hard and win my place back and in that very brief moment I achieved it.

Having clocked up just two minutes of rugby for Ireland in the previous two years, I simply had to work hard on my fitness in the close season. This I did, but I was knocked out of my stride again. I played no part in the opening game of the 1984 championship, away to France. We lost 25–12 and Ollie scored all Ireland's points. Again I sat out the next game at home to Wales in early February. Ollie was our sole scorer once more as he converted three penalties in an 18–9 defeat. It was a dismal opening to the campaign and it spoke volumes that Campbell was the only scorer in both games.

Then Ollie fell ill with a viral infection which meant another call-up for me ahead of our third game against England at Twickenham on 18 February. As I walked through the hotel doors on the Thursday before the game, Ollie was making his exit. We said hello but he seemed to be intent on going out for a walk or something, so I let him off. Then I was informed I was playing and it was such a huge thrill. My hard work and knuckling down had finally paid off. I was elated. It was not the way I would have wished to make the team. I would have preferred to win selection under my own steam rather than on the back of Ollie having to pull out through illness.

But triumph and disaster were never too far away. My return would turn out to be forgettable for a number of reasons, and especially for a huge bust-up which directly involved me. Aside from the natural nerves I felt ahead of the game, I was also feeling a lot of pressure. Ollie had scored all our points and this meant that my game – and, more to the point, my kicking – would come under the spotlight. The big moment came on the half-hour when my opposite number, Les Cusworth, conceded a penalty for a loose and dangerously high tackle. From out on the right, I slotted the kick sweetly between the posts. The nerves were gone. I was back. I slotted two more penalties between the posts, but we ended up losing 12–9 to three penalties from Dusty Hare and a Cusworth drop goal. It was cruel.

We played reasonably well but made far too many errors. Commenting on the match the following day, Hugh McIlvanney wrote in the *Observer*: 'Since aesthetic pleasure scarcely arrived in a flood, it was natural to grab at emotional satisfaction and the performance of Tony Ward was most certainly one of these.' It took me a little time to get used to the pace with the English running at us throughout. It was very fast, but I managed to sort myself out. Or so I thought. I was particularly pleased for my scrum-half, Tony Doyle, who had a great debut for Ireland. His service was first-class. Willie Duggan's play as captain and forward leader was inspirational. Despite the Dad's Army tag, our pack was still going well at the end. But the result was particularly disappointing since we gave it a go with nothing to lose – as a result of nothing to play for.

Ollie Campbell's injury woes continued and I was recalled for the final game at home to Scotland on 3 March. The Scots had won their previous three games so they needed to beat us to win only their second Grand Slam, and the Triple Crown for the first time since 1938. The build-up – and in particular the initial team meeting on the Thursday – is one I will never forget. To say it was very tense is the least of it. It was probably the most disappointing and certainly the most degrading I have ever been involved in. Before the England game I had a lot of personal contact with the stand-in captain. Willie Duggan was captain while I was leading the backs. We were both singing off the one page, or so it seemed.

Willie John McBride, the playing legend and Lions captain extraordinaire, was in charge for just that one season, and as a coach he was hugely disappointing. He had set the leadership bar as captain of the 1974 Lions, but as Ireland coach a decade later he was nowhere near it in terms of impact. I guess it was the laidback, softly-softly approach that shocked me most. This style just does not work at the highest level. Irish rugby teams need great motivating people. Tom Kiernan, 'Doyler' and, of course, 'Fitzy' spring to mind in that regard.

The team meeting before the Scotland game took place in the Constitution Room of the Shelbourne Hotel. Willie Duggan was at the top table with Willie John and Roly Meates, the then chairman. The remaining selectors were also present in the room. Duggan started to speak and suddenly I froze solid and my heart started thumping as he started to lacerate me. He stared down in my direction and proceeded to launch a verbal assault on me that lasted a good five minutes. I mean he literally tore strips off me. It was clearly calculated and he caught me off guard. He said that he wanted a performance from me where there was no 'playing to the gallery'. With hand on heart I can honestly say that I have never in my career 'played to the gallery' as he put it. Constructive criticism I can take, but this was destructive in the extreme with the captain himself playing to the gallery in the room. He stressed that I was to 'come up on your man unlike the way you did against Cusworth in the previous match'. The England out-half did play well, but it was not because I was giving him the freedom of the park as Duggan appeared to be claiming.

It was a personal attack, unwarranted and unfair. I came out of the room totally devastated. I can still remember the feeling of numbness at Duggan's tirade. This was his attempt at laying down a marker and it stank. Most, if not all, of the players came to me afterwards and said how disgusted they were about the episode. The selectors were also to blame here. What disappointed me was that not one of them had the balls to speak up or empathise as the players did. My confidence took one hell of a hit in the build-up to that final game of the season. Some captain! Like most players I thrived on confidence. While the stand-in skipper himself thrived on the 'kick up the arse' philosophy, I very much depended on the slap on the back. He had not a clue.

Apparently this was his reverse psychology at work in respect of new cap Derek McGrath, who was brought in as replacement flanker for Willie Duncan. He began his team meeting constructively by welcoming Derek and saying how the players would look after him. Then he launched into his clearly pre-ordained attack on me! It was unjust and unfair. Furthermore, in terms of team morale and supposedly setting the tone, it was self-defeating. More than that, it lacked natural leadership. To my thinking, a natural leader is someone who plays the game hard and at the same time approaches individuals in a way that elicits the optimum performance. Ciaran Fitzgerald was a great Irish rugby leader because he had the ability to get the best out of each individual. He knew how to deal with their diverse personalities on a one-to-one basis, and then how best to press the team's collective button.

Duggan knew just one way to deal with players, which was the way he liked to be dealt with himself. He and I were polar opposites. Duggan thrived on being told that he was useless and that if he did not get his act together he was finished in an Irish jersey. Then he would go out and play a blinder. If I was told that I was playing poorly and was going to be written off, then I was finished before I even went on the field. But if I was told how great I was then I always went out to try and show I was even better than people thought. As a number eight Duggan was almost peerless, particularly in terms of courage. He was a great rugby player and one of the hardest I came across. In the art of shipping punishment and laying his body on the line, he was in the Shay Deering league. But as a captain he left an awful lot to be desired. In 1984, leadership at the top was dreadful. Consequently the morale within the squad was appalling.

Ireland lost at home to Scotland 32–9, and that was little surprise after all the pre-match shenanigans. I had to leave the field fifteen minutes into the second half with concussion following a clash of heads with Scottish lock Alan Tomes. Another injured player from the match was their scrum-half Roy Laidlaw. He and I spent the bulk of our evening in the Accident & Emergency Department of St Vincent's University Hospital. But hats off to the Scots. They cut into us like a hot knife through butter to win their first Slam in forty-six years and their thirteenth Five Nations championship.

For us, 1984 ended as it began: with defeat and the dreaded wooden spoon. As a result there were serious repercussions and Willie John was given his P45 after a solitary year in charge. He was replaced by the no-nonsense and colourful Mick Doyle.

CHAPTER 15

MUNSTER CAREER ENDS

By the time the 1985 season arrived, Ollie Campbell had played his last game for Ireland, although we didn't know it then. It was not long before injury forced him into premature retirement from all rugby. The number of injuries he had sustained finally took their toll. For him, it was undoubtedly the right call as the endless battles to get fit were threatening his long-term welfare. Time and again he fought back from severe injury to help Ireland's cause. But it became too much in the end. What a legacy he left, though. Notwithstanding the honours and records he achieved, he will go down as one of the greatest Irish players of all time.

However, just when it seemed that at long last I might become Ireland's first-choice play-maker, along came my club-mate Paul Dean. It was the beginning of another saga. For 'Ollie and Wardy' read 'Wardy and Deano'. Paul got his chance due to an injury I sustained during a 1984 Leinster League game when we played alongside each other on a dark autumn afternoon at Sydney Parade. He grabbed the opportunity with both hands and was selected as Ireland's out-half against

Australia in a pre-Christmas friendly, and then for the successful Five Nations Championship that followed. I was back in familiar territory: once again peering in the window from afar.

Deano had been an outstanding schoolboy player and yet another from the St Mary's College conveyor belt of talented backs. Although there was a six-year age difference between us, my playing career overlapped with his progression from schoolboy brilliance to wearing the green of Ireland. In 1978, when John Moloney and I were the half-back pairing for the Ireland senior team, Paul and Philip McDonnell formed the half-back partnership with the Irish schools team. All four of us hailed from the same Rathmines *alma mater*. When I returned to Dublin from Garryowen and rejoined St Mary's, there was a positional clash of sorts, but no big problem. Deano was content to play in the centre where he had played in the Ireland Triple Crown-winning team of 1982. For Leinster and Ireland he wore number twelve with Ollie Campbell wearing number ten. With St Mary's it was the same combination with me as out-half and in the pivotal position I was still occupying for Munster. We had talked it over before my return and Paul was most accommodating. Ironically, I feel it helped his game enormously. If I had an obvious fault it was my tendency to drift when taking a pass, especially from a long-passing scrum-half.

Paul was, and remains to this day, the best I have known to straighten a line. He was able to run incredibly direct and it came so naturally to him. When he made the number ten position his own, his ability to straighten and deliver the most telling of passes at full tilt compensated for his undoubted shortcomings with the boot. In my view he was a much more effective centre than out-half, but mixed and matched both positions to telling effect. Deano was a player with beautiful

180

balance and a terrific hip movement. He used his natural swerve and dynamic acceleration off the mark to great effect in beating his opponent. He created space for those outside him, but he needed space to produce and show his full array of talents. He had magnificent hands. You rarely, if ever, saw him drop a pass. He was also a great tackler. So when it came to a running, fifteen-man game Paul was tops. But if he had a weakness, then it was his lack of kicking consistency out of hand. But even the greatest players have their faults. He did not influence the game as much as Campbell, but he brought a different skill set to the table, and in fairness to Mick Doyle he accommodated that in the best interest of Irish rugby.

Of course, it hurt not being involved, particularly in 1985, but I was fully *au fait* with the rationale behind Deano's selection and fully accepted it at the time. This was the 'give it a lash' era, espoused by the coach, with Deano and all-action flanker Nigel Carr the key pieces in our Triple Crown machine. The train of events which saw Deano move into pole position went broadly along the lines: St Mary's were playing Monkstown at Sydney Parade and I picked up an injury. I was due to travel to Cork that night to play for an Irish selection against a Highfield selection the next day. It was almost a trial for the upcoming friendly against the Wallabies. So I rang Mick Cuddy, the then chairman, to tell him what had happened and that there was no way I could play. But I told him Paul Dean was ready and willing to travel in my place. That is exactly the way it panned out. Paul Dean played out-half to Michael Bradley. The rest of the back-line comprised Brendan Mullin and Michael Kiernan in the centre, Trevor Ringland and Keith Crossan on the wings and Hugo MacNeill at full back. They went to town against Highfield, inspired by the brilliance of Dean. During 1985, those players just mentioned formed the backbone of one of the greatest Ireland teams. Certainly as exciting an attacking unit from nine to fifteen as we have ever fielded.

When I was struck down with that injury in late 1984, another dark cloud descended upon me. It was one of my worst periods. I had worked my ass off to get back and reclaim the number ten jersey through hard graft and determination, but now I needed to change clubs. 'It's an ill wind . . .' as they say, and on 4 January 1985, I received a letter from Ken Ging inviting me to join Greystones. He promised me three things: senior rugby at out-half, a brand of football to suit my talents, and a warm and sincere welcome.

So I left St Mary's. It did cause a fair amount of controversy and the media had a field day. There were all sorts of rumours, counter-rumours and conspiracy theories doing the rounds concerning Deano and I. The fact is that both of us now needed to play out-half and something had to give. My injury in 1984, which let in Paul for Ireland, meant that his star was in the ascendancy and, of course, he could feel justified in insisting on that position. After we agreed to alternate the pivotal slot during matches, I was suddenly dropped against Dolphin. I fully understood Paul's situation and the club's stance. After all, Paul Dean was now playing out-half for Ireland. It was only natural that he wanted to play his club rugby in that position. What possible reason was there for me to postpone my decision for a few weeks . . . months . . . years? Why hang around and feed the controversy? That is why I moved.

However, I did not want to cause anything detrimental to my new club, and in particular their out-half Jerome O'Brien, so I arranged a meeting with people at the club. On a Saturday afternoon in Clontarf Castle, I met with Jerome and club officials, including coach Ken Ging, captain Sonny Kenny and chairman Sean Fitzpatrick. The main purpose of the meeting was to ensure my arrival did not ruffle any feathers. Everything was sorted out and I was relaxed in everyone's company. Greystones were a great club, a community club, a happy club. There was an air of cordiality and friendliness. They were without doubt one of the best on and off the field. There is a beautiful atmosphere at Greystones. It feels like the entire community is involved in all aspects of running the club from the top down. I loved my time there. They were not my best days performance-wise, but they were my most enjoyable. The words of my former Greystones team-mate Johnny Murphy are very apt when he said: 'We may not be a winning team, but we sure as hell are a happy one.' Dr Hickey Park is also one of the most scenic rugby grounds in the country. I just loved driving through the Glen of the Downs on my way out of the smoky city just to train.

When I joined the Wicklow club, they were flying high. But the demons plaguing me seemed to follow and jinx the club. They had been unbeatable with eleven wins from eleven. But that all changed when I made my debut for them on 12 January 1985. We lost. To Shannon, in Limerick, of all places. It was weird to lose a game in Limerick while playing for a non-Munster side – and not just from the rugby aspect. How freaky was it that almost the entire fixture list was called off that weekend due to the weather? Apart from ours. Perhaps our game should have been postponed, too, but Shannon saw the return of this Munster and honorary Limerick man as a crowd-puller. Better still, an unbeaten team was coming into their territory and there is nothing Munster folk like better than getting stuck in and softening up such opposition. As I ran out against Shannon, I could hear distant echoes of 'Get the film star'.

When I left there with my tail between my legs, there was almost an air of infidelity in returning to the enemy province of Leinster with my crestfallen Greystones team. I had been married to Munster for the best part of a decade and all that was about to end. My career with Munster came to a head in November 1985. I was dropped for Munster's opening match in the inter-provincial series after I declined to play in a Munster trial when selected to captain the Possibles against the Probables. The trial clashed with a Greystones league match against Lansdowne. I chose to play for my club ahead of my province. I paid the penalty and Munster were well beaten.

So worrying was their performance that their selectors went into a state of panic. They bit the bullet and asked me if I would line out for them in a squad training session. After much soul-searching I agreed. It turned out to be a huge mistake on my part and I regretted it. After driving from Dublin down to Thomond Park, I remember standing in the middle of the pitch at 11.30 a.m. on a Sunday morning wondering what in the name of God I was doing there. I had left home at 8 a.m. after playing a game for Greystones the previous day. Eventually, someone brought out two sets of grotty jerseys, blue and white, and then I discovered they were going to have some sort of a trial. To my horror it was one of those 'freeze sessions' where the match was stopped when something went wrong and the error pointed out. Here we all were, amateur players, but shown very little respect. It was just a complete waste of time. In other words, there was no squad session and no organisation. I ended up playing in a 'Mickey Mouse' match.

To make matters worse, there was a bit of an atmosphere. I spoke to nobody in authority and there was no communication from anyone towards me either. Quite why I was there was beyond me. John Moroney and Jim Kiernan were calling the shots at the time so when we were finished I did not hang around. I just drove off into the sunset, literally and metaphorically. I decided, there and then, my career with Munster was over. The end had come almost seven years to the day after we beat the All Blacks. It was a sad way to go, particularly since I loved Munster and had taken such pride in wearing the red.

Very shortly afterwards, I transferred to Leinster out of convenience as much as anything. It was the right move from a personal perspective as it did not make any sense any more to travel from Dublin to either Limerick or Cork to train and play. In autumn 1986, I made my Leinster debut against Canada. It was no big deal apart from the fact that our side consisted of no less than five Greystones backs – John Murphy, Paul McNaughton, Hubie Gallacher, Tony Doyle and me – which was unprecedented. As it turned out, the game was pretty awful. When I arrived in the Lansdowne Road dressing room, someone handed me a telegram. It was from none other than Ollie Campbell who wrote: 'You have played with distinction in various shades of blue before. Hope it continues! Ollie.' A nice touch and one that encapsulated what rugby was, and is, all about. There was still a tinge of sadness and regret towards Munster when I ran out in the blue of Leinster. But common sense prevailed. From a travel, social and business point of view, I was being fair to myself. And I was being fair to Munster.

My debut for Greystones had begun with defeat, and before it got better, it got much worse: we lost the next six games. But then we turned things around and, on the strength of that, my career took a remarkable upward curve. I was never happier playing my most mature rugby than I was when at Greystones. As Johnny Murphy said, it was not about winning but about having enjoyment along the way. Having said that, Greystones

185

could meet and beat the very best, and we did when sharing the top table with the likes of Lansdowne, Wanderers, St Mary's and Blackrock. So my rugby move from Dublin to Wicklow was inspired. I could have gone to Dublin 4, but I loved my time in the Garden of Ireland in every way. If I could use one word to sum up the final five years of my playing career it would be: contentment.

CHAPTER 16

DOYLER & FITZY

Mick Doyle took over from Willie John McBride as Ireland coach. He hit the ground running making an immediate impact. But he was ably assisted by the arrival of another reliable goal-kicker in Michael Kiernan, and I guess I played a tiny part in that. Doyler's first game in charge was against the touring Australians on 10 November 1984. Lansdowne Road was packed to near-capacity. Despite missing that 'semi-trial' game in Cork I had been included in the match-day squad as cover for Paul Dean. Kiernan was picked on the left wing with Moss Finn alongside Brendan Mullin in the centre. Mullin was one of five new caps along with Michael Bradley, Willie Anderson, Philip Matthews and Willie Sexton.

We were training at Suttonians in the build-up to the game when the coach appeared at my shoulder and engaged in a bit of chit-chat. Because everything was up in the air, nobody knew who the kicker would be, least of all Doyler himself. The general feeling was that Moss Finn was the man as he had a bit more goal-kicking experience with UCC and Cork Con than

Michael, who had little or no track record at all. I watched them both kick for about twenty minutes, and then Doyler asked me who I thought should be Ireland's first-choice kicker. I said: 'Does it really matter? You probably have your mind made up already.' He answered: 'Yea, Moss Finn.' I replied: 'I think you are making a big mistake. Michael is far more natural as a kicker.'

Doyler stuck to his guns and Mossie started as his preferred kicking choice. But Michael took over in the second period and the rest is history. From 6–0 down, he kicked three penalties in quick succession to give us a 9–6 lead with around twenty minutes left to play. 'Mick the Kick', as he was soon to be christened by the lads, had arrived. But the Aussies, not for the first time, broke our hearts. In one of their greatest teams, consisting of world-class players like David Campese, Nick Farr-Jones and Michael Lynagh, Mark Ella took over. He scored a try, conversion and a penalty and they won 16–9.

That was my lone involvement that season, but what an outstanding Five Nations Kiernan had. I sat and watched in admiration. In the opener in Scotland, Ireland won 18–5 thanks in large part to two tries from Trevor Ringland. Kiernan converted both and for good measure slotted over a penalty and drop goal. Exactly a month later, he kicked all five penalties in a 15–15 draw with the French at Lansdowne Road. A fortnight on, Kiernan kept up his remarkable consistency. He slotted three penalties and converted both Irish tries in a stunning 21–9 demolition of Wales. That terrific win in Cardiff set Ireland up for a winner-takes-all match at home against England. It was a typically tight encounter, but Mullin and Kiernan emerged as heroes in a team full of them. Mullin scored the crucial try and Kiernan rowed in with a magnificent drop goal and two penalties which gave Ireland a narrow 13–10 win.

Ireland had won the Championship and also their second Triple Crown in three years.

Missing out on the Triple Crowns was not easy, but relative to being dropped in Australia all those years earlier it represented a fleeting point of disappointment. I certainly didn't lose any sleep over it. Besides, I knew time and competition for places were now against me. Kiernan was a very talented player who had originally played on the right wing in our 1982 tour match against Romania in Bucharest. He was a revelation and after that match I was convinced he was going to spend his entire career on the wing, even though centre had always been his position of choice. Along with Brennie Mullin he formed the most talented and most effective centre combination of the amateur era. Whether it was the best Irish pairing ever, I would suggest supporters of Gordon D'Arcy and Brian O'Driscoll might have something to say. Neither were the best defensively, but they organised their lines so well they covered any deficiencies in that area. Michael was a natural three-quarter with all the relevant bits.

The chat with Doyler, and winning a place on his replacement bench, made me even more determined to get back as I had done before. Above all I was now happy in Dublin playing for Greystones and, however strange initially, with Leinster, too. It was as good a place as any to start afresh. I was going to roll up my sleeves and work my socks off again to get back in the Ireland frame. If I could do that then my second big aim would take care of itself: I dearly wanted to play for my country in the inaugural World Cup to be held in Australia and New Zealand in 1987.

Injuries to Deano, and his then understudy Ralph Keyes, played their part when, out of the blue, Mick Doyle and his selectors included me in the extended squad for Five Nations training. It was fantastic just to be back and a part of it all again. It did come as a bit of a surprise, although my form for club and province had been good to that point in the season. Just under a month later I lined out for Ireland in their last game of the championship with Scotland, two years after my last full international against the same opposition. The match will be best remembered for the huge ovation Phil Orr received as he led the team out for his fiftieth cap. And because Michael Kiernan had a kick in the last minute to win the game. But from just twenty metres out his kick drifted across the face of the posts and wide. The referee blew for time soon after and we had lost 10–9. We certainly did not deserve to lose as we played really well and produced a top quality brand of attacking rugby. Even so we finished bottom of the pile, and BBC presenter Nigel Starmer-Smith summed things up perfectly when he stated: 'The Irish are the liveliest and most skilful team ever to occupy the wooden-spoon berth.'

Considering how long I had been out of Five Nations action I felt I had played well. In his *Irish Independent* column on the following Monday, Colm Smith wrote: 'Third-choice out-half Tony Ward returned after two years as a virtual outcast. His distribution of the ball was better than I have ever seen it and his presence was a source of great worry for the opposition.' A try from Roy Laidlaw and two Gavin Hastings penalties were enough to give Scotland a share of the Championship with France. Scottish captain Colin Deans was also generous to me in his post-match summation: 'He was splendid. He was like a youngster out there the way he mixed his game and moved the backline in such a way as to give his backs so much scope.' Scottish coach Derick Grant added: 'Tony Ward controlled what amounted to the best backline we played all year other than the French.' Mere words, yes, but they meant a lot. Even 'more so were the views of Ciaran Fitzgerald and Mick Doyle as captain and coach respectively. Doyler said: 'I would give back last year's Triple Crown to see another performance from Ireland like this one. Ward's skills, craft and general know-how have truly not deserted him and he proved this in the manner he returned to the international scene to play so well.' Fitzy commented: 'Our performance reminded me of the Irish teams of old and Ward, who relished so much being back with the likes of Brendan Mullin and Michael Kiernan, fitted in so well.'

The response from the public was most encouraging, too. The telegrams, telephone calls and personal messages were far in excess of what I received when I won my first cap. I found it all very touching and flattering. I guess, in a way, that taking the scenic route back into the team made it all worthwhile. It was also a huge relief because I was so nervous running out on to the pitch. I really had this sense of the public rooting for me. I knew they wanted me to do well and I did not want to let them down. I am glad I delivered. That game will always be my most memorable for Ireland.

It was great to be back, and back in such a well organised side. The parameters of the game were set by the coach. Mick Doyle was so much more than the 'give it a lash' perception attributed to him. He put the onus on the team to help me blend and not vice versa, which is what so many people had been crucifying me for in times past. I felt very comfortable in that set-up. Mick handled me and the entire squad so well that weekend. When he and Fitzy offered words of praise you knew it was earned. From that, the most important perspective of all, I knew I had played well. In rugby, more than in any other team game, the captain has a crucial role to play. In other sports he can be a figurehead. Although it has dissipated somewhat in the professional age, the rugby captain still has a key role to play. Before the game went open, the captain had the built-in responsibility of working on the psychological preparation of the team. On the field he had to be a tireless motivator.

I have no hesitation in saying that Fitzy was the best captain I had the good fortune to play under by a country mile. Those Triple Crown wins in 1982 and 1985 did not just happen by chance. The most crucial common denominator of the seven players involved in both triumphs was the man wearing the number two shirt and the captain's armband. And that was C.F. Fitzgerald. What marked him out from every other captain was his ability to get the very best out of all the very different characters and personalities in his teams. He had to handle their different idiosyncrasies. Then he had to fire them collectively with a burning will to win when they stepped on to the field of play. Never was the dictum 'all for one and one for all' better displayed than when Ciaran Fitzgerald was captain.

Also, he never asked anything of you that he did not demand of himself. His record speaks for itself with those Triple Crowns and Championships in 1982 and 1985, as well as a share of top spot with France in 1983. He was often criticised for his throw-in at the line-out, but tell me a hooker who has not shipped flak – and I include Keith Wood, our greatest hooker – for that part of their game. Sadly certain sections of the British media could never accept him being named captain of the 1983 Lions in New Zealand. But Fitzy was a brilliant hooker, an inspirational rugby player and an outstanding leader of men. It is to his eternal credit he did not allow the constant carping to affect his self-confidence. He came up with the perfect riposte by leading Ireland to great victories, and even his harshest critics had to eat their words after that second Triple Crown in 1985. The only men who came close to displaying the same qualities of leadership I so admire in a captain were Pat Whelan and Willie Anderson.

Mick Doyle's real strength was his man-managing. Yes, he was a good strategist, but it was the relationship with his captain which made 1985 such a great year. We did not just win the Triple Crown, but did so in style. Keith Crossan's touchdown in Cardiff best sums up for me that successful era of 'give it a lash' rugby. Doyler was a great motivator and had the ability to cut the cloth to suit its measure. From a personal perspective the memory I will always have of him is that final match against Scotland in 1986. He treated me with a level of respect when I came back into the side which was the exact opposite of what I had experienced just a couple of years before under Willie Duggan as captain and Willie John as coach.

What does a coach do when his side are not only facing the wooden spoon and a whitewash, but also missing key players through injury? Mick played an ace card. In order to restore sagging morale he enlisted the help of John D. O'Brien from RTE Television to compile a twenty- to twenty-five-minute video for the squad to watch in the lead-up to that game. It contained the best moments of Ireland's Triple Crown win the previous year to the music of Queen's classic hit 'We are the Champions'. It represented the power of positive thinking at its very best. Essentially the message he was evoking was: 'That was what you were capable of just twelve months ago – now go out and give it a lash tomorrow.'

While it might seem a shallow complaint, if Doyler had one failing it was his overuse of expletives. His bad language began to lose its impact after a while as the players became immune to it. In reality his macho exterior hid a very soft centre. He had a great way with television, as I knew from working with him in that capacity, and he took all the media pressure in his stride in 1985. He wallowed under the spotlight as he was a natural media man. This allowed the players to concentrate solely on the rugby.

There are so many stories that still do the rounds about Doyler, and I will relate one. Before taking up the reins with Ireland he was a very successful coach with Leinster. The night before an important match, Terry Kennedy and two other play-ers came back to the team hotel at an ungodly hour after a night out on the town. Doyler decided to crack the whip and make an example of them. Next morning the three players were summoned to Doyler's room at 11 a.m. At this juncture it should be mentioned that Mick was sharing his room with Ken Ging and apparently they had had a right bender themselves the night before. Their room was full of empty beer bottles, so Ken was ordered to tidy the room and hide the bottles. He put them behind a chair in the corner of the room. So the three guys arrived and with them was Ollie Campbell, the captain. Doyler tore into them and used every expletive and cliché in the book about how they were a disgrace to Leinster and how they had let themselves down. Ollie was feeling uncomfortable as he stood there witnessing this volley of abuse. So he pulled the chair out from the corner to sit down until Mick had finished. As he did so, the bottles toppled noisily and rolled out along the carpet. Seeing this, Kennedy burst out laughing and said: 'Fuck off, Doyler.'

Sadly, Mick passed away on Tuesday morning, 11 May 2004. He was involved in a car accident near Quinns Corner, outside Ballygawley. With his passing, Ireland lost a larger than life character and a rugby legend. Not only was he a great coach but he was also capped twenty times by Ireland between 1965 and 1968, and by the British and Irish Lions as well. Born in Currow, County Kerry – the same village that produced Moss

Keane and Mick Galwey, as well as his brother Tommy, and in more recent times J.J. Hanrahan – he had the distinction of never having been dropped from the Ireland panel during his brief career as a flanker.

With Doyler and Fitzy in charge, I at least had the security of knowing that I was very much back in the frame. I could not wait for the 1987 season and the very first World Cup. But in November 1986 my latest Ireland career could have been derailed by the 'Rugbyclass' controversy. Instead, I decided to play ball with the IRFU by being agreeable. I had learned my lessons from the past. The young Tony Ward would have kicked up a fuss and argued the toss. But in the twilight of my career what was the point? It probably would have proved counter-productive and potentially put my World Cup prospects in jeopardy. This time I bit my lip. Accepting the IRFU's take on the amateur ethos forced me into a straightforward decision: I would not go ahead with my upcoming involvement in a Tony Ward School of Rugby organised by Rugbyclass. So while Phil Bennett, Bill Beaumont and Andy Irvine ploughed on with their schools in Wales, England and Scotland respectively, I reluctantly but sensibly chose to sever my involvement here in Ireland. It left me with a clear mind and totally focused for the 1987 season.

The path was never going to be easy with Paul Dean and Ralph Keyes as my main rivals. Three into two would not go and only two specialist out-halves would make the cut. It was not going to come easily. I guess I had to count my blessings now that I was back in contention. It was a far better place to be than the previous year. More than anything, I just had to keep my head down, keep myself on-form and injury-free. That was especially true when, after returning from the Five Nations defeat in Edinburgh, I was asked to participate in a trial between Combined Provinces and the Rest of Ireland to be held in Belfast the following Wednesday evening. No one else from the team who lost against the Scots was asked to play. They were rested. This was about the best of the rest mounting a challenge to face France next up and with the inaugural World Cup just around the corner.

I had to take a day off teaching and travel up north to Ravenhill by coach. With the match played that evening under floodlights, I arrived back in Dublin much earlier than the bus thanks to a lift from Tony Doyle and Ciaran Fitzgerald. It was a meaningless match and as inconclusive as one could get. The only thing of note was my clashing heads with Ralph Keyes twenty minutes in. I played on, but Ralph had to withdraw.

For the 1987 Five Nations, Deano was out-half and I sat on the bench for the opening two games. It was very frustrating watching a record 17–0 win over England in our first match at Lansdowne Road. Two weeks later, on 21 February, we faced Scotland in Murrayfield. Again I had to sit it out as we lost a gripping encounter 16–12. Future events would show that that game was a lost opportunity in our quest for a third Triple Crown in six years.

So, in neither of the opening games had I got a run-out. Then, following that shambolic trial in Ravenhill, I was dropped from the bench and Ralph Keyes was picked as the back-up out-half to Dean. That for me was the final straw. Enough was enough. Despite agreeing to the IRFU's Rugbyclass demands, knuckling down, and travelling up for a meaningless trial, I was axed for Ireland's third Five Nations game at home to France without kicking a ball. Ireland lost 19–13.

It was a low point in my career right up there with that earlier debacle in Australia. I foolishly believed I could do no wrong from the bench. But then I was dealing with one of the duo who had hunted me out of Munster a couple of years before. An article written in the *Times* by George Ace during the same period was apt: 'The bench in Irish rugby is as dangerous as the trapdoor on a scaffold – you can disappear into oblivion mighty quickly.' When I closed the door of my home in Dublin that night, and after throwing my gear into the corner, I made up my mind my Ireland career was finally over. It was one knock too many. That was the nearest I came to calling it a day. There were other, albeit rare occasions from the past, when in the heat of the moment I considered it. But to climb back to the top of the mountain again, only to be tripped and pushed over the edge, was hard to take.

Syd Millar, who had been named as manager of the Ireland World Cup squad, forced me into changing my mind, but, boy, did I need convincing. He reassured me that this was almost like a huge test that was being handed out to me, and that those who made the decision were eagerly awaiting my reaction. If I gave in I would be doing so without a fight and letting them win. He told me that I had come this far and it was pointless throwing it all away. In tandem with Millar, Ned Van Esbeck offered the same whole-hearted encouragement. So, much aggrieved, I agreed to knuckle down and stick with it for another few months at least.

Obviously, I was not privy to the selectors' decisions or what went on at their meetings. It was suggested that Jim Kiernan might have had a vested interest in me not making the World Cup squad, but I leave it to others to make up their mind on that one. He was certainly an obstacle. He was no fan of mine and I was equally certain that whatever he had against me, it had nothing to do with rugby. That bench dropping did not just happen by chance. It was co-ordinated.

Selectors and selection committees and selections have always been a bone of contention. Well, the selection system that existed in my time stank to high heaven. It was skulduggery and party politicking at its most divisive. It was different things to different people, but transparent it was definitely not. Despite the lip service about picking the best team, human nature being what it is dictated that they do the best they can for their province or club. It was cronyism Ireland-style. I hated everything the Irish system of five full selectors and two subs stood for. If professionalism has brought one thing – and nothing else – it is a system of transparency epitomised by Joe Schmidt and the system of selection today. The old system is dead in the grave and thank God for that.

CHAPTER 17

THE RUGBY WORLD CUP

Syd Millar, Ireland's manager for the upcoming World Cup, and journalist Ned Van Esbeck were right to dissuade me from turning my back on the international team. I was named on the bench for the next international against Wales, though, to be quite frank, my inclusion on that occasion was very unfair on Ralph Keyes. It only served to highlight once more the total lack of selection logic. Nevertheless the recall offered me renewed hope and my chances of making Ireland's squad for the inaugural World Cup were looking pretty good. A place on the bench was better than no place at all. On the field, Ireland ended the 1987 campaign with a magnificent 14–11 win against the Welsh in Cardiff, a victory which meant that only the narrow defeat in Scotland had prevented us claiming a third Triple Crown triumph in six years.

Mick Doyle was the man who gave me my chance. Although it was hard to deal with certain selection issues, I just had to keep my head down. Ireland's star was in the ascendancy under Doyler and, in fairness, he had many big decisions to make. Not least was the selection of his World Cup squad. In May

1987, Mick and the selectors announced their panel for the very first Rugby World Cup to be played in Australia and New Zealand. It was as follows:

Backs – Michael Bradley, Keith Crossan, Paul Dean, Tony Doyle, David Irwin, Michael Kiernan, Hugo MacNeill; Brendan Mullin, Phillip Rainey, Trevor Ringland, Paul Haycock and ... Tony Ward. I had made it! I was so delighted and hugely relieved.

Forwards – Willie Anderson, Nigel Carr, Paul Collins, Des Fitzgerald, Neil Francis, Jim Glennon, Terry Kingston, Job Langbroek, Donal Lenihan (captain), Philip Matthews, John MacDonald, J.J. McCoy, Derek McGrath, Phil Orr, Steve Smith and Brian Spillane.

It was cruel in the extreme when Nigel Carr had to withdraw. Nigel suffered horrific injuries in the April 1987 IRA bombing atrocity which targeted and claimed the lives of Lord Justice Maurice Gibson and his wife Cecily. The bomb was detonated on an isolated part of the Dublin to Belfast road where Nigel, David Irwin and Phillip Rainey were travelling on their way to World Cup training in Dublin. Thankfully, Davy Irwin and 'Chipper' Rainey emerged unscathed from that appalling incident and made the cut.

For the first World Cup, we had been drawn in Pool Two with Wales, Tonga and Canada. The winners and runners-up from each of the four pools would go through to the quarter-finals.

There were a couple of worrying things about our preparations ahead of our departure. The media raised concerns about our severe lack of match practice. Those concerns were well founded. Mick Doyle acknowledged this and later conceded that he had almost mollycoddled the Irish players by barring the entire squad from playing for their clubs after March. In stark contrast, our first opponents Wales had played right up until the beginning of May, little more than three weeks before our match.

Another huge drawback was the tour itinerary. When we boarded our flight at Dublin Airport, it was just the first of many. I think I counted somewhere in the region of fourteen flights we took in the two countries hosting the tournament, which was far from ideal. For example, after we played Wales in Wellington, we flew to Dunedin for the second pool game with Canada on the Saturday. Then we took off for Christchurch on Sunday from where we began the second leg of our World Cup in Australia. We arrived at our base in Brisbane via Sydney on the Monday. Next day we grabbed some much needed rest and relaxation before playing Tonga on Wednesday.

Team morale was not helped by what was perceived as a clique that had developed among certain players. This first came to my attention two years before when I was chatting to Moss Finn. Moss was so easy to get along with, but when he came into Doyler's team in 1984–85 he told me he found it a very uncomfortable experience. He felt he was almost intruding in the dressing room because of a clique that was already established. If someone as easy-going as Moss was having that sort of trouble then I cannot imagine how difficult it was for others.

This situation had manifested itself after the Triple Crown win in 1985 among a group of Irish backs comprising Hugo MacNeill, Michael Kiernan, Paul Dean and Michael Bradley. Keith Crossan and Trevor Ringland were inseparable while Brendan Mullin was always his own man. On the morning of Ireland's opening World Cup game against Wales, Hugo and Michael arrived down to breakfast at the Terrace Regency Hotel in Wellington. We were all eating together in the dining hall. Both players passed around a few postcards to be signed before posting them home. The tradition among players away on tour was to get every player in the squad to sign postcards for sending home. However, Hugo and Michael had their cards numbered from one to fifteen. In other words they sought the autographs of players they perceived to be Ireland's premier XV – the 'elite' in action that day – rather than the entire squad. Those of us who were considered outsiders were only too delighted not to be signing their cards. It would have been much nicer to have enjoyed our breakfast without that distraction, but everyone had noted the symbolism of their actions. It was the first fifteen and the rest as opposed to the 'all for one and one for all' ethos of a squad.

Away from that, I was happy and extremely proud to be there. Perhaps in the early part of my career there were occasions when I took my selection for granted. Not now. After all I had been through I had come to realise that nobody has the divine right to be selected at any level. For some members of that clique this lesson would hit home hard following the opening two matches.

At the official World Cup dinner in advance of the game against the Welsh, Doyler suffered a mild heart attack. He played it down and quickly swept it away, preferring to concentrate all minds on the business of the World Cup. By the end of the tournament that health scare would have impacted on him greatly. Syd Millar may have been removed from coaching for some time, but the tour manager commanded such respect that he was able to take up the reins seamlessly.

As I took my place on the bench for our first game, I was not the only one gobsmacked when the Wellington organisers played over the public address system a James Last version of the 'Rose Of Tralee' as our national anthem. Even if it had been the right anthem, the tape was scratchy and in places barely audible. The maiden global tournament was always going to have teething problems, but with respect to the NZRFU this was 'wild west' stuff.

Wales were sharp from the get-go while we were sluggish and lethargic. They scored the only try of the game along with two drop goals against two Michael Kiernan penalties for us. We lost 13–6. It was by no means a disastrous start, but it did put us under a degree of pressure as we were expected to beat Canada and Tonga in our next two games. Perhaps if we had played either of those two first it would have stood us in better stead ahead of a match with Wales.

Changes were made for the Canadian game with Paul Dean the biggest casualty. He knew himself that he had been less than convincing in windy Wellington and took his dropping on the chin. I was brought back to replace him. In a sense it was another new beginning. That was how I felt as I approached one of the happiest and proudest days in my rugby career. I was finally getting game-time for my country in the inaugural World Cup.

On Saturday, 30 May, five days after our opening defeat, I lined out for Ireland against Canada at the infamous Carisbrook 'House of Pain' in Dunedin. Again we were far from convincing. The Canadians really shook us and the scores were tied at 19–19 deep into the second half. But we rolled up our sleeves and a late burst saw us through 46–19. There was a collective sigh of relief when Keith Crossan scored his second try of the game with ten minutes left to put us ahead and finally break the Canadian resolve. I contributed a drop goal with Kiernan on goal-kicking duty. But it was all slightly embarrassing and none of us could be proud of our performance that day. We needed to improve immeasurably.

On Monday, 1 June we left New Zealand for Australia. As our plane flew in over Sydney Harbour, and I distinctly remember listening to U2 on my headphones, I recalled that it had been eight long years since I first played in Australia on a tour. I was back. Next day, in Ballymore, Brisbane, I did a spot of training with Ollie Campbell. When Ollie first realised there was going to be a Rugby World Cup, he booked his summer holidays around the dates Ireland were due to play. How ironic. Anyone who saw us training must have been wondering what was going on. Were things so bad in the Irish camp that Campbell was sent for? Ollie Campbell and I were back where it all started. It was almost akin to the return of Butch Cassidy and the Sundance Kid. Two American cowboys in forced Bolivian exile, and we were two old kickers returning to be among ghosts of the past.

One kicker who gave it his all only for injury to cut him down in his prime; the other still hanging on and refusing a trip to 'Boot Hill', that infamous graveyard for gunslingers. My boots were still very firmly on.

Like two old codgers chewing 'tobaccy', we reminisced about old times in the outback. In fact, Ollie reminded me on that day, 2 June, it was exactly eight years since Ireland faced Australia in Ballymore. It was a very strange feeling, but to have Ollie out there beside me was in a sense reassuring. His reminder about that anniversary brought to mind another interesting fact. If Australia topped their pool, and we beat Tonga, we would face them in the quarter-finals.

Just as Paul Dean was brought down to earth ahead of the Canada game, so Michael Kiernan was then dropped for the final pool game against Tonga. Kiernan kicked nineteen points against Canada, but his overall performance clearly did not impress. By that stage I was thirty-two, going on thirty-three years of age, and yet I was about to win only my nineteenth cap in almost ten years of international rugby. Nowadays, if a player lasts that long in the game, he would have well in excess of one hundred caps.

We finally got our act together against Tonga. In a very assured and polished performance, we won 33–9. I had a reasonable game, kicking two penalties and three conversions. There was life in the old dog yet. I played at out-half and linked up well with Michael Bradley on the day. The most pleasing aspect was keeping the ball in front of our pack and, by extension, keeping the Tongans on the back foot and under pressure. The forward unit stood out with Donal Lenihan, Neil Francis, Willie Anderson and Philip Matthews dominant in the line-out. And while they were magnificent, so too was Brendan Mullin, who had a day he will never forget in registering a hat-trick of tries.

One slight drawback from that resounding win was the date of our quarter-final. We had to return from Brisbane to Sydney and a match against Australia just four days later at the Concorde Oval. It was an unbelievably quick turnaround. I was also in line for my customary shock. I guess being in Australia would not be the same without it. I felt I was in with a shout for selection. I reckoned it would come down to either a combination of me at out-half and goal-kicker along with David Irwin as partner to Mullin in midfield, or else Michael Kiernan as goal-kicker and centre with Deano back in situ at out-half.

I rang my mother ahead of the big game. The squad were to assemble at 9 a.m. for the announcement of the team, so I rang her around 8.20 a.m., bearing in mind it was still the previous evening back home in Ireland. I also wanted to say hello to my daughter Lynn and see how she was. This is the gist of our chat:

'Are you very disappointed?'
'Disappointed with what?'
'With being dropped.'
'What do you mean? The team has not been announced yet.'
'The team was announced here on the radio tonight and you are being dropped.'

Of course I found out an hour later that she was right. It was typical that once again I should learn about being dropped in such a freakish way, and from someone outside of management. While feeling naturally disappointed, I had almost expected Deano and 'Mick the Kick' to return.

We had history on our side in the shape of one very interesting statistic: Ireland had never lost to Australia in their backyard. Having played in Australia on three previous occasions, we had won the two Tests played in 1979 and also beat the Aussies in 1967. It was a sequence that wasn't to be extended. Indeed, it became apparent almost immediately that this was going to be a bad day at the office. In fact, sitting on the bench, both my room-mate Jim Glennon and I knew well before half-time that we would be on the plane home the following day. There was little to shout about as Australia coasted to victory. Mick Doyle surprised me with a comment he made in the dressing room after the match when he said: 'We won the second half.' So what did that mean? The Aussies had the game won at half-time and they could afford to go to sleep in the second period. In effect, they were saving themselves for the semi-final. They could actually have moved up a few gears in the second half had they so desired, but why bother when the game was over as a contest? We were extremely fortunate not be massacred as they declared at 33–15.

As we made our way home, four teams fought for the accolade of Rugby World Cup champions. Australia lost a classic semi-final to France 30–24, while New Zealand hammered Wales 46–6. Wales took third place by beating the Wallabies 22–21 in the play-off. In the final, at Eden Park, the All Blacks beat France 29–9. Many felt it would be just the first of many World Cup triumphs for New Zealand, but they failed to win another until 2011 when, as hosts once more, they again beat the French 8–7 in the final.

Notwithstanding our failures and shortcomings on the field, Mick Doyle stepped down after the World Cup for practical and medical reasons. I held out fresh hope that, under new coach Jim Davidson, I might be given an extended lease of life.

PERSEVERANCE

It is tough, so very tough. No matter how resolved you are to beating this ghastly illness, there are times when you want to cry. You feel so helpless. You just want to curl up in a ball on the floor and give up. Prolonged rounds of treatment are one thing but when your private life is affected that adds to the angst enormously. It is almost as if you are meant to suffer in every way and every day.

The monster and its demon army are so sadistic and cruel. As a man, the worst effect of hormone implant is loss of libido. It is an attack on your maleness and dignity, but in the overall scheme of things, specifically curbing the tumour, the treatment is essential.

Exactly three months after the initial implant I went to the Mater Hospital on 24 July 2012. I had an operation under the guidance of Doctor Michael Maher in the Mater Cancer Centre. Brachytherapy is an intensive blast of high-dose radiation and is administered under an epidural. The following month, on 28 August, I returned to the Beacon Clinic for a course of Beam Radiotherapy. This went on five days a week over five very long weeks until Friday, 28 September. It was exhausting.

The treatment I received can affect cancer sufferers in different ways. In my case the downside was one of overwhelming fatigue. For months I was zonked. While working at home from my PC, there were many times when I was literally falling asleep at my desk. Another very noticeable effect – and it still happens to me regularly – is the outbreak of hot flushes. I could be sitting with someone at a meeting, or reporting on a game, and suddenly beads of sweat would break out across my brow. This can happen without any warning and in any atmosphere. It does not have to be very warm in the room. People sitting next to me would be forgiven for thinking I had just come out of a sauna or been running as I mop my forehead with a handkerchief.

You wonder as your body goes through all these extremes if it is doing you more harm than good. You also wonder if it is going to cause any permanent damage. Above all, you wonder how much more you can take – and that is just after the first few days.

I was well into my course of treatments by late September 2012, but I also knew that the implant would be in for three long years with a new rod inserted annually. Therefore I had to bring other things into my life. I had to come up with new ideas and new plans. There was simply no way I could keep on, for want of better words, 'looking forward' to hospital visits, doctors' appointments and treatments. I had to stimulate my mind by bringing new interests which would bring much needed diversion and contentment. What I required more than anything was to put some happiness and joy back into my life. New things, new horizons, new stimuli – anything at all was required to counter the unpleasant bouts and rounds of fighting that daily struggle in an ongoing war.

It is strange to say it now but probably the biggest changes in my lifestyle came on the back of my illness. I began by doing something that had never been part of my life before: I went to the gym. I am not sure whether you term gym-goers as 'gym monkeys' or 'gym bunnies', but I never previously entertained any notion whatsoever of entering the gym culture. Eddie O'Sullivan was your original and stereotypical gym bunny back in our college days. He was not called 'Beach', as in Beach boy, for nothing. In terms of physical conditioning. and its importance, Eddie was way ahead of his time. He loved doing weights while I was the complete opposite.

When we were in college we shared a house, Eddie, Dave Mahedy, Dave Phelan, Gerry O'Loughlin and, from time to time, our psychology lecturer P.J. Smyth. But Eddie was a real fitness fanatic. Forget the 'Dagger' nickname nonsense, Eddie had well earned his 'Beach' moniker. While I was always good at jogging, more regular daily exercise was central to my recovery. It was another integral part of the internal healing process that my body really needed. Physical fitness helps the body, which in turn helps the mind. Hence the saying 'a fit body leads to a fit mind' or *'Mens sana in corpore sano'*. The gym arrived as a blessing to me. I needed to get myself right both physically and mentally.

Anyone who believes fitness to be natural is for the birds. Nothing could have been further from the truth and one story underlines that. A year after I retired, I was taking part in a fund-raising match before an Ireland versus Wales game. It was for the Ireland legends against the Welsh equivalent. Phil Bennett was playing opposite me. Benny had also retired, but a few years before me. It was not just the way that he waltzed around me. It was when he accelerated through the gap he had created, and he is six years older. The more he ran the greater the distance he put between us. At that moment I realised I was grossly unfit. It happens to so many players when their careers end. They just stop. We forget how much training and physical activity we went through, in my case, for Limerick United, Garryowen, Munster and all the rest. I was training or playing almost every day of my life. And then when my rugby career ended I downed tools. But after the personal embarrassment Benny inflicted, I decided to start jogging while also delving into a little aerobics.

Indoor football also became a big part of my life. I had not played it since college and of all the games I played, I consider that abbreviated football version to be my best. I positively love playing five-a-side soccer. Because of my physique and balance I guess I was made for it. I played indoor football into my fifties and I miss playing it so badly now. I know it would take precious little to entice me back. It was aches and pains on my joints which eventually took its toll on my body and I had to call it a day. The mind never changes, the body sadly does.

So with my illness, I went and joined a gym. Initially I joined Druids Glen and about a year after that I changed and joined Powerscourt. I absolutely love it there. I go almost every day and have a job conditioning myself to take a break at the weekends. To me it is almost like sacrilege if I miss a session. I go religiously every morning and I have been doing it now for three years. On the few occasions that I have skipped a session, it feels like a part of my day has gone missing.

I do almost an hour in the gym, but about a ninety-minute work-out in total. There is a popular misconception that it is all about weights, which I do very little of. One day current international Sean O'Brien worked alongside me and, oh, how I wished I had followed the Beach! Mostly I do the treadmill, the cross-trainer and the bicycle. I have to watch the treadmill because of my joints. Then I do twenty minutes in the pool where I swim twenty lengths. but I am not in any way an ace swimmer. Just ask my former student buddies in NCPE. Thank

God for Mr Lanaway slipping me through those end-of-year life-saving tests!

Diet became another vitally important additive to my new life regime. You are dealt the hand you are given and because of my metabolism I would invariably put on weight if I did not watch my food intake. It is something I have always been conscious of, and even more so since Doc Hubie pointed out that as a result of my treatment, and the hormonal aspect to the implants, there would be a tendency for my body to retain fluid.

Former Irish international Conor O'Shea's brother, Professor Donal O'Shea, was and is a huge inspiration. I never tire of listening to that man when he is on the airwaves talking about the importance of a good diet and good eating practices in our lives. He is wonderful for me. He inspires me to do the right things for all the right reasons. In fact, both brothers speak such sense in their respective fields that when you listen to either you know they are bang on the ball.

With specific regard to my own diet, one thing I have become very fond of is porridge. I eat porridge even in the hot months of summer. There is nothing quite like a nice bowl of porridge with berries sprinkled into it. The other thing I have become very interested in – and good at – is cooking stir fries. Fish is another thing I adore. Tony Ward with apron around his waist, wooden spoon in hand, a drop of coconut oil into the hot pan and away we go. Of course, quite aside from health reasons, my cooking is also born out of necessity because at home I am both father and mother!

As regards medication, there are new drugs that I had to take to help myself back to full health. One is Fosamax and is for bone density. Because of the hormone treatment, my bone density reduced by twenty-three per cent. To put it into context: it is similar to the condition from which a lot of elderly people suffer. It was not brittle-bone syndrome, but nevertheless it was a very significant reduction. It was shown up by a Dexa scan taken a year into my treatment. As a result I was put on this medication by Doc Hubie, who is in the process of trying to build up my bone density. Once a week, on a Tuesday, I take my bone-density medication. As for the other medications, eventually I come off some and the others are gradually winding down. The omens are good.

Another hugely important aspect of my wellbeing and recovery was my mental state. Apart from my own involvement as a campaigner for ARC House, attached to the Mater Hospital, I did not go to visit any support groups. It is an excellent medium for a lot of people, but I just did not feel it was for me. I just wanted to do things my way and try and get through it as best I could. But if it became unbearable then the magnificent set-up at ARC House was my next port of call. I cannot speak highly enough of Mairead Mangan and everybody involved in that wonderful Eccles Street-based cancer support centre.

Two other things were very important to me. Short of having a total absence of it, there was a period when I neglected formal religion in my life. I think it tends to happen to most of us along the way. But I began to reassess my spiritualism. Now I go to mass every Sunday simply because I want to. It has not overlapped with my illness, but what I have been through has provided very real pause for thought. I have long since found that this Sunday morning window of opportunity allows me time to reflect. I still believe in Dave Allen's long-established dictum 'May your God go with you'. In that key respect it certainly is different strokes for different folks. All I know is that I am mighty happy with mine.

Akin to people listening and reflecting at the end of the day to the sound and chimes of The Angelus, that forty-five minutes or so mass time each week causes me to pause, reflect, think and pray. Certainly I am no 'Holy Joe', but it makes me feel better about myself, about others and about the world. In the modern mayhem called life that therapeutic experience is surely no bad thing.

The other thing I would like to think is that the illness has made me a nicer person. The whole experience taught me to be more tolerant and I have definitely mellowed significantly on the back of it. Even something simple, but essential in the modern age, like social media provides a case in point. I cannot say I like or totally accept the social media phenomenon, but I have grown to become more tolerant of it and intend taking up a night course during the winter months.

So a whole range of changes have come into my life as a direct result of my life-changing experience. Some are mental and some are physical. Some are medicinal and some therapeutic. In the beginning you feel macho. You feel you can beat it and that you will get well again. But you are never really in the driving seat. You must lay yourself bare and in a strange way almost give in – but you never give in. You take the blows and roll with the punches. At the same time you always remain strong to yourself. To coin a well-worn sporting dictum concerning competitors forever trying to find the best way to rise above mental challenges: 'Treat it as if it means nothing but it means everything.'

The sobering reality is that it is still there. The extreme fatigue and hot flushes serve as constant reminders. But I must, and will, remain strong and fit – in mind and body.

CHAPTER 18

THE FINAL KICK

S oon after the World Cup, and leading into the 1988 Five
Nations Championship, Jim Davidson took control of the
Ireland team. Unlike so many of his predecessors Jimmy D. –
a university lecturer and former Ireland flanker as well as
hugely successful Ulster coach – was a stickler for detail.
Some felt he was out of his depth at international level. I have
mixed feelings on that one. Jim came on to the Ireland scene
on the back of a very impressive time with Ulster. I do not
think I exaggerate when I say he was the spark that lit the fuse
for the development of provincial rugby way ahead of the
professional transition that followed. Team Ulster became
very much the buzz term of the time. Ireland, however, was a
different ball game entirely.

Jim held his first meaningful international trial on 19
December 1987. It was a week before Christmas and I was
desperately hoping for the perfect present. After the honour
of representing my country at the first World Cup, I was now
up for the battle to get that number ten shirt back. For sure,
it would be no easy task to usurp Paul Dean, but that was my

Christmas wish and New Year's resolution rolled into one. By 16 January, and our opener against Scotland, I was hoping to have done enough to seal my place back in the starting fifteen.

I remember the day of the trial was a little overcast and gloomy with a typical blustery Lansdowne wind. The fact that I was slightly hampered by a niggling thigh injury did not matter. I was fully intent on giving my all and impressing those watching. Bear in mind this was still the age of the 'big five selectors'. Twenty minutes into the second half I came off injured as my leg gave way. A generous scattering of applause echoed around the ground from the few spectators who had turned up. Ralph Keyes was waiting on the sideline to replace me. I took off my blue jersey and handed it to him. Jim Davidson draped a consoling arm around me as I was given a tracksuit top to put on. Then I walked down the tunnel to the dressing room. Between a dreary day, the injury, coming off and walking alone down the tunnel, it was a dark, defining moment.

It is like that daily ritual when darkness descends in the evening and the curtains are drawn in the home. The only difference here was that when I drew the curtains, I could not find any lights to turn on. I could not see where I was going. I was lost, confused, frustrated, helpless. What was I to do next? In the pitch darkness of previous times I could always reach out and flick on the light switch. Then I could see clearly again and have the energy levels to produce the appropriate performances. Now I had no clue where the light was. I fumbled around in the dark, slapping the wall with my hands, trying to locate the switch. I thought I could hear voices in my head . . . Jim Davidson and his selectors were mapping the route forward, but there was no mention of me.

Deano initiated a brilliant move just before half-time in that trial which culminated in Hugo MacNeill scoring a try in the corner. 'Dean and MacNeill were magnificent,' I hear them say so loud and clear. 'What is the extent of Ward's injury?' I hear some murmuring voices ask. 'Does it matter?' answers one. Another shouts: 'He is finished.' The demons placing these whispers inside my head will not leave. Nor does the image of Jimmy D. with his arm around me. It reminds me of a scene from a Rocky Balboa boxing film: tired, weary, slipping off sweat bands, undoing strapping and bandages, sitting in silence on a tatty bench and then an older coach comes into the cold dressing room.

Horror of horrors, I suddenly come to my senses and realise it is not Rocky or Jake La Motta or Marlon Brando pleading: 'I could have been a contender.' No. This scene involves me and I get an uneasy feeling a fatal and final blow is going to be delivered. The wise old head sits down next to me, throws a consoling arm around my shoulder and tells me to go home. His advice is that I do not need all this hassle any more and that I should spend more time with the wife and kids. Perhaps my best days really are gone. This is a new departure for Tony Ward. It is the very first sign of resignation and an almost sacrilegious admission that maybe time and circumstance have finally caught and floored me.

Time stands still for no man and, for sure, waits for no sports person. Running around and trying to latch on to its coat-tails has now become too much hard work. It used to come easy and natural, but now it has become increasingly harder with a lethal Molotov cocktail of stress, strain, worry and pressures thrown into the mix. It is too hard to consume.

I am heading down the slippery slope past the wasteland of an abysmal 1988 season. I tell myself – and maybe even fool myself into believing – that the embarrassing losses were because I was not a part of it. Oh shame on you, Jim, and your selectors, for dropping me. Look at what has happened in my absence. Yes, you hit the ground running with a narrow 22–18 win over Scotland. But that was as good as it got. On 20 February, France thumped us 25–6. At home against Wales in March we lost 12–9. Then came absolute shame and carnage. England ran in six tries to our solitary Kiernan drop goal in a 35–3 drubbing.

One moment from that game has turned into a lasting legacy which only serves to remind us over and over again of that awful day. Chris Oti became only the second black player in eighty years to be capped by the English. But when he ran in his last try for a personal hat-trick, the English support burst into song. 'Swing Low, Sweet Chariot' was heard for the very first time at Twickenham, or so the story goes. It has been adopted as the unofficial English anthem by their supporters ever since.

I guess in a sense Jim got what was coming to him as he looked to sprint before he walked in that post-World Cup time of change. Some of the things he brought to the training ground bordered on lunacy. At one of his first training sessions, he said he wanted players who were 'bigger, leaner and fitter'. That registered. But he then proceeded to demonstrate the correct way to do a 'press-up'. He got up on the bar of the Wanderers' club house at a squad session in Lansdowne early one Sunday morning to show us. I remember Trevor Ringland was less than impressed. I will also go as far as to say that when Phil Orr heard the Davidson regime was coming to town, it spelt the end for him. It had certainly played a decisive role in Phil's decision to retire after the World Cup, just a few months previously. Perhaps he knew what was coming down the tracks.

But what happened in training before a tour to France was just farcical. Even though I had played no part in the Five Nations, I was invited to fly out with Ireland to participate in a close-season tour of France. The squad was severely depleted with only a few experienced players like Willie Anderson and Jim McCoy on board. Along with the rest of the players who cried off for one reason or another, I was not too bothered about travelling myself. It was the end of the school year, but something the principal of our school said persuaded me to go. I remember telling Jim Duke that I had little interest in going as there was no point. It was obvious that I was no longer in the pecking order and my career was all but over. However, Jim suggested two reasons why I might give it a rethink. Aside from the school's personal interest in me as their representative, he felt that, if my career was coming to a close, then what better way to end it than playing an inter-national away match against the French.

Before departing for France we had two days of squad train-ing on the back pitch at Lansdowne Road. For one of those sessions, Jimmy told us all to take off our tops. He videoed the session and then played it back to us. His objective in going to these extraordinary lengths was to show us our differing body types. For guys with the metabolism to put on weight – and who were self-conscious about it – this was the last thing they needed. I felt it was degrading and insensitive. That type of thing had me shaking my head in disbelief and I was left won-dering why we did it. It was also the first introduction to an Irish squad for players like Mick Galwey and Nicky Barry, and they had to endure that glorified form of degradation among the so-called elite of Irish rugby. In fact, Nicky was quite liter-ally just out of school.

Being fair and balanced, and to give Jim some credit, his great legacy to the Irish game is the changed attitude to fitness.

He was also beating the right drum when advocating province over club as the way forward for Irish rugby in the event of the game going open. There is no doubt about that. But in 1988 he was most definitely in the wrong place and at the wrong time for what amounted to a complete change in culture. He had an admirable vision to put Irish rugby on a par with the rest of the world. But as Irish coach, he was in the wrong position to be trying to implement this new way forward. Jim was trying to change things from the top down whereas, in my opinion, what was required was to change things from the bottom up. He was in the wrong position but with the right ideas.

We played four games on that French tour and the key match was against France in Auch. Neil Francis was superb and not just in the line-out. He gave us the perfect start with a brilliant try just two minutes in. Penalties from Didier Camberabero and Jean-Baptiste Lafond put France back in front. But then just before the interval I kicked a penalty from halfway to put us 7–6 ahead. I landed a drop goal and a penalty in the second half, but the French responded with a try to lead 18–13. With around five minutes left on the clock, I picked up a loose ball and started a counter-attack which, to my astonishment involved so many of our players that it could have come from the French textbook on flair and support. Not only that, but somehow I popped up at the end of it all to go over for our second try. It may only have been a tour game, but as I dusted myself down to attempt the conversion to win the game, the French crowd entered into a chorus of noise to try and unsettle me. Thankfully, I was the old dog for the hard road at that stage in my playing journey. There I was trying to attempt a conversion in the twilight of a career – and a kick for a win – that I had found so hard to carry off when I was younger. I slotted it sweetly between the posts for a 19–18 win.

It was an unbelievable performance. We were really up against it, but we played with such fire in our bellies the French just could not handle us. Also, and because of the adverse conditions, including the booing at the end, I do not think I was ever as happy with a result. Ned Van Esbeck, my great friend and *Irish Times* rugby correspondent, came into the dressing room at the end. It was the first time in my career that I had seen him do that. It was raw emotion. He was then followed by the entire posse of Irish journalists over for the game. This was unprecedented and said a lot about the magnitude of our achievement. All of this got to me. I became very emotional. People were slapping me on the back and telling me about what I had done and what others were saying.

French coach Jacques Fouroux told the press that I was the difference between the sides. While I was flattered by his kind remarks, I was uncomfortable nonetheless. For if ever there was a victory for a band of brothers in adversity this was it. Willie Anderson, as captain, was the key. Both on and off the field big Willie was a leader apart. On that tour of France he came of age. Irish manager Ken Reid declared: 'I have never in my life been as proud of Irish rugby as on this occasion. They stood up to everything.' An IRFU official echoed the chorus of plaudits, adding: 'This was the best performance I've ever seen from an Irish team, bearing in mind the circumstances.'

These were no idle words or clichés. Those 'circumstances' were born out of Ireland's dismal display in Paris earlier that year. France had won then by nineteen points. But this turnaround on French soil was a record-breaker of sorts. It was the first win by an Irish side on Gallic territory since 1972. The line-out went particularly well. To anybody not present it is difficult to explain what a magnificent performance and occasion it actually was. My heroic colleagues who brought off that courageous win were as follows: Phil Danaher, Johnny Sexton, Vinny Cunningham, Paul Clinch, Pete Purcell, Tony Ward, Fergus Aherne, Tom Clancy. Steve Smith, Jim McCoy, Neil Francis, Willie Anderson (captain), Don Whittle, Mike Gibson, Denis McBride. Replacement: Pat O'Hara for Whittle, on forty-five minutes.

The euphoria of the moment eventually got to me. I could not control my emotions any more and I let it all flow. I cried in the dressing room. It was the first time, the last time and the only time I cried after a game. The final tour match took place at La Rochelle when we played a star-studded French Barbarians team. Not surprisingly, in the conditions, we were beaten 41–26, but it was another fabulous effort. Irish teams were not used to playing in ninety degree heat on a rock-hard pitch as we did that day. We were also missing two crucial players from our hitherto dominant line-out in Neil Francis and Michael Gibson.

Jean-Baptiste Lafond was the undoubted star on show as he scored twenty-nine points. Serge Blanco was not bad, either. Throw in All Black World Cup-winning captain David Kirk and Franck Mesnel at half-back and I think you get the drift. To our immense credit we scored a whopping five tries ourselves with Rab Brady and Peter Purcell scoring two apiece. Mick Galwey scored the other and I converted three of the five.

La Rochelle may have ended in valiant defeat, but that French tour was such an astonishing success that it provided the perfect way to draw the curtain on my representative career. It was the last time I wore the green of Ireland. When I arrived home from France, and just short of my thirty-fourth birthday, I announced my retirement from international rugby. What

Jim Duke had said to me before I went made everything crystal-clear.

For sure, there were pangs of sorrow, but I had made a decision and there would be no return. I had come in out of the cold and it felt warm inside. At last I had found the light. I turned it on and shut the door.

CHAPTER 19

REACTION

As I closed the door on my international career by announcing my retirement, tributes poured in. Of course, there was plenty of comment from the media. But what really mattered to me was what genuine rugby fans, players, coaches and the public had to say. Legendary England captain Bill Beaumont was one of the first to give his reaction with a simple: 'But why?' Bill seemed surprised that I did not carry on for another couple of years. He went on: 'He proved on the tour to France that he was at the top of his form. Tony has been missed by Ireland in the last few years. I can't understand how they left him on the sidelines. At least he had the satisfaction of proving them all wrong by the manner in which he performed so well in France. I don't think he should be retiring – he still has a place in international rugby.'

I did play on with my club, Greystones, until 1991 when I was thirty-seven. But in terms of international rugby, thirty-three going on thirty-four is in most sports considered the 'veteran stage'. It is certainly thought of as old in rugby. There are not many international players playing for club, province and country – and who train for all three as well – who play on past the age I retired. You do get the odd exceptions, but such players are really blessed. Avoiding serious injury is one of the biggest factors aiding longevity. To put it in perspective, the great Brian O'Driscoll was also thirty-four when he retired from playing for Ireland in 2014. On the flipside, Ronan O'Gara continued to play with Ireland until 2013 when he was thirty-six. Paul O'Connell will be thirty-five when he leads Ireland into the 2015 World Cup. He also has two years to run on a contract with French club Toulon.

The Welsh people were always kind to me. For instance, in the late 1970s Carwyn James was quoted as saying: 'I wish Tony Ward was born a Welshman.' When I hung up my boots, there was no shortage of Welshmen saying nice things about me. Legendary Welsh scrum-half Gareth Edwards weighed in with his thoughts about my packing it in when he said: '"We have always believed that if he'd been born a Welshman, he would have played far more internationals than he did for Ireland. Sometimes we could not believe that he wasn't in the Irish team.' For the record, I deem Sir Gareth the greatest all-round rugby player there has ever been. Impossible to measure, I know, but I defy anyone to come up with a more complete game-influencing rugby player . . . ever.

There was a flood of responses from the public, and the vast majority of it was very kind. Of all the tributes paid to me via television, radio and newspapers, I have to mention this letter to the now defunct *Sunday Tribune* newspaper. It was written by a Mr D.A. O'Donnell from Malahide in County Dublin. Headlined 'Thanks for the memories, Tony', the following are extracts from the letter:

Only recently he did what Ireland hadn't done for years. He beat France and he didn't chicken out on that tour either when he had nothing to gain from it – unlike some of our other lauded internationals. If Ireland continues to produce outside halves of the calibre of Ward then she has nothing to worry about.

Tony Ward graced the international scene for ten years or thereabouts. He did so with dignity which is more than can be said for some who were involved with our national team in recent years. He was, if nothing else, an outstanding sportsman and a fine example to the youth of the nation inside and outside the rugby environs.

If a player's reputation was to be judged on just one match, then Tony Ward can point to Thomond Park and the day Munster beat the All Blacks. He made the Munster team beat New Zealand and that is meant to show no disrespect to the other fourteen team members. In Limerick, like in Cardiff, they know a good fly-half when they see one.

'Enjoy your retirement, Mr Ward, and thanks for the memories.'

In truth I have always felt and known the great love shown to me by Irish sports fans from my early days in Limerick. It was also shown when I came on to replace Ollie for the last few minutes of an international, when I returned against Scotland in 1986, and right up to my retirement and through to the present day. Writing for Independent Newspapers and reporting for RTE has always provided me with feedback from the public, and much of it has been supportive and positive. Yes, of course, it is gratifying when people stop me, be it in the street or wherever, to 'thank me for the memories', but much more than that is their ease in doing so. They clearly feel comfortable in approaching me and that, I can assure you, means more than anything. I repeat, I never, ever played to the galleries, but it is comforting to know that those galleries approved. I frequently get this attention and, no, I never tire of it. I made a point of always making time for people right from the very beginning of my career. That Pelé lesson was never lost. Without supporters we would not exist.

But then there was the negative response to my retirement. My old friends within the IRFU reared their ugly heads again when they threatened to issue legal proceedings over some rugby pieces I was assigned to write. Very shortly after retiring, I agreed to write a series of 'tell all' articles for the *Irish Independent*. The newspaper began advertising them on their front pages and on the airwaves. In terms of marketing and selling copies of the newspaper, this was their way of getting the message out to the public. In effect I would spill the beans about the IRFU and the battles I had with them throughout my career. They were clearly livid. My heart bled.

On the front page of the *Irish Independent,* dated Tuesday, 31 May 1988, under a headline 'Worried Rugby Chiefs call in tell-all Ward', journalists Sean Diffley and Gene McKenna wrote the following:

> *Controversial rugby star Tony Ward, who announced his retirement from international rugby last week, is on collision course with the game's rulers yet again.*
>
> *Ward could be in hot water with the IRFU over a new series of articles he is planning to write for the* Sunday Independent *about life at the top in the rugby game.*
>
> *The colourful out-half has hinted that he will lift the lid on the incidents during his career which led to searing controversy over his omissions from the international team.*
>
> *Ward was always the darling of Irish rugby fans who loved his exciting style – but not of the rugby hierarchy. And the IRFU are obviously worried about the revelations he may make, for they are asking him if the articles are in accordance with the rules of the International Rugby Football Board.*
>
> *Ward said: 'Now that I have retired, I feel free to talk about the controversial issues during my career. I intend to talk plainly and frankly and to hold nothing back.'*

The IRFU meets on Friday and is expected to discuss the proposed Ward articles. Under the rules and regulations of the amateur game, he will be asked by them to give a sworn statement that he is not being paid for the articles or that he has arranged to give any monies he gets either to the IRFU, his club or a charity.

An uneasy relationship between the player and the IRFU has existed for a long time.

Nine months later, on 21 February 1989, the following letter arrived from Paddy Moss, secretary of the IRFU:

The Committee of the IRFU is concerned that some prominent members of the rugby fraternity in Ireland may, perhaps unknowingly, be putting their amateur status at risk by writing or broadcasting about the game.

In general it is an infringement of the regulations of the IRB relating to Amateurism to 'communicate for reward'. This term covers written, oral and visual communication.

I should be grateful if you would let me know if you have, during the current season 1988–89, received any payments for writing or broadcasting about rugby football, and, if so, how these have been disbursed.

Furthermore, I would like to know if you intend to continue with these activities so that you may be advised how your amateur status would be affected.

Those irritants aside, one of the finest tributes of all was paid to me by a real celebrity giant. Comedian Dermot Morgan was a genius. More to the point he was a great friend. He was the founder and creator of the famous Irish comedy satire *Scrap Saturday*, but he will always be known to his legions of followers worldwide as

Father Ted. Tragically Dermot died of a heart attack in 1998, aged forty-six. Apart from his comedy, Dermot loved his football, too, both indoors and when lining up alongside me, clad in pink (his choice, of course), and representing Stillorgan Park in so many charity and celebrity games over the years. He was special.

Many of his skit songs from *Scrap Saturday* went on to become hugely popular with the Irish public, such as classics like 'Thank you very much, Mr Eastwood' (about boxer Barry McGuigan), 'Get outta that saddle, Stephen' (cyclist Stephen Roche) and 'Do you know Bono?' Not a lot of people may know that he penned a song about me entitled 'Don't Pick Wardie'. Some lines from the song still bring a smile to my face and here are some excerpts from it:

> *You can pick Joe*
> *With the broken toe*
> *But don't pick Wardie*
>
> *You can pick Dean*
> *Or any human being*
> *But don't pick Wardie*
>
> *Wardie always went too far*
> *He behaved like a superstar*
> *He appeared in his swimming trunks!*
>
> *He's not my choice mister*
> *He's not even a bloody solicitor*
>
> *You can pick mother*
> *Or even A.N. Other*
> *But leave Wardie off the team*

He'll never get my vote
He doesn't even wear a sheepskin coat

You can pick Trevor
It doesn't matter whoever
Wardie's not my style

You know I'm no knocker
But he used to play soccer

It makes me sick
He's far too slick
Let's bring back Jack Kyle

We don't mind Mick Kiernan on
We knew his dad
And his Uncle Tom

But it makes me histrionic
Wardie doesn't even drink gin & tonic

You can pick a one-legged midget
But leave Wardie off the team

What better way to encapsulate my career than in those humorous words of the late, great Dermot Morgan. Yes, they are funny and said in jest, but ultimately they disguise the harsh realities of the truth. Perhaps forgiveness can be a long time coming, but to reconcile with the truth sometimes humour is needed to soothe the healing process.

CHAPTER 20

MY LIBEL CASE

I had always been very affable and media friendly. So it was no surprise really that I eased into the role of sports journalist towards the end of my rugby career. I had built up a lot of experience from dealing with the print and broadcast media during my playing days. Apart from giving interviews to the press, I occasionally popped into the commentary box to offer my thoughts for radio or television. Also, I caused a bit of a stir upon my retirement when I agreed to 'tell all' about my controversies with the IRFU. So, if not a natural progression, then the field of journalism certainly beckoned for me.

The Independent News and Media Group, based at the time in Middle Abbey Street in Dublin, approached me in 1987. The then sports editor of the *Sunday Independent*, Adhamhnan O'Sullibheain, asked me to do a rugby column. Initially I agreed. Raymond Smith was a brilliant and long-standing journalist and we worked together on my column. He would ring me to find out my thoughts on all things rugby and then ghost-write the piece under my name and photograph. After writing the article, Raymond would ring me to make a few alterations and then it would go to press. In the beginning it was great. It worked well and I was paid for it while teaching during the day. But then my feelings began to change. This bore no reflection on Raymond or his work. He was a first-rate author, compiling many great sports books such as the highly acclaimed *Better One Day as a Lion* with champion Flat jockey Mick Kinane.

It just got to the stage where I hated the nature of what I was doing. I did not feel in control. When I picked up the paper and read my column, it was just not me or the way I would say it. It was partly my fault as well. If you are going to do a column I believe you have to do it properly or not at all. I wanted to give my opinions, my words, my way. I stand by what I write, but I will not stand by someone else's spin on what I write. So in 1988 I began writing my own stuff on a part-time basis for P.J. Cunningham, who at the time was sports editor at the *Evening Herald*.

In 1995 the 'Indo' approached me to ask if I would be interested in taking over from another admirable and long-serving scribe, Sean Diffley, on a full-time basis. I thought seriously about it, but politely declined because at the time I was really happy with my teaching career in St Andrew's. P.J., along with group editor Pat Courtney, who was a boyhood hero of mine when he played for Shamrock Rovers, wanted me on board for two main reasons. Firstly, they wanted a high-profile replacement for the great Diffo, who was retiring, but they also wanted someone from within rugby now that the game had just gone open.

I declined their first approach but continued writing for the 'Indo' and specifically the *Herald* on a part-time basis while still teaching. Then in 1997, P.J. Cunningham, in his new capacity as sports editor of the *Irish Independent*, backed by Courto, asked me again. By this stage the game had turned professional and they wanted gravitas and serious opinion from someone with rugby knowledge and who had the relevant contacts. The offer was generous and instead of saying 'No', I decided, to borrow from Mick Doyle, 'to give it a lash'. I held on to my teaching job by way of a five-year sabbatical. I never went back to teaching and have been at the *Irish Independent* ever since.

There was a touch of irony, too. Everyone knew Tony O'Reilly was the owner of the INM group and so he was, in a sense, my boss. Yet, as one of Ireland's all-time rugby greats, he had been a hero of mine when I was growing up. For his last Ireland cap in 1970 he arrived in a chauffeur-driven car at Twickenham. It underlined his stature within the game. That game also marked his comeback as he had been out of the Irish side for the previous few years. His playing days were a decade before mine and it was disappointing that I never got to play with or against him. He played with Old Belvedere, Leinster, Ireland and the Lions. He was physically powerful with a personality to match. When he walked into a room he oozed charisma and charm, but he also commanded respect.

In a 1979 issue of *In Dublin* magazine, for whom I gave a question and answer interview, one of the questions was: 'Who would you most like to meet?' I replied emphatically: 'Tony O'Reilly.' Very shortly after that interview I was over in Edinburgh with the Ireland team at our base in the North British Hotel on Princes Street. It is an old colonial hotel which is now better known as the Balmoral. Next thing I knew Tony O'Reilly was standing beside me in the hotel lobby. He had been told about my magazine interview (I suspect by Paddy Madigan) and as he was in Scotland to watch our game at Murrayfield the following day, he felt it only right for him to make my wish come true. It was a gesture much appreciated and we hit it off immediately.

Little did I know then, that ten years later I would be writing for the *Irish Independent*, owned by him. But while he was revered by everyone as this multi-millionaire owner of the paper, and had been knighted by the Queen, he and I never saw it like that. There was no red carpet or bowing or deferring to 'Sir Tony'. There was none of that nonsense between us. He was Tony and I was Tony and that was it. I loved that. It made me feel more comfortable within the walls of Independent House. Another thing I loved was the annual summer's eve party with gala dinner he held in a magnificent marquee attached to his house Castlemartin. The black tie event coincided with the race meeting he sponsored at The Curragh nearby.

From a personal perspective it was nice to be included and it left me in little doubt that my switch from teaching to full-time journalism was appreciated by the boss. Certainly that was how Sir Anthony made ordinary Anthony feel. We spoke a lot about rugby on those party nights as well as in private conversations over the years. A deep regret we shared was never winning a precious Leinster schools senior cup medal. I think it bugged Sir Tony more than it did me. I lost a semi-final as captain in 1973 and he lost in the 1954 final, also as captain, In that final, Niall Brophy, another great and future Lion wing, led Blackrock to an 11–3 victory over O'Reilly's Belvedere.

So my friendship and rugby links with Tony helped give me a great deal of confidence within the newspaper as I had not come through the standard school of journalism. I came through the back door, so to speak. I had trained in PE, with a degree in History and Geography, but English was never one of my strong suits. I was all right at it, but I came into full-time journalism through a very circuitous route and my rugby links with Tony O'Reilly certainly did me no harm. His son Gavin took a more hands-on approach within the newspaper when

Tony entrusted him with overall control. It made a lot of sense as Tony was jet-setting all around the world, so much so that the joke back then was that his plane never landed.

Anyway, that was all before the bombshell fell. I was on the Heathrow Express train coming out of London after the England versus Ireland game at Twickenham on 15 January 2000. With me was RTE sports broadcaster Jim Sherwin as we headed to catch the last Saturday night flight home to Dublin. My mobile phone rang and I could see it was the newspaper office back in Dublin. I thought it had something to do with my copy, or perhaps they were asking me to do something else about the game. So I answered immediately. With all the commotion on the train, the noise of the wheels on the tracks and what have you, I was totally confused and could not quite get a handle on what the guy on the other end was talking about. Something about my opinion or quote on something or other. Then he started going on about 'an article' and the word 'gay', and I became even more confused. I genuinely thought for a few brief moments that this was a prank call and that the joke and jokester would be revealed. Was it an early April Fool's joke? Who is this? What is the angle on this joke? I am not familiar with it. All these things and more were going through my mind on a speeding train. Jim was clearly intrigued by my bemused reaction to the phone conversation. It was difficult to get my head around the thrust of the call, but then came the shock.

In the Saturday magazine issued with the London *Times* earlier that day, a feature appeared about a team playing in a London league. They claimed to be the world's first 'gay' Rugby Union side and the following are extracts from it:

As the world's first gay rugby team gets changed, the support – a gay couple, a couple of gay men, two injured players and a shrieking girl – mill about the touchline making small talk about half-time refreshments.

'Oranges as usual – that catering manager has no imagination,' mutters one.

'Let's run out with a load of bananas, that'll scare them,' titters another.

'Or plums,' someone giggles.

'Canapes!'

'Fruit salad!'

'No, no, no!' stutters another. 'Quiche!' and they all fall about laughing.

Fans of the Kings Cross Steelers have every reason to be cheerful, for this season is the team's first as members of the Rugby Football Union.

Formed four years ago in Central Station, a gay pub near Kings Cross Station in London, the Steelers have spent the last three years campaigning for acceptance into the League.

The injured captain, who prefers to remain nameless, bemoans the lack of quality players in the side. He said: 'There are so many professionals – internationals even – who would join us when their careers are over if only they weren't afraid of being outed. You just can't put gay and first class together – *look at Tony Ward, who played for Ireland in the 1970s. He was "international player of the year", "Lions' player of the year", "Ireland player of the year" and "Five Nations player of the year", but after he was outed he never even played for his club first team, Munster, again. Times have changed since, true, but that stigma still exists.'* (My italics.)

Those words exploded off the page like a machine gun spraying bullets into me. I had been totally unaware of the magazine or its content. I was still in transit to Heathrow Airport when the guy at the *Sunday Independent* rang again. He asked me for a reaction and in a moment of anger and frustrating impulse I told him that whatever had been written was absolute nonsense. It backfired badly because that simple and honest reaction was reported. In that instant I was on the record. But this was my own employer for God's sake. On page two of the *Sunday Independent* next day, the following appeared:

Ward denies gay claim

Former rugby international Tony Ward described as 'utter crap' a claim in a London *Times* magazine article that he was one of several international players who was gay.

Mr Ward said he had 'nothing to say' about the article which he hadn't read and he said it was 'absolute rubbish'.

The article quoted the captain of a gay rugby club in Britain who claimed there were so many professionals and internationals who would join the club when their careers were over if only they weren't afraid of being outed.

I was furious with Gavin O'Reilly, with Tony O'Reilly, with the *Sunday Independent*, with the editorial staff, with Independent News and Media. It was a very long time since I had felt such anger and a feeling of utter betrayal. This was my own employer and they were willing to exploit one of their own employees. Me! All of this was despite my clear and unambiguous denial. I was fuming. The entire episode and the behaviour from within INM still makes me angry now. What I could not understand – quite apart from the scurrilous piece in the *Times* – was how my own employer could run with it. It was an absolute disgrace exacerbated by the fact not one of the tabloids went anywhere near it. If it had come from a Sunday or maybe one of the Monday tabloids I would not have been surprised in the least. But *my own newspaper group*! I went through the full gamut of emotions and constantly shook my head in disbelief that this could happen.

On Monday morning, after arranging a meeting with my solicitor and instructing him to start the ball rolling immediately with 'a solicitor's letter' to both newspapers, I rang Gavin O'Reilly. In no uncertain terms I told him that I had a family to think of with children at school. I was livid as I tried to explain the gravity of the situation. Even having to do that stuck in my craw. At any time, any one of my four kids could be taunted by other kids with a 'your daddy is gay' comment and I asked him for an explanation. He sympathised and apologised to me, but that was not enough. Then I rang Tony as I wanted it to go to the very top and nowhere short. To his immense credit he took all the time I needed so that nothing was lost in translation. He was as sensitive and as attentive as he could possibly be. At least I felt I was getting somewhere. At the best of times it was difficult to tie him down as he was seemingly forever in the clouds. As one of the world's leading businessmen he had his minders so it was probably easier to infiltrate the KGB. In fairness to him, he said:

'Tony, I'm not sure of my schedule but I'll be in Dublin on Tuesday or Wednesday of next week, so if it suits you to pop down to the house we can talk in guaranteed privacy.'

In the meantime we got in touch with the *Times* of London and reached agreement on a settlement almost immediately. They knew full well that I was going to sue for libel. But this was not about the money. It was never going to be. First and foremost I sought a written apology to appear in their sports pages the following week. I also received a financial settlement.

The apology appeared on page forty-one, within the sports section, of the *Times* on Saturday, 22 January. It read:

Mr Tony Ward

Our article 'Out To Win' (*Times* magazine, 15 January) about the world's first gay rugby team wrongly stated that Tony Ward, the distinguished Irish rugby player of the 1970s and 1980s, was homosexual, and that his playing career came to an end after he was 'outed'.

We fully accept that these statements were completely untrue, and acknowledge that Mr Ward is not, and has never been, homosexual.

We reservedly apologise to him and his family for the distress and embarrassment caused by our article, and we have agreed to pay Mr Ward damages and legal costs.

The *Sunday Independent* once again printed what the *Times* had said in their issue of Sunday, 23 January under another page two headline stating: 'London Times Apologises to Ward'. This angered me further as my own newspaper colleagues were in effect making big headlines of their own on this whole gay saga. To that end I put my solicitor on standby to sue Independent Newspapers. He just awaited my final instruction.

Michael O'Loughlin is not only my solicitor but a very dear friend. He and his wife Pamela are godparents to my youngest daughter Ali. Michael was advised by his barrister Paul Murray that there were two cases of precedence in England whereby a ruling by Lord Denning could find the *Sunday Independent* libellous as well. This was precisely what I had been arguing and why I was so angry with my own colleagues and bosses in the 'Indo'. In effect, the original libel from the *Times* only received significant coverage in Ireland when the *Sunday Independent* ran the story.

But before I took any action I needed to get Tony O'Reilly's reaction. When I met up with him in Castlemartin he was upfront and honest with me about what happened. He had obviously spoken with Gavin and been briefed fully on the whole horrible episode. He said to me: 'Tony, I can only offer you my sincerest apologies on behalf of Independent Newspapers and it is obvious that we got this one badly wrong.' I accepted his apology and at the same time conceded that the culpability could not be levelled at him. Owner or not, he was out of the country and unaware of what was going on.

During our conversation, what made his apology more meaningful was when he likened my situation to his own. He told me he knew exactly how I felt as he had been in my shoes on numerous occasions with his own legal team acting on his behalf. I am not sure the context was the same but I got the message and the sincere manner in which it was delivered. In other words, there was so much stuff written about him – particularly in the Sunday papers – and not just about his business affairs, that come Monday morning he was always briefed first thing by his legal advisors. Inevitably, untruths and libellous content arose regarding his private life and he had to take action himself. He also felt hurt. It soon became very clear to me that we were both singing from the same page. In my case it was the unfairness of what the 'Indo' had done in repeating the original slur perpetrated by the *Times*. It was most reassuring to talk to him about it because he got it and understood exactly where I was coming from.

One other thing I wanted Tony to hear was that I was not in this for any recompense or financial settlement. This had been suggested to me in my conversation with Gavin when he said:

'Don't worry, Tony, we'll compensate you for this.' That was never in my mind. It was never about money. I mean, for God's sake, why would I even consider biting off the hand that fed me? This was purely about my person, my character, my standing and, above all, the feelings of my family. So I took no money. While I wanted no more newspaper coverage, not even an apology in print, both Tony and Gavin provided me with that in private, and with a guarantee that nothing remotely close would happen again.

However, we did agree a nice perk of the job going forward. For the next World Cup in 2003 in Australia, and for all subsequent travel outside Europe, INM would fly me business class. This proved to be an unexpected, but most welcome bonus. In addition, I was allowed to take my partner with me as well. So for the final three weeks of the 2003 World Cup, they flew my then wife Louise to Sydney. It was a gesture she and I really appreciated.

To this day, and whatever people say or think about Tony O'Reilly and everything going on, particularly with AIB Bank and his businesses collapsing, at least he tries to tackle things head on. That is the nature of a very proud man. You can best form an opinion of a person by how they have treated you. In the case of A.J.F. O'Reilly I have nothing but good to say about the man. I have always – and will always – have the utmost respect for him. He was a giant and a tycoon in business. But he was a giant of a person in terms of integrity and honesty. And to that let me add sensitivity.

He was also one of those people who walked into a room and immediately evoked an aura of charisma and energy. He had a powerful presence, similar to other people I met like Charles Haughey and Nelson Mandela. Princess Diana was another of that stature who I encountered briefly. Fred Cogley and I stood with her on the platform at Cardiff railway station as we returned to London from an international in the Principality. There is no doubt about it but there are certain people in this world who are just blessed with a clear and obvious gift. Tony O'Reilly had it by the bucket load. One further point I would like to make about him was that, if there is, or was a better after-dinner raconteur than him, then I am not sure I can recollect them.

Tony handled my situation regarding the gay slur perfectly, and had this knack of reassuring me and putting me at ease. That is the way he could deal with people. I just hope that he comes through his own current difficulties successfully. For sure, I will be there on the sidelines shouting him on – just as I did when I was a kid.

CHAPTER 21

THE PROFESSIONALS

The Irish Rugby Football Union had to be dragged kicking and screaming into the 'Professional Era'. They had a fixed mindset back in the day and would have been very content to stick with their 'Five Nations' format. 'If it's not broke why fix it?' was their attitude. The real fear, however, was in sharing or losing control. But all that changed in 1995 with the Paris Accord. I remember getting a call from Pat Kenny asking me to go on his morning show on RTE radio the day the Paris Accord became public. He wanted me to discuss the changes that were hurtling towards us. Like everybody else, I had no idea just how seismic the transformation taking place would be.

The rugby-playing Southern Hemisphere countries of South Africa, New Zealand and Australia were so far ahead of the four home unions in terms of professionalism. They were going down the pay-for-play route regardless of whether the home unions were with them or not. The signs had been there on our trip to Australia in 1979, but especially so in New Zealand for the inaugural World Cup. Frankly, players from north of the zero line, and specifically Irish ones, were wet behind the ears.

We saw high-profile All Black players like John Kirwan and Andy Dalton advertising products on television with brazen regularity.

Given what I had endured, just imagine the thoughts going through my mind as I watched the new age evolve before my eyes. Bear in mind this was 1987, still eight years and a couple more world cups before the starting gun actually went off. Ironically, GAA players had been doing similar deals in a nonchalant and relaxed fashion for some time, but it was a 'no-no' in rugby. So while I agree with how the GAA gradually evolved with little fuss into a modern professional machine – save for full-time playing employment – rugby was different. Going 'open' meant one thing and one thing only: that the game as we had known it would never be the same again.

There had been a few attempts at what might be termed 'professional sporting circuses'. This concept was peddled by Australian media magnate Kerry Packer with groups of hired hands being bought up and remunerated for their efforts. It began with cricket, but that was already fully professional anyway. Rugby Union made for a different process entirely. The cricket model found its way into rugby, most notably in South Africa and New Zealand. I was approached to take part in two of these proposed events, but I stood by my stance on South Africa and apartheid and declined.

Naturally the transition was not without its share of controversy. The New Zealand Cavaliers' tour to South Africa in 1986 was a case in point and it caused ructions. So even ahead of 1987, and the first global tournament, minus the outcast South Africans, the seeds to professionalism had been well and truly sown. The IRFU did not want any part in it. In fact, with the game still amateur they voted against the concept of a world cup close to when the deal was done. Despite cracks appearing, the Home Unions were happy to keep their hands on what they had. They wanted to remain in control of the game on their own particular patch, but that train, too, was already leaving the station. When reality kicked in for Ireland in 1995, the 'Wild Geese' syndrome returned.

Irish players, like geese flying to more exotic and warmer locations, flew to England to join clubs. London Irish, for self-evident reasons, was the most popular port of call, and they swept up the best Irish players, like David Humphreys and Malcolm O'Kelly. Keith Wood went to Harlequins, the Wallace brothers went to Saracens, while others like Paddy Johns scattered to the four winds. Who could blame them? In those early years many top-quality Irish players went to English clubs. It was catastrophic for our domestic rugby. It was soccer being repeated. And that was the last thing the sport in this country needed. It was a disaster for the international game because it meant the IRFU had no control over Irish players travelling and playing abroad.

In total contrast to those years of turmoil, our game is now in rude health. The reason we are performing so well internationally is down to what we have come to know as 'centrally contracted players'. The IRFU is paymaster in chief. In the vast majority of cases players now play at home with Connacht, Leinster, Munster and Ulster, but they are all contracted to the IRFU. Our governing body also introduced the 'player protection policy', whereby players are only allowed to play within strict playing guidelines that dictate their game-time. It can seem a little over the top to be wrapping players up in cotton wool. The days when I would play and train with several teams most days of the week have been consigned to history.

But the bottom line is that when you can control players who are contracted here in Ireland, and playing and training at home, they are much easier to oversee. In 1997, Ireland training sessions usually took place on a Wednesday at the Aer Lingus Social and Athletic Association close to Dublin Airport. Players could fly in, train and return to their London bases. Despite being a crazy set-up it was the best available at the time. But to their immense credit the IRFU took control. They made a conscious decision to bring all their players home. In doing this they upped the ante by offering them significant contracts as well as limiting the number of games they played. This was in marked contrast to France and England where guys can still play between thirty-five and forty games a season.

There was, of course, the odd exception who opted to play overseas. Keith Wood stayed in the UK after coming home for one year to Munster. Geordan Murphy remained at Leicester and Tommy Bowe with the Ospreys in Wales. But most came home. For that, the IRFU deserve great credit. So much so that the idea has now become the template for many other unions worldwide. At the moment, Wales are trying to apply the Irish model of centrally contracted players. New Zealand and Australia have gone down the same route. In England and France the tail wags the dog, although the club owners definitely do not see it that way.

There is much controversy in England at present where Stuart Lancaster will not pick players who ply their trade abroad, most notably with Delon Armitage and his brother Stefan who play for French club Toulon. Warren Gatland has the same policy with the Welsh players, and so do New Zealand. Because of the resources these countries have, they are in a position to do that. On the other hand, Australia have followed South Africa's lead in bending the rule to suit their needs. Michael Cheika, the Wallabies coach, has made a conscious decision to play the best. Mark Giteau and winger Drew

Mitchell play in France but that is no bar to their international selection. Not picking the very best players just because they play overseas, would further weaken the Wallabies who are currently at an all-time low in the world rankings.

Philip Browne, as CEO of the IRFU, has handled the situation brilliantly in steering a steady but proactive course. The IRFU is a much different body, although still with some old-time flaws, to the one before he took over. Old ways and old junkets die hard. Today's otherwise efficiently run body 'pays the piper and calls the tune'. The Union governs and overrules all the branches which means they can say who can and cannot play. This was a big issue for Leinster with their twenty or so players involved in the Ireland set-up. Matt O'Connor, in particular, was very much the victim of the national elite, being mollycoddled following the 2015 Six Nations. By contrast, Johnny Sexton had no choice in the matter. While other Leinster players in that victorious Irish team were given a break, Sexton had to return to France to train and play with Racing Metro.

Another serious issue is how our club game has been massacred by the advent of the professional era, post 1995. Today, clubs and their academies are trying to fast-track young talent through for professional contracts and it is affecting our bread-and-butter club rugby. I was talking to former All Black out-half Doug Bruce, who I met recently for coffee while he was on holiday in Ireland. He is also in despair at what has happened to the club game in his country. You cannot buy match experience and that sadly is being lost to the modern-day professional as they are fast-tracked through the academy system.

One positive aspect is rugby spreading its wings way beyond the elitist territory of times past. 'Go to the right school' and all that nonsense. The game still has a way to go, but is getting there. Bear in mind that after a couple of decades we are still in nappies relative to the rest of the professional sporting world. Transparency is another welcome addition, not least in terms of selection, and amen to that. Joe Schmidt, the Irish head coach, has the most angelic face and lovely smile, but underneath he is absolutely ruthless. He has to be to survive.

If there is a drug issue in rugby then I have never seen it. I have no doubt there are some, as in all sports, who will attempt to cheat the system. Whatever it takes in terms of testing, and investigative journalism, to keep rugby clean then count me in. And for the record, I abhor 'taking supplements', but I know I am rowing against the tide.

I have been asked many times: 'Do you regret missing out on the professional era?' I do not begrudge any player taking advantage of everything they can today, but I am envious of the opportunity they get to maximise their potential. If ever a player fulfilled his potential to the 'nth' degree, it was Brian O'Driscoll. I know I had a God-given gift, but given the chance to develop that talent would have been Utopia. The only thing I would not have liked about today's game is that the players are brought up to run at bodies. I was never a physical player and was taught to run into space. Now they are primed and robotically trained to run at their opponent and in the process break the gain-line. Jack Kyle and Mike Gibson just shake their heads when I talk to them about it. Everything now is about 'systems'. You listen to coaches today and if they are not happy about a performance they put it down to 'individual error' or 'the system' breaking down. I hate that terminology.

Some coaches are so controlling that everything is done in accordance with the system. In our time we attacked space when the opportunity arose. Now that is termed 'heads up' rugby. How the hell are you supposed to play rugby if you have got your head down and you are ploughing headlong into bodies? With that in mind, concussion is now more frequent than ever. Players and coaches are at fault. So was I when I played. I was concussed several times during my career and all I wanted to do was play on, and did. Now, thankfully, the word of the doctor rules.

Two other bugbears of mine relate to the scrum and physical size. The scrum is a huge area of concern and is causing much headache and debate. We have gone from the refereeing command of 'crouch, touch, pause, engage' to 'crouch, bind, set'. It might sound little but it means a lot. That said, far too much time in a professional sport dictated by bums on seats, is being lost to the scrum. In our day the only call came from the scrum-half putting the ball in with a simple 'ball coming now'. The art of hooking, too, has been lost. In my playing time, the scrum-half fed the ball into the middle of the scrum when the hooker flapped his hand. Today hookers cannot be bothered for the simple reason they do not strike. God be with the days of channelled ball. Now the ball gets stuck in the middle of the scrum and it is going nowhere. It just remains static on the ground until one or other pack drives over. It is all about power. The modern hooker is afraid to strike the ball because if he does he fears his scrum – as in all eight forwards – will lose cohesion. More often than not the scrum collapses and as any front row forward will tell you, it is really a case of 'tweedledum, tweedledee' as to which side will be given the penalty. Sadly I do not jest. It is a real headache with no obvious solution. Stopping the clock when the scrum collapses for a reset would help for starters. There is much too much time lost to the mind-numbing element that is the scrum. And I say that with the greatest of respect to my forward friends, past and present!

The scrum cannot and will not be abolished or de-powered as in Rugby League. Nor should it be. It is an integral part of the game. But, frankly, it has become a boring mess. On current evidence it is not going to improve anytime soon. I have genuine sympathy for the World Rugby governing body on this one. The scrum, just like the line-out, must always be central to Rugby Union, but in a much less interfering and time-wasting way. Coaches and players know what they are doing. They milk penalties and they kill the clock. These are the real issues in need of address and, no, I do not have the definitive solution. The scrum is out of control and we have to make it more manageable.

As for the 'penalty try' on the back of scrum collapse, let us not even go there. Prop forwards do not know the answer, and some of the greatest brains in rugby do not know. Luke Fitzgerald's dad Des is a real scrum guru – an expert in whom I trust – and he will confess to not having a clue any more. It all comes down to 'referee interpretation' and over the course of a game these things tend to even themselves out, hence my 'tweedledum, tweedledee' comment. One penalty is given to one side followed by another penalty for the other and so on. Players do want consistency, but consistency without rationale is difficult to comprehend. Referees make decisions not knowing for sure if they are right. In their defence, however, I will say the object is to at least try and keep the game flowing. In professional sport, there is a natural win-at-all-cost mentality, so a certain cynicism and cuteness has come in. Where once it was the defending eight mainly culpable for collapse, now the attacking scrum is equally capable of eliciting a penalty or a penalty try under that guise.

That brings me to another issue, one that is not all that obvious to most rugby fans: the thick, square, pillar-like padding around the base of the posts. The law for a try dictates that the attacking player only has to touch the base of the padding with the ball for a try to be awarded. I know the fat pads are there in the best interests of safety for players but I hate this ruling. The rules of rugby are quite clearly defined in the book, and to score a try a player must cross their opponents' try-line and touch the ball down on or over the whitewash. Touching the padding is not the try-line. Furthermore, when the padding was first introduced, it was merely wrapping around the posts. Now it is a monstrous size. And, no, we will not mention the advertising on that padding.

For the first time in the history of rugby we are seeing players and coaches question and argue with refereeing decisions. Rugby always prided itself on an absence of dissent and players just got on with it. To question the referee bordered on sacrilege. As I have long told my under-age charges when coaching: 'The referee may be blind, but he is also right . . . period.' But to be fair, there is still that core respect in rugby that soccer has long since lost. Gaelic Games is still hanging on in there despite many problems, but it is struggling. No rugby referee has yet found himself smuggled away from the ground in a car boot. Rugby still has its in-built respect, but elements are creeping in. Bear in mind, kids are watching their role model's every move.

Touch judges and other officials have to take more responsibility and must exercise greater authority in helping the man in the middle. The need is for them to be more hands-on, and in fairness this is beginning to happen. But I would like to see much more. Some are also suggesting that more ex-players should become involved in refereeing, like Alain Roland and John Lacey have done. I happen to share that view. That said, irrespective of background, the best referees are the ones you hardly notice. They just let the game flow.

Nigel Owens is the best referee in the world who also happens to co-present a chat show in Wales with an old mate, legend and man I greatly admire, Jonathan Davies. This could lead to an element of celebrity which is not necessarily in the best interest of the game or the individual involved. For all that, I do think Nigel Owens is exceptional in the art of refereeing and on-field communication. But, if anything, the wiring-up of referees with a microphone so the viewer can hear what he is saying does more harm than good. We are hearing referees communicate with those around them on the pitch more and more. It might add to the entertainment value, but it is also adding to the celebrity value of the once inconspicuous man in the middle. The spotlight is fixed very firmly on them and some – though I emphasise not all – have lost the run of themselves. So less vociferous referees please and let us all just get on with the game.

One of the biggest threats to Rugby Union, I fear, will come from rugby sevens, which will form part of the Olympic Games in Rio 2016. People in China, elsewhere in Asia and the Americas are going to be introduced to sevens, this incredibly quick and skilful game. There will be non-stop action, tries all over the place, minimum scrums with just three players each side, a 'get it in and out' mentality, and on the whole it will be a far more vibrant, all-action game than the fuller version. It is just around the corner and be under no illusion, Union will face a very real threat from sevens. Can we learn lessons along the way? Perhaps. Look at Rugby League. It used to be a fifteen-man game, but when they took the two wing forwards out, and reduced it to thirteen, it became more open.

League has six forwards instead of eight, but Union will not go down that route. The common denominator is that when the codes were first invented, players were smaller and scrawny.

Now they are bigger, fitter, faster, stronger and heavier. Since the Paris Accord in 1995, players have become massively powerful athletes in the space of just twenty years. They are huge specimens in terms of physique. The knock-on effect is that room or space on a pitch is at a premium. Therein lies one of the core issues going forward. I can only see the situation getting worse. With stadiums already in situ around the world, we cannot reduce the size of pitches so, however reluctant we are, the question of numbers of team personnel appears a logical way to go.

It is incumbent upon our great game to address its problems. The authorities may eventually have to, and move with the professional times. In my heart of hearts I certainly would hate this to happen. But I would like someone to explain to me just where are we going to get the badly needed space on a pitch? You cannot make Twickenham bigger. You cannot make Lansdowne Road bigger. So how are we going to address this obvious problem as our rugby athletes get bigger and stronger? There is no other obvious way unless I am missing something entirely.

There are aspects to the professional game I hate. Many of my contemporaries feel the same and, no, it is not part of the 'ah, but in our day' attitude. While we are losing touch with our roots and how it all began with William Webb Ellis, that in itself is no bad thing. But give me schools rugby and club rugby for a different 'fix' entirely. There is room for both, but I know which I prefer. Perhaps the way forward is to look back at the past. As we enter the third decade of professionalism, perhaps we should define the split between the amateur and professional strands far better than we have done to date.

CHAPTER 22

MY IRELAND SQUAD OF THE PROFESSIONAL ERA

In picking my best Ireland squad of the last twenty years, I am leaving myself wide open to debate. No doubt it will generate plenty of discussion, but one thing I am sure we will all agree on is this: the professional era produced the greatest Ireland player of all time. Brian O'Driscoll. If ever a player maximised his potential it was Brian. He would easily make most people's World XV never mind the national side.

What went before bears little comparison to the present professional set-up. It would not be comparing like with like. So without further ado these are the best I have seen in their specialist positions from 1995 to date:

1 – Cian Healy
I played with Nick Popplewell who was the trailblazer and the complete prop forward. Apart from scrummaging and lifting at the line-out, Poppy was effective all over the field. He was a great ball-carrier as I experienced first-hand when playing with him at Greystones. He will be in my replacements, but I

have to go with the modern-day Poppy and that is Cian Healy.

Cian is everything Poppy was: explosive, dynamic, a gain-line breaker and built like an absolute tank. He is a ball-carrying forward capable of establishing forward momentum, which is the lifeblood of the modern attacking game. His role for both Leinster and Ireland is priceless. He filled all three front-row positions as a schoolboy in Belvedere so he can cover all bases.

2 – Keith Wood
There were a few players in the frame for hooker: Sean Cronin, Shane Byrne (a latecomer to international level), Frankie Sheahan, Rory Best and Jerry Flannery. But it has to be Keith Wood. Pound for pound as good an Irish forward as there has ever been. Great attitude to the game and born a winner. In that respect you could liken him to Roy Keane in soccer. Woody was a complete all-rounder and while accustomed to being at the bottom of a ruck, he could just as easily be found on the left wing. He had a remarkable ability to read the game and to appear in the most unlikely places on the back of that extra rugby sense. There were some who criticised him for this adventurous streak, but that is nonsense. Not once did he neglect the basics of his trade as a hooker.

3 – John Hayes
Tight-head has long been a problem position for Ireland. Nowadays it is Mike Ross, who is our Mr Reliable and in many ways we cannot do without him. But, for me, it has to be 'The Bull', John Hayes. He was simply outstanding and over an extraordinary period of time. People used to question his long back and scrum technique and although I am no expert in that area, you must be doing something right to win over one

hundred caps. The fact he was a late convert to the front row, born of necessity with Shannon and Munster, made it an easy line of attack in terms of wanton criticism. As a lifter at the line-out, and in anchoring his side of the scrum, he was a pillar of strength and reliability.

4 – Mick Galwey

He comes from Currow, County Kerry. This has to go down in Irish sporting circles as one of the most amazing villages in the country. You would think it is most famous for GAA. They won a county novice championship in 1982, a Kerry junior football title in 1988 and the intermediate championship in 2013. But this tiny parish has produced rugby players of the calibre of Galwey, Mick Doyle, Tommy Doyle, Moss Keane and, most recently, J.J. Hanrahan. It is quite extraordinary.

In my opinion, 'Gaillimh', as we nicknamed him after the west coast city, bridged the gap between amateurism and professionalism in a very romantic way. He did this while still managing to carry on the fun element and equally embracing the professional transition. He was an outstanding Munster leader and captain. He was also at the heart of the movement that set the southern province on the road to their great and successful Heineken Cup adventure. That European platform built up a wider interest in Irish rugby like never before. Galwey was the fulcrum. Quintessentially, he was what an amateur player should be and what a professional player should aspire to be.

5 – Paul O'Connell

With the greatest respect to all, 'Paulie' owns this shirt. He is a veritable 'totem pole', not just in physical terms, but in the way he carries himself. Similar to big Moss Keane, he is the type of leader you want in the dressing room. Like Ciaran Fitzgerald, too, they are the type of guys players would simply die for. Munster were extremely fortunate to have had two in succession with Paulie following Gaillimh at the heart of their pack. More to the point, they were blessed to have two guys of such quality. Of all his obvious traits – out of touch, in the scrum and around the field – the outstanding quality for me is Paul's honesty in adversity. Let me be more specific: when momentum is with the other side, and the tide flowing heavily their way, Paul is the player who pops up just about everywhere. I do not know what the word is to describe someone who is the polar opposite to the so-called 'sunshine player', those who deliver in buckets when the tide is in their favour and the hurricane at their backs. But Paul O'Connell personifies it. He is the definitive team player and a hero of heroes within Munster and Irish rugby. He is actually uncomfortable in that role, and that pushes him even higher in my book.

6 – David Wallace
Picking an Irish back row in any era has always been nigh on impossible. We have always been so strong in that area. Two spring to mind: Jim McCarthy's era which reached its zenith in Jack Kyle's 1949 Grand Slam-winning side, and, in my time, the 1982 Triple Crown-winning side with John O'Driscoll, Fergus Slattery and Willie Duggan.

To pick a modern-day back row is so difficult. The list is endless. And I mean endless. On it would be outstanding players like Alan Quinlan, Anthony Foley, Denis Leamy, Stephen Ferris, Iain Henderson, Jamie Heaslip, Peter O'Mahony, Victor Costello, David Corkery, Eric Miller, Keith Gleeson, Trevor Brennan and Simon Easterby.

I will plump for David Wallace to cover the blind side. He was such an intelligent player and another dynamic ball-carrier who read the game so well. Along with Paul and Richard, the Wallace family – and, remember, all three represented the Lions – are the most talented in Irish rugby history. Take the power of prop Paul, the pace and swerve of winger Richie and the prototype wing forward in David, and that is some family. But David was the best of them all. A class act in every way.

7 – Seán O'Brien

The arrival of mole-like midfielders – and I am thinking specifically here of Brian O'Driscoll and Gordon D'Arcy – effectively led to the removal of the all-action open-side flanker from Irish rugby at the highest level. It is not stretching it in the least to suggest their impact as ball-winners at the breakdown effectively finished Keith Gleeson's Test career in that role. For Gleeson was a traditional breakaway player, similar to Slattery, Nigel Carr or Denis McBride. But progress did away with the need for an out-and-out number seven.

So while I am probably playing this guy out of position, I make no apologies for doing so. But I just could not pick a team without Seán O'Brien in it. I make the same point as I did about Cian Healy: he is so dynamic and a gain-line breaker. He is as tough and uncompromising as they come. What you see is what you get and I love his attitude and *modus operandi*.

8 – Jamie Heaslip

This was such an easy choice for me. It goes against much of the criticism and crap written just because he is no flash merchant making juicy breaks and what have you. He does so much more unseen and understated work. Jamie reminds me so much of Willie Duggan in terms of work ethic. But mix in the best of Victor Costello and Axel Foley and you have the real deal in our current number eight.

The guy is not a natural leader when compared to some, but when it comes to walking the walk he is in the top bracket. My greatest fear, given the flak he most unfairly ships, is that Jamie Heaslip will not be fully appreciated until he has gone. For me he is the most complete rugby footballer to wear the number eight shirt.

9 – Conor Murray

When I look at Conor I see a future Irish captain. He is so composed. Nothing seems to faze him. He is quite tall for a scrum-half and reminds me in physical terms of Welsh greats Mike Phillips and Terry Holmes. His box-kicking game – such a key component for the modern-day number nine – has improved out of all proportion. He works so hard at his game and, much like Simon Zebo, is a very definite product of the club system. He has got where he is through hard graft, and it is clear that off-field ethic will never change. And much like Michael Bradley, he is also an extra wing forward in terms of defence and general reading of the fringe breakdown. His pass may not be in the Peter Stringer league – few are – but it is nonetheless right up there in terms of speed and accuracy.

10 – Johnny Sexton

This is another hugely tough call to make. It boils down to four candidates: Eric Elwood, David Humphreys, Ronan O'Gara and Sexton. In their pomp and at their best, Elwood and Humphreys are right up there with the other two. They were that good. In fact, if I was to pick my most complete out-half at his very best, I would surprise many in opting for Humphreys. He seldom got the appreciation his skill set deserved. Elwood, meanwhile, is without any doubt the greatest Connacht player pound-for-pound ever. Some statement I know, but I defy anyone to come up with anyone better. He also laid the groundwork for Pat Lam to take Connacht to where they are today on the European stage. Eric was fundamental to that initially with Michael Bradley, and later as the main man. Not only was he a fine tactical kicker, but he had a real presence. What probably sets him apart from the others was his natural leadership and that steely desire to win.

But it comes down to 'ROG' or 'Jonno'. Both are similar in so many ways. They are blessed with tunnel vision, but I feel Sexton has more to his game in terms of threat. Ronan's great forte, so under-rated, was his hands and that innate ability to put players into holes or gaps. Just ask our greatest rugby player, Brian O'Driscoll, who played most of his career alongside. He was by extension a beautiful distributor off either side. But because people were so obsessed with his kicking, we lost sight of that fundamental part of his game.

In a journalistic and coaching capacity I have watched a great many of these players come up through the under-age system, specifically the schools. I first came across Johnny in 1993–94 when he was on the St Mary's senior team at under-16 level. My initial impression was that he kicked much too much as the St Mary's tradition, generally born out of necessity, was to run everything. I could be wrong on this, but I suspect that Felipe Contepomi had a huge influence in attacking terms on Jonathan at Leinster. Like O'Gara, he always seems to take the right club out of the bag at the right time. And like his immediate predecessor he has an edge. He is now pretty much the complete out-half.

12 & 13 – Gordon D'Arcy & Brian O'Driscoll

When you think back to the 1980s, Brendan Mullin and Michael Kiernan were a class combination as our centre pairing. Then, into the professional era, we had the likes of Kevin Maggs and Rob Henderson. The last two were effective but they were more of an abrasive A to B, route one, ball-carrying combination.

But for most of us, the D'Arcy and O'Driscoll partnership at its best stands alone. Gordon was without hesitation the best full-back bar none I witnessed when covering schools rugby. He could not kick snow off a rope, but in every other respect he was top notch and destined for high places. For the switch from wing (where he had started out for Leinster upon turning professional) he can thank the then Leinster coach Gary Ella. The former Wallaby great only lasted for a year, but his legacy was in switching D'Arcy from wing to centre. The rest, as they say, is history. D'Arce turned out to be a phenomenal success as well as the ideal foil and partner for O'Driscoll.

Do I need to say anything about O'Driscoll? What can I add that has not already been documented about this remarkable athlete? Well, perhaps I was one of the first of the posse to predict his future. The following is what I wrote for the *Irish Independent* on Tuesday, 1 June 1999. I was in Australia to cover his first overseas tour when he helped Warren Gatland's Ireland blow away New South Wales Country 43–6:

SOMETHING SPECIAL

Mark my words, O'Driscoll is something special and I would have no hesitation in giving him his first cap against the Wallabies. Forget talk of his age and experience. There is simply no substitute for skill and he has that in abundance.

O'Driscoll has all the vital ingredients to play at the top level – especially the one precious commodity you simply cannot coach. Call it flair if you will but this kid has it in abundance. And, more to the point, he is not afraid to express it.

Beauty is in the eye of the beholder when it comes to the best of all time, what with Jack Kyle and Mike Gibson, to name two, up against O'Driscoll. But as I said at the start of this chapter, the professional era gave all modern-rugby players the chance to fulfil their potential. And, by God, did Brian do just that.

11 – Denis Hickie

Just before the advent of professionalism, Simon Geoghegan would have been my choice for this position. I just loved the way he played, loved his competitiveness and his derring-do. He just never got the chance to come remotely close to fulfilling his full potential. Unfortunately for him, he came on the scene during a very poor era of Irish rugby when we could not buy quality possession for love nor money. The 'blond bombshell' was a special talent, in the right place at the wrong time. How good would Geoghegan have been if he had been part of the professional era? He was just a fabulous rugby player.

But my choice for the left wing is Denis Hickie. Denis came from the same nursery as me in St Mary's and when I saw him play around the age of thirteen or fourteen I said then, all things being equal, that he would definitely go on and play for Ireland. It was so obvious. In his pedigree, his father Tony was the unluckiest full-back never to play for Ireland. His uncle Denis won seven caps at number eight for Ireland in the early 1970s. So it was in the genes. But what Denis junior had was a burning and blistering pace, similar to Brendan Mullin. Give Denis the ball and he was gone. He was a natural left-sided player, but most notable was his unbelievable speed, swerve and acceleration. He was so balanced, so good, and deservedly gets the nod ahead of Shane Horgan, which in itself indicates the exceptional standard set by our wide players in recent times.

14 – Tommy Bowe

I first saw Tommy in his early days at Royal School Armagh. He hails from Emyvale in Monaghan and I know his mum Anne and dad Paul quite well. His dad was a towering lock and won a Leinster Schools medal with Newbridge College in 1970 when they shocked Blackrock College in the final at Lansdowne Road. Tommy's sister Hannah is an international hockey player. So, like the Hickies, it is in the DNA.

Tommy's outstanding qualities are his deceptive pace, his strength and off-loading in the tackle, plus his obvious brilliance in the air. What is not too widely known is that when coming up through the under-age ranks, specifically at Queen's University, Belfast, Tommy played full-back, and like Gordon D'Arcy he was outstanding in that role. So when he eventually reverted to the right wing, where he is a natural, he was bringing all the relevant bits and pieces into the equation.

15 – Rob Kearney

Jim Staples bridged the gap between the amateur and professional eras, but I would narrow my selection down to four players: Girvan Dempsey, Geordan Murphy, Conor O'Shea and Rob Kearney. Hand on heart I find it really difficult to pick one, but I just favour Kearney. They were all outstanding. What I loved about Geordan Murphy was his moral courage. He was willing to try anything from anywhere at any time. And again from my experience of the schoolboy scene, many people will probably not realise that Geordie was an out-half and only changed from number ten to fifteen when he went to Leicester Tigers. What a transition.

Girvan Dempsey and Conor O'Shea both came from Terenure College. One was as good as the other. They were similar in style and outlook and both were blessed with a wonderful facility to read the game. Little wonder, therefore, that both are making their way as coaches with Leinster and Harlequins now. Like his brother, Donal, who I spoke of earlier in terms of nutritional knowledge and articulacy, the same is true of Conor: he is a great rugby pundit and talks so much sense. He played that way too, just like Girvan. The only difference between them was that Girvan was right-sided and Conor very much favoured the left. Like a magnet, wherever the ball was played, one or other was underneath it as they read the opposition out-half so well.

Rob Kearney was from Clongowes Wood College. He succeeded Gordon D'Arcy, which was a difficult act to follow, but, boy, did he do it well. He was the exact opposite of Gordon. Rob can kick the ball seventy yards downfield with a spiral or torpedo kick, whereas Gordon struggled in that department. He could kick but he was inconsistent and it was always as a last resort. In contrast, Rob is a beautiful kicker of the ball, and like Conor has always been left-footed. Like Gordon, he stood out as one who was destined to make it big. Their backgrounds – like the O'Shea brothers from Kerry – was steeped in GAA with Rob representing Louth and Gordon Wexford.

Rob was a slightly slower developer than D'Arce, but what he had, and still has to this day, was that moral courage to run at the opposition. Watch him. The second the ball drops into his hands, his natural instinct is to counter-attack. Geordan had it in abundance and Rob has it, too. As a full-back you are the last line of defence. You are the goalkeeper. Make a mistake and you are exposed with nowhere to go. You must be brave and assured. As my first-choice full-back, Rob fulfils all of that.

REPLACEMENTS

16 – Rory Best
I considered a very much under-rated hooker in Jerry Flannery, but will side with Rory Best. Rory seems to be maturing like a vintage wine despite injury problems plaguing him over the years. His biggest attribute, over and above the basics, is his work-rate at the breakdown where he is second to none at pilfering ball. It is almost his trademark now. Time and again he translates a 'mere' tackle into possession.

17 – Nick Popplewell
Rob Andrew took him over to England as one of his earliest signings of the professional age to play with Wasps, and subsequently Newcastle. That was a statement in itself. Poppy was the real deal and a ball-handling front-row forward way ahead of his time. At his best, Cian Healy is now what Poppy once was.

18 – Paul Wallace
Wally really came of age on the Lions Tour to South Africa in 1997. With great respect to Jeremy Guscott, Paul was the key cog and single biggest difference between winning and losing that Test series. Not by any means the biggest prop ever, but the proverbial battleship in every way.

19 – Malcolm O'kelly
Big Mal is a product of Father Noel Redmond and Templeogue College. He is their most capped international and they are immensely proud. I pick Mal ahead of Donncha O'Callaghan, Devin Toner and Paddy Johns, who captained Ireland. A great big beanpole, with an incredibly laidback attitude, but scratch below the surface and therein lies an incredibly competitive

forward. Big Mal was a natural and it showed in his play. He was so comfortable on the ball and was another who maximised his potential through the professional game.

20 – Eric Miller
Eric gets my vote ahead of Stephen Ferris, David Corkery and Peter O'Mahony. He was the most talented schoolboy forward I have seen come through the under-age system, where he played with Wesley College. A multi-talented sportsman, he also played soccer at my old schoolboy club Rangers as well as turning his talent most proficiently to Gaelic football with Ballyboden St Endas. He was the complete back-row forward and was so versatile he could play at numbers six, seven or eight, much like David Wallace and Seán O'Brien now. He is currently coaching in Sri Lanka.

21 – Peter Stringer
Prior to Peter Stringer's arrival on the scene – when I remember seeing him alongside Mick O'Driscoll winning a European Universities title with UCC at Donnybrook in 1998 – Colin Patterson was the best passing scrum-half I had seen or played with in this country. Now that mantle has fallen to Stringer, who continues to be the best passing scrum-half the game here has seen. Quite how, and why, Munster let him slip away to England when they did, I will never know. There was one loser and it was not the player. His level of fitness to this day is testament to a consummate professional.

22 – Ronan O'Gara
No added icing necessary. One of the all-time greats whose legendary status for Munster and Ireland is guaranteed. 'ROG' is a true icon of the professional age.

23 – Shane Horgan

The candidates for utility back included Geordan Murphy, Simon Zebo and Luke Fitzgerald, but there is only really one for me and it has to be 'Shaggy'. He grew up playing his rugby in 'The Valley of the Squinting Windows', namely Delvin, now Boyne, RFC. He started out as a centre when I first saw him play alongside his great mate Brian O'Driscoll for the Leinster under-19s. Once he moved to the wing, and accepted that position as his best way forward, it was win-win all round. He was a huge success and his ultra-competitiveness proved a nightmare for every wing opponent. Whatever else he achieves in the game he will always be remembered for scoring the Triple Crown-winning try against England at Twickenham, and that unforgettable touchdown against the same opposition at Croke Park on the greatest Irish rugby day of all.

CHAPTER 23

THE SEARCH FOR 'MELODY FAIR'

At the beginning of the book I talked at length about my mother and how I was brought up by her, her sisters and my grandma in Harold's Cross. I have hardly mentioned my dad and for two very good reasons. Firstly, I was only five years old when he died and I have precious few early memories. Secondly, I knew very little about him or his family. For whatever reason, my mum never discussed anything to do with the other side of the family. As a consequence, I never pushed her beyond what she might occasionally bring up in casual conversation over the years. It was not so much that I did not want to know. I just knew she was uncomfortable with certain family matters.

I left it alone, but my daughters did not. Nikki and Lynn decided as part of a Christmas present to do some serious digging through a professional genealogical research company called Ancestry Made Easy. They came up with some amazing findings that I had never known about for the best part of six decades.

For starters my father, one Danny Ward, or so I thought, was born on 16 August 1909 and registered as Saul Solomons. His parents were Harris Solomons and Jane Cohen. Harris worked as a tailor and lived with Jane at Great Garden Street, Whitechapel in east London. Saul (Danny) had three siblings: Sadie (Fanny), Sydney (Syd) and another sister Sarah. Sarah died soon after birth. The three surviving children were all born in London, but their nationalities were noted as Russian on the census return. Saul was also listed as Solly. Saul went on to change his name to Daniel Ward. Sydney and Sadie also changed their names, but I do not know their present names as I didn't even know they existed until recently.

As a family the Solomons were victims of their time. Following the assassination of Tsar Alexander II in 1881, the persecution of the Jewish population in Russia, Poland and Finland became severe. As a direct consequence of the assassination, anti-Jewish programmes and legislation were introduced across Russia and neighbouring countries. This led to a life of economic hardship with increasing and ferocious persecution. As a result it is estimated that more than two million Jewish people left Eastern Europe between 1881 and 1914. Many saw the UK as a stopover on their way to America. However, research indicates that approximately 125,000 stayed in the UK, the vast majority settling in London in areas like Spitalfields, Whitechapel, Shadwell, Stepney and Mile End. They were attracted by the cheaper cost of living and the fact that those areas had been home to a Jewish population from the 1880s. Many of these settlers found work in the 'Rag Trade'.

My grandparents, Harry and Jane, had apparently been married for six years before arriving in London and their birth places were both registered as Poland (Russia). I knew my dad had been married before meeting my mum, and that there was a connection with Russia, but beyond that I was in the dark. However, as the girls discovered, Danny (Saul) met and then married Lily Gross in the Philpot Street Synagogue in 1934. They both worked in London as hairdressers and had a son Derek (my stepbrother, I guess), who was born in 1935. Their marriage was later dissolved.

It is thought Danny then moved to Ireland where he settled in Dublin in the late 1940s. It seems he met my mum around 1952, and there was an eighteen-year age gap between them.

By late November 1953, having changed his name from Saul Solomons to Daniel Ward and converted to Catholicism, my parents married in Cardiff Registry Office. I was born almost a year later. Then, on St Patrick's Day 1960, he suffered a heart attack and died in Leeds General Infirmary. Our return to Ireland and to Dublin was almost immediate, and so began an upbringing that would always have a pronounced female influence in my life.

I have talked about that in depth as well as my active involvement in rugby and soccer. Therefore one could be forgiven for thinking nothing else mattered in life, but it is very untrue to intimate that my social life was non-existent. Being a sucker for mushy movies of that time like *Love Story*, *S.W.A.L.K.* and, whisper it, *Gone With The Wind*, I was a romantic right from the start . . . a normal red-blooded male who loved female company. Yes, of course, I went to see *The Exorcist*, *Soldier Blue*, *The Godfather* and films of that ilk. But give me a gripping, feel-good, romantic movie and I was in my element. It does not quite fit the macho rugger-bugger image I know, but we are what we are, and for better or worse that is me.

I have already outlined the impact an innocent movie like *Love Story* had on me, not least in relation to my recent bout of illness, but so, too, did *S.W.A.L.K.* What was that you might ask? *Sealed With A Loving Kiss* was a coming-of-age story of young, innocent, puppy love with the lead roles played by Mark Lester and Tracey Hyde. Mark Lester will be forever remembered for his portrayal of Oliver in the 1968 musical of the same name. In the film *S.W.A.L.K.*, with music by the Bee Gees, Tracey Hyde played the part of Melody Perkins. Like Ali MacGraw – Jenny Cavalleri in *Love Story* – Tracey became a love of my life. How sad and innocent was I? At least I have the consolation of calling on the early teenage years as a definite line of defence.

That said, the search for Melody Fair was up and running. I would like to think I came close twice when making what we are all brought up to believe is the ultimate commitment. The 'it' to which I refer is, of course, matrimony and twice I have taken that step. Unfortunately in the marathon that is marriage, neither union made it close to the stadium, never mind into the final straight.

Maura and I were kids when we got married. I was in my first year out of college and she was in her second year of a four-year course at the same college. It was infatuation on both sides. She was strikingly beautiful and I was the 'athletic jock'. I was in the prime of my playing career and she was making her way towards a teaching degree and a life in education. However, we drifted and, after five or six years, went our separate ways. Along the way we were blessed with our beautiful daughter Lynn. Lynn Catherine came into the world in the Coomb Hospital on 31 July 1983. I am glad to say she has an equal and loving relationship with both her parents to this day.

Maura remarried and moved on with her life and is based in the UK. She has been very supportive, particularly through my health scare, and I know I speak for both of us when I say we remain friends. She has a great dad (Pat O'Regan) and brother (Brian) who remain hale and hearty and living in the family home in Dublin. Of course, everyone could have done without the trauma of the break-up. But time heals and, in retrospect, it was as smooth as it could have been given the circumstances. We were kids, wet behind the years, and ready for anything but marriage. At that age there is no tomorrow. Oh, for 20–20 vision and the massive benefit of hindsight. Did it put me off relationships and marriage? Not in the least. If anything it whetted my appetite. Despite the perception peddled throughout my career, I do not think I could have been termed a womaniser. I did not have a roving eye and when I was in a relationship, whether in marriage or outside, I was loyal to a fault.

Louise Cole came into my life as my rugby-playing career was winding down. She, too, was stunning in appearance with a warm and affectionate personality. Immediately I was smitten. We met in Greystones Rugby Club where her dad Eric (sadly no longer with us) had been a former president and her mum Angela – a fantastic woman – was a hard-working member of the ladies' committee. We will not go there, but the female role within rugby clubs was very different back then. Like so much else in life if we had known then what we know now. Anyway, the chemistry was electric between us. Here we had a single mum to Rich, who was four years old when we met, and a separated dad. Lynn was also four and there was just three months in age between the kids. It was not a factor in our getting together, but in so many ways it seemed just right. We had first laid eyes on each other at a reception in Jim Doyle's Bar on Bray seafront for Tony Doyle and me just before the 1987 World Cup.

We clicked in January 1988 and moved in together later that

year. Two years on, in 1990, we were married in Newtownards. While Father Brian (D'Arcy), a really good friend for so many years through our common links with Mount Argus, could not perform the marriage second time round, he was still actively involved in almost every other way. He spoke passionately and reassuringly at the reception in Avoca, County Wicklow, to celebrate the union. Brian is an extraordinary man with an extraordinary zest for life. He baptised Lynn and Nikki and to all intents and purposes married me twice, insisting on a special mass for both families in Mount Argus on the eve of travelling to the Registry Office – organised by Colin Patterson – in the North of Ireland. I could fill a book on Brian and the amazing work he does.

Nicola Jennifer (Nikki) arrived a year later in 1991 and Alison Louise (Ali) in 1996. They were great times, loving years and for the best part of our two decades and a bit together life was good. Nikki and Ali were both born in Mount Carmel and, despite all the cups and caps, being there for the birth of both girls was the most exciting, and equally the most humbling, experience of my life. I had to stay outside the room for Lynn's birth. They were different times with different norms.

There was a rugby connection with the arrival of Nikki and Ali through Hubie O'Connor, our official obstetrician, and Karl Mullen, who was there for the birth of Ali. Both were great Irish forwards of their time. Karl led Ireland to Grand Slam and Triple Crown glory in the late 1940s and early 1950s, and Hubie, while studying medicine in Trinity, featured as flanker in all four games of the 1957 Five Nations Championship, two of them under the captaincy of Jack Kyle. The multi-talented gynaecologist was an avid painter, golfer, writer and lover of everything French. Having safely delivered

Richie as well – some eight years before – this doctor-patient relationship was special. Hubie O'Connor was a great man sadly missed.

While Louise had little interest in sport our relationship was strong for the best part of our marriage. In the last few years we did drift with the fault equally shared. Other factors came into play and a different dynamic developed. Such is life and without wishing to sound flippant, however traumatic the impact, we learn to move on. Do I miss the intimacy of marriage? Well, for starters, I sure did not plan on being in this position at this stage in life. What I miss most I guess is not the romantic dinners, not the adventurous holidays, not even the more placid ones. No, the real loss was, and is, in problems shared. I miss no longer having that ear in which to whisper or that shoulder upon which to cry when things get rough. And, yes, it was tough paddling the canoe through the most recent health-challenging years.

While my dice with cancer was not caused by marital difficulties, the stress and anxiety resulting from the break-up running parallel certainly did not help. But through the love and support of those closest to me, including an extraordinary circle of friends, but most of all my girls and Rich, we live to fight another day. The changing circumstances could be put down to many things, but only the two central characters know the truth of what actually transpired. Those factors are private and that is how they will remain.

I listened recently to an old tape of former Wallaby greats Nick Farr-Jones and David Campese talking about the modern game and whether or not they would push their kids into rugby. The principle behind that question is intriguing. For the record both World Cup winners initially answered by way of an automatic 'no'. A response revealing in itself, but Farr-Jones on reflection said that if a young lad or lassie of his showed interest then in his view 'whatever they want to do it is up to them'. And therein, after the best part of forty years' teaching and coaching, lies the only message one still involved in schools sport at the cutting edge – as director of rugby in St Gerard's School – tries to transmit. The bugbear and biggest problem confronting teachers and coaches is the parent who, quite frankly, wants his son or daughter to be the sporting genius he or she never was. The lengths to which some will go is scary. So to Farr-Jones and Campese add the name Ward.

Of my four children, only one – Lynn – had the prowess and, more importantly, interest to pursue her sporting involvement at under-age after leaving school. Her mum had been All-Ireland Universities champion in 100 metres, 200 metres and long jump, and she was also a top tennis player. Lynn picked up many of those traits, being particularly talented at hockey which she still plays socially.

I feel that is the real satisfaction to coaching involvement at under-age. Yes, it is great to see a Jack Conan – along with pop singer Hozier, our most recent star turn at St Gerard's – make his way in the professional game. But when I meet young men or women I once taught or coached still playing (as I did at a recent tag rugby event held in aid of Aoife Beary, one of the victims of the horrific Berkeley balcony tragedy), I get a good feeling inside. Sport should be for life if the formative interest is there.

There is a good case in point with Andrew Hozier-Byrne. Andrew – or Hozier as he is now globally known – loved his rugby, but unfortunately he did not quite make the cut for the senior team in his final year. But his commitment was every bit the same as every other squad member that year. With the full support of coaches Joe McDonnell and me, he became official touch-judge and never let us down. Therein lies a dual message for parents. In whatever direction their interest goes, encourage your children to the full, but let it be their interest and not yours. Secondly, as with Hozier, room for active involvement can be found for everybody, and that is as it should be.

And lest I do him a disservice, Richie was a promising soccer and rugby player in his youth, but only on his terms. I never once pushed him where I knew he did not want to go. He had other interests, but at least he had the opportunity and that was good enough for me. Not for a minute would I profess to have all the answers, but a lifetime's involvement in under-age sport has taught one simple lesson which I try and pass on to parents in the most inoffensive way. That is, to paraphrase Farr-Jones: 'Whatever they want to do should be up to them.'

As regards my own brood, Richie is now an established electrician in Melbourne. Lynn is married to Stuart Dempsey, her childhood sweetheart from St Andrew's schooldays. Indeed, Stu, a son-in-law of whom I am immensely proud, is a case in point. A little like Hozier, he was just outside the starting fifteen, but he stuck at it through thick and thin and eventually made the Senior Cup squad. He and Lynn are still very actively involved in tag rugby, while Stu can fairly burn it up on the golf course, too. Lynn is in HR and loves what she does. Nikki is making her way in child care, to which she is to the manner born. She is absolutely made to measure for the career she is pursuing. Ali, my baby (she will always be that) has just completed her Leaving Certificate and hopes to take a third level degree in business and maybe Spanish.

Like most parents I love them all unconditionally and, yes, I would have loved it if that sporting spark had been there. But *c'est la vie*. Despite my own prowess between the white lines, they knew they were *never* under any pressure just to please the auld fella. They did their thing their way, and whatever or wherever the interest, they had full and unconditional parental support. They are not by any means perfect, but are as close as is humanly possible in my eyes. No, I lie, they are perfect . . . Perfect with a capital P.

Meanwhile, the search for Melody goes on.

ACCEPTANCE

I have shared my thoughts on most things I have been directly involved in during my life. I have revealed my opinions on so many players, people, teams and organisations. I have talked and passed judgement. It is high time and only fair that I talk about myself. Just how does Tony Ward see Tony Ward? Am I bitter, resentful and angry at the way certain areas of my life turned out? Am I embarrassed about the way I handled certain things? Am I proud of what I achieved? Will I forgive those who trespassed against me? Above all else, if I can forgive and forget, am I happy and content with my life? In evaluating everything it is best to start at the very beginning and go back to my childhood.

Do I resent not having a normal or regular paternal presence like most of my friends? Resent is probably too strong a word. But regret, yes. I would love to have grown up with both parents hale and hearty. I would love to have experienced that father-son, man-to-man thing. Even when I was making my way on the football and rugby fields of Bushy Park and Kenilworth Square, I missed not having that direct male support on the sideline, and the feedback that would have followed. Given my father's interest in almost every sport, he would have broadened my horizons beyond the round and oval balls. I am sure he would have taken me along to other sporting events like he had my mum in the years before I was born.

Alas, it was not to be. You can only play the hand you are dealt. At that age anyway it is all about friends. Living with five women – my mum, her sisters Renee, Bernie and Ann, as well as my grandma – just seemed so natural. It was the way it was. We just got on with life. Naturally, being surrounded by women impacted on my personality and I will concede to being overly sensitive ... probably too much at times for my own good. Rightly or wrongly, I put that down to the massive female influence in my life. It is no different today than ever it was.

Was I unlucky in love? Perhaps yes, although I would qualify that by saying in life and love, as in sport, we make our own luck. To borrow that oft-used quote from golf legend Gary Player: 'The harder you work the luckier you get.' Do my marriage break-ups sadden me? Yes. Do I regret the road taken? No. We all make what we believe to be the right decisions at any given point in our lives.

People can gossip and see it as a glass half-empty. I prefer to view it as a glass three-quarters full, especially with the beautiful children I have been blessed with from those unions. All four of my children occupy an equal place in my heart. Indeed my stepson Richie is but the mere touch of a button away from decision-making and family involvement, which is regular and natural. He is my male advisor and I am his. He stayed on in Australia following the now mandatory global tour in 2007. As a qualified electrician studying engineering, he has set up his own business which, thankfully, is going from strength to strength. His work ethic is second to none and is a great example to the girls, particularly the younger two, Nikki and Ali. While Rich is making his way nicely in Melbourne, for Renee, Bernie and Ann (all now deceased), read Lynn, Nikki and Ali. My girls make me tick, and not for a moment would I pretend anything otherwise.

Perhaps I was spoilt by getting to see the world through sport. But, much as I loved Australia after five tours there, I never had the urge, like Rich, to stay on. Even as a student, when trying to find employment post-graduation, emigration was never an option. Of course, I love travelling, but I still adhere to the principle that the best thing about going away is coming home. I am immensely proud of my place of birth. For all its faults we live in the best little country on earth. I hate the perception of us in relation to drink and all that 'sure aren't the Irish great craic' nonsense. I can live without that.

As for Tony Ward in 2015, it has been a time for considered self-examination. I have looked myself in the eye in the mirror and reflected on what I saw. I might just draw a morbid parallel. Whenever I attend a funeral, and particularly one in which a life has been less than fully lived, it seems to give us all that invaluable time to pause for thought. For a while at least we can move out of the fast lane. As we all know, it is only too short a respite and back we go into that outside track, competing with the best of them at a million miles an hour. I guess what I am trying to say is that, when confronted with the 'Cavalleri moment', a moment when the word 'mortality' takes on a meaning like never before, you do get a real sense of what life is all about. That perspective extends way beyond the days in the immediate aftermath of a funeral, irrespective of how sad the circumstances surrounding the deceased might have been.

Acceptance

So, on my own personal reflection, I would like to think I am a nicer person on the back of the most challenging period in my life. For sure I feel I have mellowed in outlook. Of course, I still worry far too much and I am too sensitive for my own good. But in respect to my general attitude to life I think my prostate cancer experience has been a coin with a very definite flip side. And a flip side I very much like and feel proud of.

I am involved in various cancer societies. These include the Irish Cancer Society, Arc Cancer Support Centre, Marie Keating Foundation, Mater Hospital Foundation, Men's Cancer Alliance (MCA), Cancer Focus Northern Ireland, and Movember Foundation Ireland. I also sit on the board of the Heartbeat Trust, which supports services and research at the St Vincent's University Hospital Chronic Cardiovascular Disease Unit.

Quite apart from contributing in practical terms, the overall objective is to get the message to men everywhere: get checked. I was that macho male who ignored the danger signs to my detriment. 'Sure I'm grand, I'll get it checked tomorrow.' But tomorrow comes and goes all too quickly. And as we all learn in that deadly fast lane of life, days turn into weeks, turn into months, turn into years.

For Men's Health Week 2015, coinciding with and finishing on Fathers' Day in mid-June, I worked as the 'face' of Men's Health Forum Ireland (MHFI) in a cross-border initiative jointly funded by the Health Service Executive (HSE) in the Republic and the Public Health Agency (PHA) in the North. Its aim was to create a revolution in men's health with a simple and self-explanatory theme: 'Creating Culture Change – it's time for a new script.' The reasons are both clear and stark:

287

Men in Ireland die, on average, almost four and a half years younger than women;

Males have higher death rates than women for all leading causes of death, and at all ages;

Poor lifestyles are responsible for a high proportion of chronic diseases;

Late presentation to health services leads to a large number of problems becoming untreatable.

This high level of premature mortality among men in Ireland has far-reaching repercussions – far beyond the life satisfaction of men themselves. It affects not only industry and commerce, but also impacts upon the social and financial positions of families. However, it is not a lost cause and much can be done to change the current situation and macho attitude. But I repeat clearly and starkly: the bottom line message to men everywhere is *get checked*. I did just that and thankfully my own life has settled back into something of a normal routine, but one underpinned by priorities in relation to health and fitness.

As they say: 'This ain't no dress rehearsal.' I got a second chance when at 11.30 a.m. on 29 April 2015 I finally had my hormone implants removed. Less than a fortnight later, on 11 May, I had a full-on consultation with Doctor Hubie Gallagher. Following three torrid years of treatment and intensive medication the results were good. My PSA reading had come down close to where my doctors and I wanted it to be. I had followed to the letter everything my professional carers had instructed me to do. On the back of that my medication was eased out over the summer. Now, both physically and psychologically, I felt like a man reinvented.

Sadly no such rehabilitation applies to the rugby part of my life. That cannot be fixed.

To bend Brando's words from *On the Waterfront*: *I know I would* have been a contender. Those close to me know I am not precious or conceited in any way. I do not do arrogance, and particularly not about myself. I am uncomfortable talking about me in a sporting context, so I think it best to leave that to others.

Vincent Browne, who presents TV3's *Tonight*, was also a former journalist and newspaper editor. In the March 1979 issue of *Magill* he wrote a paragraph about me in a piece entitled 'Irish Rugby's Slow Progress'. It read: 'Ward is of such class that is foolish not to build the side around him and the selectors have doggedly refused to do this.' Not only Vincent, but players, coaches, journalists and fans alike all expressed the same opinion. They cannot all be wrong!

Therefore, while I have long since forgotten, and to some extent forgiven, what was done, I still find it very difficult to accept. While holding up my hands to naivety in some of the things I did, I hope I have shown throughout this book that there was no malicious intent in any shape or form. The cages my media profile and public persona rattled in the corridors of power, I still do not get.

In the end, the blazers won. I dislike that description and seldom use it because it portrays disrespect. But the bottom line here is that the young rugby player oozing with confidence, and in his playing prime at twenty-four years of age having just been voted European Player of the Year, had his legs cut from under him. It is an appropriate metaphor because in the international honours that followed for Ireland and the Lions, right up to my retirement from representative rugby in 1988, I was never the same player again. Yes, I had my moments and, for sure, each subsequent return to the national team was almost as good as the first given the backdrop.

There is no need for me to repeat in minute detail the Australian debacle again now. All those who were central to my axing, and the manner in which they behaved in the immediate aftermath, have to say is: Ireland 2, Australia 0. We won the Test series, the first by a Home Nation in the Southern Hemisphere. Not only that, but in my replacement, Ollie Campbell, they had the player of the series and one who more than merited his selection. So, in their view, the end justified the means. They are difficult arguments to counter.

Am I bitter all these years on? I think the answer to that is self-evident. With hand on heart, it is not being dropped that gets me. That comes with the territory in team sports. Look no further than Brian O'Driscoll, who was dropped for the final Lions Test 2013 in the same country for the most recent evidence of that. My issue is with the lack of empathy. I was a young and very promising rugby player who wanted to play rugby, nothing more, nothing less, and despite the perception peddled then and since, nothing beyond that. Like most I suffered from nerves in the build-up to big games, but put me on a football pitch on the big day and I was transformed into Superman on Speed. That was taken away in an instant in Australia.

Thanks to the game going open it should not happen in rugby again. But let there be no room for complacency. If there is one message I want to leave in this book it is precisely that. Whether it is a Henry Shefflin, Gooch Cooper, Brian O'Driscoll or whoever, no player, no matter how bright a star, has a divine right to selection. What they should be given, however, is a level of compassion in how their situation is handled and in ensuring they are provided with the relevant knowledge, opportunity and encouragement to work at, and find, a way back.

Despite being dropped in 1979 my career at the highest level lasted the best part of another decade. However, nineteen caps by today's standards is a rather pitiful return. Does that bother me? Not in the least. Just proving myself to me was motivation enough. I have loved my lifetime in sport to date, but Australia 1979 I could clearly have done without. So, all these years on, while I can forgive and forget, I accept my true potential was never realised.

God forbids it will ever happen to another talented sports person. In telling my story that is the message I wish to convey most of all. Sport mirrors life and life, for all its trials and tribulations, is precious. So, switching the channel from sport, I hope that the suppression of a talent or of potential will not happen to anyone in the most important sphere of all . . . LIFE.